.D

The Great Typo Hunt

Jeff Deck and Benjamin D. Herson

The Great Typo Hunt

| Two Friends Changing the World,
One Corr∤ection at a Time |

 Crown Publishers / New York

Copyright © 2010 by Jeff Deck and Benjamin D. Herson

All rights reserved.

Published in the United States by Crown Publishers, an imprint of the Crown
Publishing Group, a division of Random House, Inc., New York.
www.crownpublishing.com

CROWN and the Crown colophon are registered trademarks of
Random House, Inc.

Library of Congress Cataloging-in-Publication Data
Deck, Jeff.
  The great typo hunt : changing the world one correction at a time / Jeff
Deck, Benjamin D. Herson.—1st ed.
      p.   cm.
1. United States—Description and travel.   2. Deck, Jeff—Travel—United
States.   3. Herson, Benjamin D.—Travel—United States.   4. Editors—
Travel—United States.   5. Spelling errors—Social aspects—United States.
6. Punctuation—Social aspects—United States.   7. Signs and signboards—
United States—Editing.   8. Written communication—United States.
9. United States—Social life and customs—1971–   10. National
characteristics, American.   I. Herson, Benjamin D.   II. Title.
E169.Z83D43 2010
302.2'244—dc22   2010004505

ISBN 978-0-307-59107-4

Printed in the United States of America

Design by Elina Nudelman

10   9   8   7   6   5   4   3   2   1

First Edition

To Henry Collins
and the grammatical world he'll inherit

or·thog·ra·phy (ôr-thŏg'rə-fē)

n. *pl.* **or·thog·ra·phies**

1. The art or study of correct spelling according to established usage.

2. The aspect of language study concerned with letters and their sequences in words.

3. A method of representing a language or the sounds of language by written symbols; spelling.

—*The American Heritage Dictionary of the*
English Language, Fourth Edition

CONTENTS

The Great Typo Hunt

1 | How to Change the World

June 8-10, 2007 (Hanover, NH)

Wherein Jeff Deck, unassuming Editor, has his measure taken by a flurry of his peers and learns that his Destiny is to serve a Higher Cause; whereupon he recognizes the Sign of his quest in an errant sign which warns 'gainst either geographic indiscretion or trading locks of hair.

On a fine June weekend in 2007, in the verdant reaches of northern New Hampshire, I decided to change the world.

The world needed changing—that I knew. Global warming threatened to give us all a lethal tan; war and poverty decimated whole nations; crops worldwide were shriveling; even our brethren beasts menaced us with their monkeypox and bird flu and mad cow disease. I just couldn't figure out what *I* could do for our troubled civilization.

Those thoughts echoed in my head as I drove into the idyllic little town of Hanover, New Hampshire, for my five-year college reunion. I'd been toying with the idea of a road trip. Oil addiction and carbon emissions aside, I had to count myself among the many Americans who regarded their cars as a signifier for freedom itself. Any day I could get into my iron steed and—escape. I hadn't, so far, but I could. I could explore the country, embark on towering adventures, and simultaneously fulfill some noble purpose. Yes, a road trip seemed like a fine idea, but I didn't know what was worth seeing and, more crucially, I didn't know how to infuse the trip with the sparkling sap of magnificence. How do people blunder into conditions that their unique abilities alone can resolve? I couldn't trust that I would wander into a situation where only my intimate knowledge of Final Fantasy lore would defuse a standoff between two rival video-game-obsessed street gangs. I pondered that as I pulled into a parking spot and ventured off to find my classmates.

To exacerbate the matter, it turned out that five years was more than enough time for my fellow graduates to work miracles in the public and private sectors. My heart beat at techno tempo as I listened to tales of the most astonishing exploits and ennobling acts of virtue. I talked with one woman who was slowly restoring ecosystems damaged by the rapacious engines of industry. Another guy, a lawyer, sought to break up harmful corporate monopolies. Others were doctors, bankers, and politicos, all positioned to alter the great trajectory of civilization. And then there was me.

"So, Jeff, what have *you* been doing?" they'd ask, with the unspoken postscript: ". . . for humanity?"

Unlike my classmates, I hadn't erected any schools for Balinese orphans or wrested any kittens from death's blasting maw. After graduating, I'd moved to the Washington, D.C., area to see what I could do with the skills I'd picked up from a creative writing degree. The chief export of the nation's capital is, of course, paperwork, so I reckoned I could land some kind of writing or editing position at one of the many nonprofits and associations in the area. An academic publishing house in Dupont Circle took me in and nursed me on the *Chicago Manual of Style.* I burned a few years there as an editor, managing two strangely divergent publications: a magazine about rocks and minerals, appropriately titled *Rocks & Minerals,* and a New Age-y journal about consciousness transformation and other inscrutable bits of pseudo-academia. Neither topic was exactly my area of expertise. My qualifications for the job rested mainly on my ability to ferret out spelling and grammatical mistakes in text. I found that I was a natural, spotting typos with idiot-savant-esque regularity. I hadn't had this kind of chance to show off my geeky prowess since winning consecutive junior-high spelling bees. In high school I'd branched out from mere spelling perfectionism to the full gamut of editing delights on behalf of my school paper. At the publishing house, I could water my little patch of textual earth, checking that *fluorite* was spelled with the *u* before the *o,* and that the names of Norse gods had the ðs that they required.

This sufficed for a while, but eventually I noticed the distinct lack of influence that my little labors had on the world outside my publications. I felt the call to return to New England, and I traded D.C. for Boston to be closer to family and old friends. Now I worked as an administrative assistant for a center at MIT that studied climate change, but my heart remained that of a reviser and corrector.

Outside the reunion tent, I bumped into Kevin, an occasional buddy in our college days; he was one of those genial and imperturbable people you wish, upon crossing his path later, you'd known better. I related my minor publication successes, a short story here and there, and that I had at least found work in my field (for a while) as an editor before moving to Boston. Then I asked him, "You'd been doing all that sports broadcasting for the college radio. Did you ever do anything with that?"

"Sorta started to," he began. It had been difficult at first. Even before he'd left Dartmouth, he'd begun sending out tapes of his broadcasts. A year out of college, he was still sending them out and had gotten a job selling suits to pay his bills, and he decided he needed a new plan. While keeping his job in the evenings, he took a broadcasting class at a local trade school, which got him access to an internship at a television station. This was his ticket back into broadcasting. Over the intervening years, he'd proven himself through the internship and had become a key player at the news station. "So, now I'm in charge of the ten-o'clock news, Monday through Friday nights."

"Wait . . . you're the guy picking which stories go on the air?"

"That's part of the job. I mean, that goes hand-in-hand with assigning the stories to people."

"Which you do, too?" He nodded. Kevin's story brought the rest of my classmates' stories into perspective. Determination seemed to be the factor that elevated an ordinary destiny into a life of impact.

That night the reunion featured an event on the upper level of Dartmouth's sprawling arts center, usually known as "the Hop." While old comrades, crushes, and foes merged into a perspiring mass on the dance floor, I mulled the question of my destiny outside on the rooftop patio. There I could gaze at the campus quad, the Green, and, beyond it, the eternal phallus of Baker Tower, our *axis mundi*. As I leaned on the rail, cooling under the Hanover moon, I couldn't fathom how an editor would go heroically forth among the populace. While medical school or law school served as a straightforward way of approaching a concrete goal, I just didn't see myself taking up a stethoscope or a gavel. I had to hew to my own talents and strengths, but what instrument could I wield in the great clashes of our era? A red pen? I realized that no matter how I angled my approach to this problem, I'd need to strive beyond my daytime duties as an administrative assistant. Even if the professor I worked for were to go on to win the Nobel Peace Prize (which he did manage to do later that year, with Al Gore), I could not be satisfied with "administrative assistant" as the apogee of my career.

The next day I returned to my apartment in Somerville, Massachusetts, close to some revelation but unable to quite pin it down. In the glaring light of my reunion, I retook an inventory of my current situation. I had plenty of friends nearby, and my aforementioned job at MIT at least paid well. My rent remained cheap, since the landlady's parents had plastered the house with religious propaganda, scaring off general interest in the property. Things were, all in all, not so bad.

The breezy summer afternoon beckoned to me, so I ambled outside. Maybe I'd seek out a hot dog in Davis Square. But *fate* intervened between me and that dog. Halfway to my destination, a large white and red object—appalling to any sensitive eye—froze me in my tracks!

NO TRESSPASSING.

The sign had been taunting passersby with that loathsome extra *s* for who knew how long. It hung on a wooden fence around a vacant lot next to a dentist's office. Sure, I'd noticed this sign before; dozens of walks to Davis Square had occasioned dozens of silent fist-shakings at this very spot. This time, though, the sign's offense struck deeper. How many spelling mistakes had I noticed over the years in shop windows, street signs, menus, billboards, and other public venues? Countless, I thought. *Not an enterance. NYC Pizza and Pasta at it's best! Cappuchino! Pistashio! Get palm reading's here!* To/too, their/there/they're, and your/you're confusion, comma and apostrophe abuse, transpositions and omissions, and other sins against intelligibility too heinous to dwell on. Each one on its own amounted to naught but a needle of irritation thrusting into my tender hide. But together they constituted a larger problem, a social ill that cried out for justice.

For a champion, even.

I stared at that NO TRESSPASSING sign, and I wondered: *Could I be the one?* What if I were to step forward and *do* something? The glare from the extra *s* seemed to mock me. Sure, others before me had recognized that there was a problem afoot in modern English. Plenty of people had made much hay of ridiculing spelling and grammatical errors on late-night shows and in humor books and on websites weighted with snark. But: *Who among them had ever bothered with actual corrective action?* So far as I knew, not a soul. A lambent vision descended upon me, like the living wheels revealed unto Ezekiel. In it, I saw myself armed with Wite-Out and black marker, waging a campaign of holy destruction on spelling and grammatical mistakes. The picture widened to describe not just my neighborhood, not just the Boston area or even the august span of the Bay State, but the entire nation.

There was my answer—typo hunting was the good that I, Jeff Deck, was uniquely suited to visit upon society.

I would change the world, one typo correction at a time.

I turned back toward home, abandoning thoughts of hot dogs, and locked myself in my room, as typo-free a warren as one would expect. Typos might leap out from anywhere—were, in fact, everywhere. How should I go about this quest? And would I be alone in my fight, against the whole world? Then it all clicked into place, and the vision stuck. I already had one ally, the Sleipnir to my Odin: Callie, my car. That road trip I'd wanted to take! This would be the motivational engine that I'd been missing. I think I collapsed onto the bed, the force of revelation knocking me unconscious, the proverbial lightbulb blinding me with its incandescent flare. Of course, I had also missed lunch.

When I came to, I decided I should attempt another outing, but this one with much more purpose. I immediately bought a sizable wall map of the United States and tacked it over my bed. With the sunset casting an eerie glow through my apartment, I stood enraptured by the sheer span of the nation. So many tiny names, so many *roads.* Quite a profusion of territory over which to spread the gospel of good grammar—at least several thousand miles. I'd make a loop of the country's perimeter, since that seemed the best method for (a) seeing the most of this mammoth republic and (b) avoiding covering the same ground twice.

Are you sure about this? quoth the doubting raven in the dark aerie of my mind. *Are you sure, are you sure?*

"Shut your beak," I growled. True, my history did not especially glimmer with derring-do. First off, I had been terrified of driving at least until my early twenties, and my travels to date had never taken me west of Ohio; much of the country, *most* of it, lay beyond my ken. That in itself could argue for the adventure, but I wondered if I might be getting in over my head, setting too many new challenges at once. I'd been shy growing up, not prone to speaking out of turn or, well, speaking much at all. Once I started going around the country trying to correct typos, I'd inevitably have to *talk* to other people. The more I thought about it, the more I realized that this mission of mine would force me to continually confront strangers—oftentimes over their own mistakes! How far did I honestly estimate that I had come from the meek days of yore?

I chose to put these worries aside. I had plenty of time to address them, while other, more tangible items needed immediate attention. Certainly I wouldn't be able to take a vacation from work for long enough to travel across the country, correcting typos as I went, so I'd have to leave my job. I'd need to set my sights on loftier concerns than income. Spider-Man always had money trouble, after all. If I took the leap for typo hunting in the pursuit of a better, more grammatically correct world, so be it.

I could still be sensible in my preparations, though. The trip itself would cost some serious bread. I had a savings account with some starter funds hoarded away, and I earned enough that I could save much more. If I cut costs by not going out as much, packing my lunch more often, and refraining from any extraneous purchases, I could probably save a significant chunk of change. I wouldn't want to travel the nation in the winter anyway, so I figured I could stay at my job through December and then take a couple of months to organize full-time all the little details of the trip. Not only would I have the chance to build up a respectable bank account, but I could also take more time to analyze the various aspects of this trip and decide if I really and truly could pull it all off.

I reached for a pencil on my desk to start jotting down some notes, and somehow I grabbed a Sharpie instead. It felt right in my hand, as though it had always belonged there. This, I thought, could be the tool to make a hero.

2 | Allies

Finds our sleepless Hero amassing Allies for the impending orthographic onslaught across the Nation. For this auda-
cious Cause, he must call upon all species of Persuasion,
from breathless verbal sparring to cyberspatial communication,
and even climbing unto that very pinnacle of heroics: donning
Eighties attire in public.

I discussed my cross-country typo-hunting notion with barely
anyone, cradling it close and secret lest the scrutiny of others burn
mortal wounds into its gossamer body. This passive strategy worked
fine during the daytime, but at night I lay awake and sweating underneath the giant map of the United States. I felt the weight of the
nation hanging over me, from San Diego at my feet to the Florida
Keys at my crown, with lower Texas thrusting accusingly at my neth-
ers. In the hazy borderlands between sleep and wakefulness, America
morphed and mutated, enlarged and anthropomorphized, to alternatively admonish me to action or cry that I hurtle to its rescue. My
orthographic duties could not be delayed. I had to begin planning
now, which conveniently left ample time for chickening out.

I mused over the details on extended lunch breaks that summer,
sitting on the lawns beneath the glistening central dome of MIT.
With my route already roughly mapped, I turned to temporal questions: when to go, and for how long. I'd first envisioned an odyssey
of six months, but that'd be pricey and exhausting—three months

would do fine. I could hold on to my apartment while I was gone and tailor the route to the seasons. I had a horrific vision of driving through the northern states fighting blizzards and treacherous ice the whole way. I also wouldn't want to head through the South and Southwest anytime after April, lest I and my car melt into a blasphemous puddle of man-machine on the highway. Come March, I'd head south and then west. By April 1, I'd hit the bottom of the West Coast and work my way up. Late April through May would carry me homeward, east through the northern states.

In August I made the strategic purchases of a laptop and a GPS. The former would help me to keep in touch with those back home and assure them on a regular basis that I had not been garroted by a disagreeable shopkeeper. The latter would compensate for my dismal sense of direction. They would be my constant electronic companions, boons of our dawning technological age. Yet, what about companions of the actual human variety? Would Frodo ever have reached the heart of Mordor without the devoted companionship of Sam? Where would White be without *Strunk*? I needed somebody to stride with me into stores or restaurants or municipal buildings, our two pairs of eyes simultaneously scanning the walls and aisles for rank lexical foes. Someone to cause a diversion in front while I snuck around back, someone to mop the dew from my dampened brow as I raised my marker for the glory of all humankind. Someone who could take the wheel once in a while, and pay for half of the hotel rooms.

It was time to go public with my intentions. I hoped my trip idea had grown a sufficiently leathery shell.

To recruit allies, I'd have to somehow thwart the considerable barricades thrown up by practical, responsible life. Most of my friends were gainfully employed and thus not likely to accompany me on the road for a dozen weeks. I could try for a rotating lineup of roadmates, but taking off work for even a third or a quarter of that time would be out of the question for normal folks. The standard clauses of the American dream only included two weeks of vacation a year. Still, I knew at least one person who would risk it all for a stab at true adventure and righteous action.

"Dude!" Benjamin hollered into the phone without preamble. "I'm so done."

"Hi?"

"That's it; I've had enough. I'm quitting my job."

Benjamin D. Herson had skipped our reunion, but I already knew what *he'd* been up to the last five years. Back in D.C., we'd been roommates, holding down jobs while we co-wrote an epic novel about two ordinary guys beating up evil frat boys. He would come home from his night shift at the bookstore as I was heading off to edit *Rocks & Minerals,* and slip me the day's bus transfer, which I would dutifully return that evening before he left the apartment for more overnight shelving. My only regret about moving back to New England had been leaving my old friend behind.

"You're leaving the bookstore?" This shocked me to the core. When asked once why, if he loved his job so much, he didn't marry it, Benjamin had replied that he proposed to it late one night, in the hallowed aisle between the Architecture and Household Repairs shelves. It had played coy, and now it had broken his heart.

"Yes, and I'm going to hike the Appalachian Trail next year."

"Really? I'm planning on taking a road trip next year." I wanted to ease sideways into discussing my idea.

"Cool, so we're both heading off on adventures."

"So speaking of our adventures," I said.

"Oh yeah! My brother was going to come on the trail, but he's married now. So he's out. Want to hike New Hampshire with me?"

"Hm."

"That's okay, Deck. You've got time to think about it."

"The thing about my road trip is that, while I'm going around, I thought I could also—"

"When are you going? What time of year?"

"Probably around—"

"Because, you know, if you want any company, and you plan it right . . . I won't hit the trail until April, so I could potentially do a leg of your trip with you or something."

Capital! I thought. He was so raring to go, I hadn't even had to ask him. Then it occurred to me that Benjamin didn't drive, had never even bothered to get a learner's permit. So much for sharing the wheel. Now I merely had to mention that in addition to taking in the sights of our comely nation, we'd also be harassing people about spelling mistakes the whole time.

". . . time to see the country, you know, before it's gone," Benjamin was saying.

"Before the country's gone?"

"What? No, the opportunity!"

"Yes, the opportunity," I replied, determined now, "and I thought I'd *also* take the opportunity to correct typos while I'm traveling around."

"You want to correct typos around the country?" Benjamin asked.

"Yeah."

"Didn't you write a story about something like that?"

"No," I said, "that was just one typo."

"On a homeless guy's sign!"

Benjamin, as usual, had excellent recall (another desirable trait in typo hunters, who would need to summon the musty old rules of grammar on the fly). A few years back, I had written a short story called "The Missing R," about a well-meaning editor with a warped sense of how to aid his fellow man. The story had ended with the editor inserting a missing *r* into a homeless man's sign (HOMELESS, HUNGY, PLEASE HELP). Obviously the character and I had divergent priorities, but now that I thought about it, perhaps the story had tapped into my subconscious more than I'd realized. That sign, after all, had been based on a real one I'd spotted long ago.

"Right," I said. "I don't think I'd bother with the typos of the destitute."

"Because sometimes I think those are intentional."

"But what do you think?" I pressed.

"About what?"

"The typos! And going around the country fixing them!"

"I think a road trip's a great idea," Benjamin said.

Someone in the background asked him a question on his lunch break. As Benjamin patiently explained to his co-worker how to go about some arcane inventory procedure, I attempted to mentally regroup.

"Sorry," he said. "And I'm not even the inventory supervisor!"

"Right. So do you think someone could sustain a trip around the country correcting typos? I'm pretty sure they're everywhere."

"Sure. Yeah, typos, man. So this'll be cross-country, right? As in, all the way across? As long as you can get me to Californ-aye-yay, count me in. L.A.'s stolen a good half dozen of my friends."

Benjamin's endorsement of the actual mission was lukewarm at best, but no matter. I steered us instead toward the proverbial brass tacks. We discussed the dates and found that my plans to head down the East Coast and west across the South in March fit well with Benjamin's plans to hike the Appalachian Trail. He'd come along until Los Angeles and then come back east to strike out on the Trail (it would be early spring, an ideal time for a northbound hiker starting in Georgia). I'd signed on my first sidekick for almost a month's worth of trip.

I savored this initial triumph for a moment or two, then decided to attempt recruiting friends for the latter legs of the trip. I tried to picture the more unconventional types, the ones who would be as open as Benjamin was to exploits and escapades. Then I remembered that my friend Josh Roberts, who lived down in New York City, had been talking about a West Coast road trip for years now. His perfectionist tendencies would have him typo hunting with gusto. He'd jump at this opportunity! I instant-messaged him.

Sometimes, in the oft-long stretches between seeing each other, I kind of forgot what Josh was like in person. His online persona became the reality, a living screen name that hid the red-haired, bespectacled figure typing away behind it. To some extent, we *are* our own text, which is why my mission would be important—erroneous signs confer their blemishes on their very owners. Still, the images we project with IMs and social network profiles are hardly a substitute for genuine, three-dimensional people.

After I'd finished describing my proposed journey, Josh was silent for a moment. Then he said, "Oh my god. You'll be killed within a week."

I feigned indifference, trying for a different angle of appeal. "Probably, but it could at least be funny."

"Okay, I *do* find unintentional misspellings funny," Josh allowed. "I saw a diner calling itself the 'All Night Dinner' once, but I can't remember where."

Yes, I thought, come along for the yuks if you must. Once we were on the road, carrying out actual corrective action, I could train him to focus on the higher goals of the journey. Right now I only had to get him into the passenger seat.

"Who are you road-tripping with?" he asked.

"Whoever wants to come along," I said. Then, cautiously: "So . . . are you in?"

"Definitely!" he fired back, to my delight. "I've never been to the West Coast. I want to do the leg of your trip that'll encompass Los Angeles to Seattle. I'd even go up to Vancouver if that were possible. And hey, when we're in L.A., I can network."

Josh worked as a film editor and production assistant in New York. He had some decent gigs with commercials and friends' projects, but I could picture the greater opportunities that Left Coast connections could produce. Judging by the high-quality editing that I'd seen him do, he deserved a shot at loftier glories. I imagined he would bring the same exacting discipline to interstate traveling. True, now that I reflected on our past adventures, Josh could also be obnoxious sometimes, but I figured that would be a plus in places like L.A.

We discussed the financial considerations. Money would be tight for him. Living from gig to gig takes a dire toll on one's bank account. I'd lit the watchfires of the idea in the turrets of his brain, though, and he would not see them extinguished for anything.

"I may have to live off ramen, but I will make it happen," said Josh.

Now both Benjamin and Josh were on board—no longer would I be a lone typo maverick. We were a team, and we needed a catchy name. Something that captured the scope of our ambitions and that would also look great on a T-shirt. Something like TEAL: the Typo Eradication Advancement League.

Autumn fell, and I discussed my ambitions openly and frequently now with friends, family, and hapless seatmates on the subway. Their questions helped me realize that *typo* described some of the errors I would be looking for, but not all. Some errors would be caused by ineducation, not carelessness. Some errors would be scrawled by hand, not typed. They were all worthy quarry, so I would expand the definition of *typo* for my purposes, to include all types of textual errors. I had emerged from the typo-hunting closet. I began to set up tentative sofa-surfing arrangements with people I knew in various corners of the country. It turned out there were certain geographic limitations to the Jeff Deck social network. I had the West Coast, the Midwest, and the Northeast/East Coast pretty well covered, but there'd be giant housing gaps in the South, the West, and the Great Plains. I needed cheap shelter options or I'd burn through my travel stash in a hurry, so I picked up a guide to reputable U.S. hostels (it was a short book) and Benjamin and I went halfsies on a tent. Hotels would be a last resort, and definitely not resorts.

In late September a friend invited me to a party down in Allston, near Boston University. I almost didn't go. It was an eighties occasion, and I had grown weary of such things, having already attended two eighties parties that year. Though I was a child of the decade myself, I never wanted to see parachute pants again. But I was always looking for excuses to talk about my impending mission, so at the last minute I threw on a Nintendo T-shirt and headed for the subway.

My friend greeted me at the door, wearing a dyed side ponytail, glammed-up eye shadow, and a tied-off Aerosmith shirt. Perhaps, I thought, I should have tried harder. She led me into the living room of her apartment, where the revelers had congregated. In the midst of them, a pretty, lanky brunette corralled chairs for guests. Like me, she had made little concession to the eighties part of the evening, opting for a jean skirt and tights. She threw me a thoroughly genuine smile with a goofy tinge, and I froze. My friend said, "Jeff, this is my new roommate, Jane! She's from Maine!"

"Uh," I said. All the glittering turns of phrase available to me had, in that moment, collapsed into a verbal slag. I had to tear myself away from those wide, warm eyes before I could regain conscious thought.

"Hi!" said Jane, taking my hand, which I had apparently extended.

It's all in the opening line, I thought wildly. Snare her with a brilliant observation or offhand witticism, something that will, in ten words or less, perfectly position you as a captivator of mortal hearts, an unalloyed ingot of allure. What came out was: "What do you do?"

Jane responded by typing on an invisible keyboard in the air. A web designer, i.e., a geek girl. My heart soared still higher. Then she asked what I did, and I found my stride.

"At the moment, I am but a lowly administrative assistant," I said. "But soon, very soon, I will be embarking upon a road trip to correct typos around the country!"

The room quieted. Or maybe I stopped listening to everyone else as I awaited her response.

"Sounds like a fun idea," Jane Connolly said, tacking on an anime-character-like, high-register "uh-huh!" Dazzled by her gracious smile and those hazel eyes, I launched into how I envisioned the trip playing out, burnished with heroic embellishment here and there. She tossed me thoughtful questions, such as what tools I would need to bring with me, how I planned to deal with hostile reactions, and whether I would get people's permission every time (I hadn't even thought of that). I thrilled at her attention. She was really *listening* to me, I thought, not just waiting for someone handsomer or more interesting to wander her way.

I may have been flattering myself a tad. Asking a lot of questions, I learned later, was a common Jane tactic to mitigate her own shyness. She did loosen up after a while, though, and told me more about herself, about her favorite mystery books and her experiences at a women's college in western Massachusetts. I ended up talking with her pretty much the whole party, and I snagged her phone number before I left.

We enjoyed two dates in downtown Boston during the next few weeks. On our third date, Jane came over to my apartment for Chinese dumplings and a screening of some embarrassing videos that I had made during a film course in college, including the adventures of the Phantom Purifier, a hygiene-obsessed superhero portrayed by me in a bathrobe with a tie around my head (also featuring Benjamin as my sidekick, the Soapy Ghost). Then we retired to my bedroom—to play the engaging card game Phase 10, of course. After a few strenuous rounds, we took a break, and Jane's eyes wandered to that giant map of the U.S. over my bed. I'd slathered the map with a rainbow of sticky notes. Yellow ones indicated places where I knew people. Blue marked second-degree connections. Purple was for hostels. Most of the sticky notes lay along the circuit I'd be taking around the perimeter of the country.

"Dang," she swore. "I don't think I know that many people even in New England."

"A lot of them are friends from school," I demurred. "I could only keep track of them through the wonders of Facebook, honestly."

"So this is all for planning your trip?"

I nodded. "Going to try to crash on as many couches as possible." Divans, futons, davenports, and settees were also a possibility; anything to keep expenditures down. But I didn't want to come off as a cheapskate this early in our courtship, so I didn't elaborate.

"You'll have such an amazing adventure," Jane said. She looked a bit wistful.

She couldn't be missing me *in advance*, I thought. Could she? I chided myself for vanity, but the thought remained. However, I never stopped to consider the perils of missing *her*. "There's going to be a website that you can follow," I blurted.

For the sake of the greater mission, I had to pave the way for TEAL in the meadows of the InterWeb. I envisioned keeping a blog of the trip so that interested net-trawlers could track my progress. Merely fixing the typos was not enough; I wanted people to know what I'd be doing, and to have a record of every vile typo vanquished. I'd post before and after pictures of each typo and update my kill count at the close of each entry.

"I see," she said. Then, casually: "So who's designing it?"

This time I got the message. Jane did ply the innards of websites for a living. With her considerable expertise in Flash, she could build an attractive site around the blog. It'd be a much better production than whatever awkward code I could paw together. "Nobody yet," I said, keeping my tone neutral. "Say, what's your going rate?"

"Ten Twizzlers an hour!" she proclaimed, and went off to raid my candy supply.

After we'd been dating for about three months, I realized that my *Weltanschauung* had undergone a subtle but measurable shift—Jane was now in everything I saw. No one else had ever cut such a finely limned cookie on the dried batter of my heart. Taking a three-month journey without seeing her at all would be a swift invitation to madness. This became ever clearer as I got down to planning the journey day by day, stop by stop, and I gained a visceral understanding of how long seventy or eighty days straight on the road would really be. When I'd sown the seed of this typo-hunting idea in the black soil of my brain, I'd been prepared to abandon every aspect of my former life. But as 2007 yielded to 2008, I found that I needed to drag Jane across the boundary with me. One early January eve, as we were playing Phase 10 again, this time at her apartment, with the green-line trolley screeching on its tracks outside and soused frat boys screaming along to "The Final Countdown" on some nearby fire escape, I said, "Come with me."

"Hunh?" Jane had thrown down a Skip card.

"You should come with me," I said again. "For part of the trip."

She gave me a big grin, and finally I saw that I should have asked her a lot sooner. "When, where, Jeff-Bear?" she sang.

"From Seattle to, uh, somewhere east?" Josh would be parting ways with me right at the last critical turn of my compass, and I'd be left alone to face a three-thousand-mile eastward journey. "In late April. Time-wise, it would be about the middle of my trip."

"Sure," she said, adding gamely, "I love road trips!" Jane would have preferred to go to California. She was such a good sport, though, that it didn't ultimately matter to her where we went, be it Mission Street or Missoula. She was sure we'd have fun anywhere. That kind of optimism tends to be self-fulfilling, and contagious. *Wouldn't* it be a touch romantic, I thought, or at least Romantic, to experience the wide and unblemished Western plateaus with this shyly smiling nymph beside me? We could dare the plains and the mountains together, under gray skies and fair, our two tiny islets of warmth shielded all around by a sea of empty miles.

"*Hurrkk!*" One of the frat-boy revelers outside was evidently unpacking the contents of his stomach.

"Can you take a week off?" I asked. Jane's webmistressing skills were in high demand, but she hardly ever took vacation time, so I figured she could squeeze five days out of her employer. "That could get us from Seattle to Minneapolis."

"Uh-huh! I'll talk to the project manager tomorrow." She got rid of her last card and did a little dance. I had lost the hand, but I'd won a new traveling companion. Jane could now consider herself the fourth official member of the League, and first in my heart.

Somehow I'd suckered three other people into this demented trip, securing companionship for the majority of those thousands of miles on the open road. The final part of the trip, homeward across the Midwest and into the East, I'd have to do on my own, but by then I'd be back in familiar territory with folks that I could stay with along the way.

I'd made commitments. I'd secured arrangements. Now there was no denying the trip—the *mission.*

3 | First Hunt

February 23-March 4, 2008 (Somerville and Boston, MA)

Commences—with repast, drinks, and assorted merriments—the adventure of our Hero, Who boldly, singly, launches himself amidst familiar streets with unfamiliar steps. Though carrying forth his righteous Banner, yet our Knight of Orthography stumbles, beaten back by a disquieting storm of uncertainty.

I threw a going-away party for myself in February, about a week before my departure date. By combining it with the celebration of my twenty-eighth birthday, I created the can't-miss event of the grim winter season. Kids love a themed birthday party, but my friends were in their twenties, so I skipped the He-Man party hats and centered on grammatical foibles instead. I set up a Typo Creation Station in the living room, where guests could make their favorite typos with alphabetical stickers, and I provided construction paper for cutting out states, real or metaphysical. I heard the back door slam as my reticent roommate fled the apartment, hours before the party was slated to begin.

Twenty-odd (or maybe just twenty odd) friends showed up, and they proved to be generous souls, showering me with gift cards and road tunes and other items useful for long months on the road. Jane and her sister gave me a snakebite kit and an exquisitely ugly dashboard hula dancer, both of which I would carry all the way around the United States without actually using. By the end of the evening my living room teemed with choice erroneous samples and all manner of cutouts, such as penises, snowflakes, and the obligatory silhouette of a naked lady. From the typos on the walls, apparently my friends expected me to run into a lot of *teh*s and *you loose*s.

Jane took me aside during a lull in the revelry and squeezed me in her long arms. "Tell me again why Jeff-Bear is leaving me for so long," she said.

"Somebody needs to fix America," I said. The look on her face said she thought I was being facetious. I leavened my argument with specifics. "I think that I'm the only one who can ferret out these mistakes consistently, day after day. Or at least I'm the only one who *cares* enough to make it happen. I know that there must be hordes of typos skulking around out there, and that's a big problem for everybody."

"*Why* is it a problem, exactly?"

"It's the creeping menace of carelessness!" I said, not even understanding the question. To me, the iniquity inherent in typos was as plain as a swath cut through virgin forest, or dog feces upon a white beach. It was like asking why armed robbery was a problem. "It's a malignancy for which I am the lone salve."

She sighed.

I knew in my marrow that the trip could make a palpable difference, perhaps even as much as the deeds of my old classmates. The specifics of how it would do that remained beyond my grasp. Maybe I'd need a few days on the hunt to figure it all out.

"Just get to Seattle safely, okay?" Jane said. "I don't want to be all alone at the airport when I arrive."

A couple drinks into the evening, the madness of what I was about to do struck me. I was about to leave all of these excellent friends behind for two and a half months, and my girlfriend for a month and a half, in the service of wiping out errata that probably nobody had ever noticed anyway. My concerned mother had asked me, "Are you sure that you'll be able to find a typo *every day*?" Though I wasn't worried about the hunting itself, I feared the greater trials that were sure to accompany it. I would likely encounter resistance the whole way from truculent shopkeepers and restaurateurs. I could even be arrested if I rankled the wrong folk. Plus I'd be blowing several thousand dollars in the process, money that could be spent in far more constructive ways, each now helpfully passing through my mind: exploring the far corners of Europe; a writing sabbatical for finally finishing my half-dozen half-completed novels; lots and lots of video games; or even, hmm, bolstering my pitiful retirement fund. What in the samhail was I doing?

Somebody encouraged a shot down my throat. A hurrah went out to the birthday boy, and it's possible someone slapped my bum. My doubts dissipated: the renewed glimmer of the mission's importance shone into my bleared eyes. This was virtuous work. Suddenly the vision shone bright, and I could see the future unrolling before me like a majestic throw rug, though its fringes were blurred. It would begin one typo at a time, each correction brightening the world a bit more. As each day went on, I'd meet more people, exhorting them to mindfulness of their p's and q's (along with any other relevant letters and punctuation marks). The cumulative effects of the multitude I'd inspire along the way would send ripples of proofreading across the land. As the legend of my deeds spread, people would come to my website, the one typo-destroyer in a sea of passive typo-patrol boats. I could inspire them, exhorting them to take up a marker and take their neighborhoods back. This could be the beginning of a true League beyond the humble quartet that I'd cobbled together.

The next day, once I could move my limbs again, I started gathering survival supplies for the road and cramming clothes into suitcases and bags. I bought a forty-eight-count steamer trunk of Pop-Tarts, reckoning that the abundance of toaster pastries—two dozen brown sugar cinnamon and two dozen frosted strawberry—would account for a major portion of our sustenance on the road.

I also began to assemble a rude collection of tools for fixing typos. The initial lineup consisted of

- elixir of correction,* standard-sized
- a thick black marker
- a black Sharpie
- white and colored chalk
- vinyl stick-on letters

All of which I thrust into a plastic shopping bag. It didn't stack up to, say, the Dark Knight's utility belt in either efficacy or glamour, but I thought my tools would be able to handle most typo situations. I'd already written my first blog entry about my preparations, and I wrote another about the party. The blog had launched quietly, without fanfare, for Jane was still working on the official front page of the website, with its animated doodads. I didn't expect very many people to be looking at the site at this pupal stage, anyway. As it turned out, my mom wasn't my only reader; a couple of my friends posted encouraging notes. I felt nearly ready to depart. With three days left before the Typo Hunt Across America began, I had two things left to do: load up the car with my suitcases, and try my first typo hunt.

It did occur to me (rather late in the process) that I had never actually corrected a typo. I mean, sure, I'd corrected thousands of my own and those of classmates, colleagues, and magazine and journal authors, but they'd been *looking* for my help. Now I would need to confront strangers about spelling, punctuation, and grammar. These people would not necessarily share my zeal for such things, particularly in regard to their own errors. How could I, no extrovert by any measure, face them without wilting in fear? I could probably sneak in and make the correction myself in certain cases, but that wouldn't work all the time. I had created a mission that forced me far out of my comfort zone.

I could work up to it, though. I had three days. I began at home.

---

* To avoid sounding like a commercial, I will generally use this term, which is what I tended to call it in my head.

On Sunday, March 2, I corrected my first typo. One that I'd noticed while on the john.

A year ago, while preparing for the GRE, I'd brought home a shower curtain festooned with mathematical principles. Though I enjoyed the reminders for binomial multiplication, the definition of an obtuse angle caused me acute pain. This first text in need of correction actually featured two for the price of one: a wandering comma, and a *that* for a *than*. I uncorked my new vial of elixir, took out a black marker, and went to work. Two downed typos later, I'd cleansed the errors from the tapestry of knowledge.

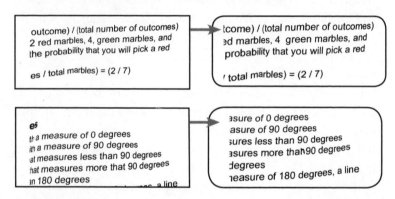

I'd bounded off to a great start, two for two. Or, wait—I set the marker and elixir of correction on the sink and took a step back. I ought to be conservative in my counting of typos, so that no one could accuse me of inflating my numbers. Each sign corrected would count as one typo, regardless of how many typos existed within the same sign. Thus, in my dim and dingy bathroom, I established the official policy for the League's reckoning of typos. I would maintain two totals: one for total typos found during the trip, and another for total number of those typos actually corrected. The ratio of the former to the latter would become a source of statistical obsession for Benjamin throughout the trip.

The next day I hit the pavement to seek out grammatical malefaction wherever it might lurk. Though not exactly renowned for its politeness and good cheer, Boston served as my home turf, so I figured it'd be safe territory for learning as I went. With typo correction supplies unceremoniously stuffed into my backpack, I headed out for my first mission. Plus I had a doctor's appointment in Brighton. As I surrendered my wallet to the rapacious gullet of the Massachusetts health-care system, I noted a stack of business cards with a troubling interpretation of the word *referral.* "Referal"!* To think that one little letter could mean the difference between directing someone to the help they needed and . . . returning to savagery?

I steeled myself, preparing for battle. My first time talking to someone. About typos, that is. "Excuse me," I said to the young, earring-bedecked man behind the counter, "there's a typo on these cards."

He checked for himself, as I had hoped he would. The guy sounded genuinely embarrassed on behalf of Brighton Marine Medical Center as he mentioned that he'd never noticed the missing *r.*

I paused, and not merely in anticipation of a further response. I had a terrifying vision that he'd give me the go-ahead and then watch, intrigued at first, as I inserted the *r* into each and every card. He'd forget all about me until a few hours later, when I'd hand the stack back to him, and he'd produce a box from behind his desk with an innocent smile and say, "Oh, hey, I found a couple more." I'd start the trip two days late and with a sprained correcting arm, only to find a comment from Josh on my blog the next day: "NO, THAT'S CHEATING. You can't count that as five hundred typos found and corrected. They're the same error!" So violently taken aback by this condemnation was I that I broke my reverie with a stumble, jerking back as though I'd caught a kryptonite bullet in the shoulder.

A puzzled stare met my eyes. Right, he'd never noticed the missing *r* before, and now awaited either our next topic or my graceful departure. I shook my head, as if clearing away any last hopes that

---

* When presenting erroneous text within quotes, we've left the punctuation outside ("Referral"! rather than "Referral!") in the interest of precise quotation.

my mission would be simple, then offered in a resigned (but hopefully sane) tone, "I suppose this will never be fixed."

No. There were thousands of them, the young man assured me. Thousands of errors found, none corrected. No way would I type that into the blog. The Josh-like commentary inside my head had it right. It could only count as one error, no matter how many times it had been printed. The ultimate goal would be to have the next print run corrected (assuming the clients could still read after they'd all been re-feralized).

Fine, so now I had another rule that could help ward against accusations of inflating my count. Multiple copies of the same typo-sporting document, like multiple typos on a single document, would count as one typo.

After my appointment, I headed for Back Bay, choosing a path along Boylston Street, under the upthrust of the city's twin spires, the Prudential and Hancock towers. Today, as usual, moderately well-off shoppers bustled across the Boston thoroughfare, popping into its chain apparel stores and grabbing a bite to eat at pseudo-Italian cafés. The mild weather had put complacent smiles on many faces, including my own. I weaved through various stores, but I found precious little signage to inspect in many of them. I began to wonder if my mother's fretting had been more sensible than I'd realized. Sure, I *thought* I saw typos all the time, but now that I was seeking them out, maybe they wouldn't turn out to be so numerous.

Then the East Coast's favorite bargain clothing store, Filene's Basement, rebuked that thought with near-biblical force. As any decent otherworldly omen should, the typo appeared above me: MENS CONTEMPORARY. And below it . . . MENS' BOXED TIES! Two varieties of error on the same word. I'd had a suspicion during the birth of the League that apostrophes would turn out to be a problem area for people.

Then the doubting raven's dread prophecy came to pass: I walked on out of the store without saying anything, leaving the blasphemous MENS hanging in my wake. *Men* is already plural! You can't put the *s* on without the apostrophe, that's simply wrong, but that wrong I could not work up the nerve to right. I didn't know how. Stealth was the strategy that appealed to my present cowardice, but this one hovered too high for that to be tactically feasible. I didn't know whom to ask, or how. Yes, the struggle for grammatical uprightness begins not on the printed page, but in the soul. Caught under the piercing glare of that errant sign, I conjured every excuse I could fathom. The common sales clerk wouldn't care enough to hear me out to the end of a sentence, right? Oh, and that one passing by seems busy with something else. Even the appearance of the sign seemed reason not to interfere; if not for the grammatical chicanery, a shopper could consider these signs professionally wrought. How could I possibly get anyone to heed my call for justice? Why, again, had I chosen to embark upon this insane trip?

Though not accosting anyone did eventually turn out to be a prudent choice, I concluded that day's blog with a note of defeat, scolding myself for having made such vaunted plans and then retreated so easily. I felt I'd joined the ranks of truly miserable failures, falling somewhere between the impotent strivings of Wile E. Coyote and Michael "Brownie" Brown's FEMA. I didn't even count the MENS' BOXED TIES as an official typo find, since those signs seemed to have come as a set. The tally for my early days of hunting came to a mere three typos, only one of which I'd corrected—the one hidden in my bathroom, which I'd meant to be a warm-up. The spirit of TEAL focused on text directed toward many people, words that were open and asking to be read and reread by the masses. My bathroom received far too few visitors to meet those standards.

Tuesday morning, on a break from packing, I made a quick trip into CVS. After yesterday's debacle, I didn't have the heart to go out typo hunting, and so I made the mistake of leaving home without my corrective supplies. Of course, just as neglecting one's umbrella acts as a dare to the storm gods, my oversight ensured that I'd stumble onto quarry—a tchotchke featuring an apostrophe for a plural: PINA COLADA'S. I snapped a crude picture with my camera phone. I should have known that I couldn't turn my heightened senses off, or even down to a simmer. O Weird Sisters, O Fates, you had stricken me with a typo in the very store where I'd purchased my elixir of correction! Something in me awakened then, and I loosed a growl of outrage at punctuation used in error. I tore off a corner of the label sticker from some nearby mouthwash, big enough to plant over the needless apostrophe. Without consciously deciding to, I'd pulled off my first stealth correction. I'd vaulted a country mile toward overcoming my inhibitions—for the world's sake and that of the three or four people following my adventures at that point. Fresh stores acquired, I returned home to finish packing Callie.

That night, Jane finished the front page of the website. Now we could show our visitors a visual representation of our route, bios, and a statement of our mission. Not only would our little cartoon avatar heads travel around the map of the United States—they *bounced* when you hovered over them. I loaded Jane's superior handiwork online, and with that, the Typo Eradication Advancement League was in business. Oh, the lives we would touch!

That is, once people actually stumbled across the website in the first place.

I spent an hour making the little Jeff head bounce when I should have been making a final inventory of my supplies. Then I sent an e-mail to my friends and family announcing the official launch of the website and my imminent departure. I figured a few people might be interested in following along; possibly one of the Boston alt-weeklies would do a piece on the journey when I got back. Though the goals of TEAL were lofty, I didn't expect many folks to truly understand. I stayed up late ripping my entire CD collection to my laptop and then went to sleep, one last time, in my own bed.

TYPO TRIP TALLY

Total found: 4
Total corrected: 2

4 | Benjamin Joins the Party

March 9. 2008 (Rockville, MD)

Veteran and rookie grammatical Champions find themselves immediately hemmed in by typos when first they set rubber soles to the
hunt. Even this opening Gauntlet is but a dwarf, however, when
compared to the Golem of apostrophic misappropriations to come.

On a chill and dank early morning in Silver Spring, Maryland, a
lone figure stalked through a parking lot and up the walk to a girl's
apartment. The wind gusted again, and he braced himself against
the frigid splatter of rain as he made his quiet way to the door, hoping through an alcohol-induced haze that he'd come to the right
place. The first rap-tap-tapping went unheard, so after a short pause
the visitor banged louder.

Benjamin D. Herson winced at the cold as he opened the door, his
short, slight frame nearly nude. He wore only a scraggly beard and a
pair of boxers, neither of which proved sufficient protection against
the onslaught.

"Sorry," I whispered, "to come back so late. We decided—"

"Shhh! It's nearly four a.m.! Get in here!" he whispered harshly,
and hauled me inside. I had fortunately already unrolled my sleeping bag before I left to hang out with some D.C. friends from the
old *Rocks & Minerals* days, so I was able to feel my way into it in
the darkness. I'd overdone the booze a bit in an effort to burn off
the stresses of my initial few days of typo hunting. Benjamin and
his girlfriend, Jenny, had the heat cranked up in her tiny efficiency,

and I felt glad but confused. My watch had 2:40 a.m. Pretty late to return from an outing, but still not quite 4:00 a.m. Then I recalled today's date, and tetrominoes in my addled brain snicked together as I glanced at the glowing red numbers next to Jenny's bed: 3:40. No wonder Benjamin had been about ready to *spring forward* for my throat.

I heard the thump of my head falling back against the sleeping-bag pillow, and then it was time to get up already, Benjamin informing me that I'd slept plenty. Through bleary eyes I gazed up at my new sidekick. This time he was fully dressed, sporting one of his trademark rock-band T-shirts. An old, battered Dartmouth hat perched on his head. Pretty much as I remembered him from our days as roommates. He bobbed up and down, impatient for action.

Today the proverbial rubber would meet the road. I'd have no more excuses for tepid typo-snaring. After departing from Boston, I'd meekly hunted alone in New York and Jersey. Only in Philadelphia did I have company, a college friend who also kindly hosted me. So far, the results had not been promising. Often I couldn't summon the nerve to approach proprietors about the errors in their midst, and stealth corrections had occasionally proved more difficult than I'd expected. Would I be emboldened by the presence of Benjamin, my comrade on late-night walks and adventures of varying significance in years past? Benjamin suggested that we begin with a late breakfast in Rockville, where we used to share an apartment, giving me hope that familiar surroundings would also help to smoothen our road.

"The Silver Diner's in the same shopping plaza as another Filene's Basement," he said. "Jenny and I were thinking that those signs you found in Boston might have been sent from corporate. If we find the same signs in this one, we'll know." I started to sit up. "I mean, it'd be a cool mystery to solve, assuming you're still doing this typo thing or whatever today." My elbow on the sleeping bag slipped out from under me. "Do you need another hour to sleep?"

"No! No . . ." I struggled to pull myself up and get moving. I had to write the blog entry that I hadn't gotten to last night. That might distract me from the profound unease that Benjamin's words had provoked. Had he implied there might be *days off* on this quest? Or, worse yet, did he not understand that this "typo thing" of mine served as the foundation for the whole quest? I might stay in the same place two nights in a row and thus take a day off from driving, but never would there be justification for forsaking, even for a single day, the primary, sacred duty undergirding my entire journey. Had I somehow left this unclear to Benjamin? I needed to know now, but I feared the answer.

Last night's typo yield had been meager. Storms had harried me all the way from Philly, making for a stressful drive, so I'd let my desire to kick back for an evening trump the typo hunting. Dining with my friends, I'd found three different spellings of *raspberry* (none of them correct) on the same menu, but nothing beyond that. What if Benjamin had fully understood the mission but, upon observing how casually I went about it, figured the terms were somehow negotiable? As I worked on the blog, my thoughts drifted back to when I'd first invited him along. I'd never explicitly said he'd be typo hunting with me every day, had I? I should have set the tone immediately yesterday when I came out of my car to meet him, should have shouted something like "Prepare yourself for transpositions!"

By the time the three of us made it to breakfast at the retro-style diner on Rockville Pike, they were serving lunch, but the wait promised to be short. "How many?" the host queried.

"Three," Benjamin answered.

Three people walked in right behind us, and the man asked, "Are they with you, too?"

"No, we're only *this* three."

Benjamin's plan had been to get a good meal in and then typo-hunt; however, my typo-sensitivity has no off-switch. Ahh, the chalkboard, its transience inviting typos to breed like larvae in old provisions. Sure enough, their dessert special left something to be desired, namely the second d in *pudding*. Glorious! I'd found one

already, and I could demonstrate to
Benjamin both how serious I was about
my mission and how easily—

"Dude, I got one!" Benjamin whispered in my ear.

While I'd drifted over to my target,
Benjamin had carefully examined the
very first piece of text he'd encountered, a sign I'd walked past on
my way to the chalkboard. No longer would I need to show him how
distressingly common these reeking flotsam were in the tidal flats of
our language: he'd just reeled in his first error.

Adding to the serendipity of our simultaneous find, Benjamin's
first collar turned out to be a double offender. The announcement
listed the rotating events of a weekly local program for kids. We
saw that the first event night of each month had its own problem.
First they'd have "a Coloring Contests" and later they'd be "making
Rocket Ship." They'd put the article in for the plural and left it out
for the singular! (The sign also evinced a consistent disdain for commas, but hey, let's not be *picky*, right?)

I grabbed photographic proof for the blog as the line moved forward. We had to make this correction thing happen in a jiff. There
wasn't a lot of extra room, and surely our ministrations would call
attention to ourselves if we gummed up the queue. I lent Benjamin
a black pen and a draught of elixir. "We're surrounded by typos," he
whispered to Jenny as the line moved again.

Guessing that each child would be getting his or her own Rocket
Ship to take home, Benjamin didn't hesitate to add in the *s* to elimi-
nate the second error, but the potential coloring contest configu-
rations made the resolution of the other more questionable. Sure,
they might have a single contest, but kids who wanted to color could
easily color through pages upon pages. There could very well be a
second contest, and a third, later in the evening. Or maybe they had
separate contest categories: most creative, best use of color, most
realistic, most surrealistic, best evocation of the Old Masters. He

could be overthinking it, but only one version could be true; they could have either "a Coloring Contest" *or* "Coloring Contests." And, as is writ in the Book of the League, what profits a man if he gain a typo correction but lose the true meaning of the words? This was an object lesson in how typos foster chaos and confusion. He'd need to know more to complete his first correction, but how?

Meanwhile, I asked the host if I could add an extra *d* to the chalkboard. Before he could rebuff me, I produced my little cylindrical trump with a flourish. "I have a piece of chalk right here." A pair of teenage girls, waiting in front of us, burst into hysterical giggling. While field orthography is a serious matter, I can understand their reaction. *Quelle coincidence,* a man spotting an error and happening to have on him the proper instrument for its destruction. The host allowed me to proceed as the tittering teenagers were shown

to their table, peeking back over their shoulders. As I inserted the *d,* I realized how smoothly and unconsciously I had spoken up to the host, my former hesitations and inhibitions all but forgotten. Just having a friend *nearby* had helped me find my voice.

"What should I do about the first one?" Benjamin asked us.

"Three?" said the host. Three typos, yes, but also the size of our party. I'd completed my chalk-work none too soon.

Like a mongrel latching onto ankles, Benjamin had taken various pursuits between his teeth over the years: religion, politics, slam poetry. I watched carefully to see if he'd show the same tenacity in typo affairs, considering all those other causes already lodged in his bicuspids. How many legs could conceivably fit into one mouth? As I pondered this, Benjamin queried the young man escorting us to our table about the notice out front, with uncharacteristic subtlety. "I saw that you have a Kids' Night here. One night they have a coloring contest? Or is it a series of contests, like for most original, most realistic . . ."

While gesturing us into our booth and handing out menus, the man replied that, to his knowledge, the night in question revolved around a single coloring contest. Benjamin and Jenny huddled together in a conspiratorial manner. I wondered if he'd really attempt this daring super-spy stealth correction or if, perhaps, the novelty of his first typo correction would fade at the sight of a stack of pancakes. I still hadn't fully decided on my rules of engagement: when to ask permission, and so forth. I seemed to be leaning toward stealth corrections in minor cases when it didn't seem worth troubling anyone, or there was no one around to trouble. I never really set specific guidelines for myself. And I might have already broken a minor rule; I'd made a correction at an eatery before I'd been served my food. I didn't think I had to worry about the diner staff concealing sputum in my meal, though—nobody had taken offense at my *pudding* correction.

Benjamin chuckled and pointed at our server's name tag. Now that I'd gotten him to look out for typos, my former roommate had become hyper-aware of all written words to cross his path. Thus, being served by a man named Victor Hugo was the height of hilarity. In the spirit of our friend's namesake, I decided to go with the caramel French toast.

Before our drinks arrived, the man who'd seated us returned. He'd taken Benjamin's inquiry at face value, thinking he must have a son or cousin or some other eligible urchin in his life, so he now dropped off some literature on the weekly Kids' Night. Or Kid's Night. Kids Night? Uh-oh. What a magnet for error my companion had turned out to be! So soon after Benjamin had spotted one typo, he'd now been *handed* another. Every possible rendition of Kids' had been attempted somewhere on the flyer. Due to someone's lack of, shall we say, *apostrophic confidence*, they'd decided to try putting the apostrophe before the *s* here, and after the *s* there, and over in that corner we can try it without one. I.e., the kind of approach to punctuation one might expect from that notable pair of flip-flops back home, John Kerry and Mitt Romney.

We weren't sure, though, which rendition we ourselves would

vote for. The more we talked it over, the muddier the question became. They offered a Kid's Party Package: a single package deal for a singular kid's birthday party. Or should it be Kids' Party because there would be plural kids attending? Then again, it could be Kid's Party, using the archetypal Kid to stand for all kids. Like Mother's Day, which referred not to a day for all mothers (Mothers' Day) but the day that *you*, Vic Hugo, had best scrounge up a carnation or two for your *own* mother.

We can argue over the logic, but the U.S. lacks an overarching authority or consensus on generic possessives.* So the Mother's Day argument makes sense in isolation, but the government yanked the apostrophe out of Veterans Day. Let's not get started with Presidents' Day . . . Presidents Day? President's Day?

I have a confession to make. I don't care whether you go with Kid's or Kids', Presidents or President's. There isn't some apostrophe god reclining upon an ancient, pitted throne, clutching one single answer to the conundrum. What's more essential is that you make a decision and *stick with it*. Consistency is the key, and unfortunately also the area in which so much signage fails. Some days later, in Charleston, we'd see a store announcing "Phillip's Shoes" on its awning, while "Phillips Shoes" adorned the building itself. You can't even make up your mind about the name of your store? Isn't that kind of an important decision? The Filene's Basement problems we'd be investigating further after brunch were another telling example of apostrophe confusion. "Mens' boxed ties" was an easy one to make, arising from someone knowing a basic grammatical

---

* Maybe that's for the best. In 1890, President Benjamin Harrison formed the U.S. Board on Geographic Names, to regulate the names for the astonishing number of cities, towns, and natural features that America had come to encompass. They decided that the less punctuation, the better, particularly in place names containing a possessive. So they went and blasted the apostrophe out of Pike's Peak, making it Pikes Peak, and so on. The policy remains to this day, with only a few exceptions being granted by federal largesse (and, here and there, rebellious communities such as the Fells Point neighborhood in Baltimore—its residents insist on *Fell's*).

rule (plural apostrophes go after the *s*) that happened to be broken in this particular case (since *men* is already a plural noun, there's no need to distinguish between the singular and plural. It's *man's* and *men's*). But then another sign had decided to skip the apostrophe altogether, resulting in the MENS department.

Your teachers were right about the apostrophe always standing in for a missing letter or letters. A millennium ago, instead of using an apostrophe and an *s* for possessives, English used a genitive case that added the suffix *–es* to the possessing noun (e.g., Benjamines beard, kides night). Within a couple hundred years, that practice fell into disfavor as English became the preserve of the lower classes, after English-speakers got stomped on by French-speaking Normans from across the narrow sea. But we'll hold off on the edu-tastic voyage through history. Suffice it to say that in the case of possessives, the apostrophe stands for that lost *e,* from a grammatical convention that no longer exists.

Further maligning the logic of apostrophes is the fact that the possessive nouns often *sound* the same as the plural noun. Spoken language came on the scene long, long before the written symbols that corresponded to it; the oral form of language often guides the written. In the case of possessive apostrophes and plurals, in so many cases verbally indistinguishable, the written distinction becomes increasingly confused for a growing segment of the population.

We enjoyed an incredibly good meal, I treated, and we departed, but not before Benjamin made one last change. Thanks to his inquiry, we now knew that a single coloring contest took place. I handed him the elixir and got my camera ready, and we rolled out according to plan, Benjamin leading our procession and pausing, as Jenny and I passed slowly between him and any probing eyes. He struck with a quick splash of the elixir and took Jenny's arm, leaving me to flash a picture and scurry out the double doors after them.

We triumphant three strode out into the parking lot, cool as cantaloupes. My first successful venture with my new typo-hunting ally Benjamin. I felt suave and in control, action-movie cool, except that I couldn't figure out how to walk in slow motion.

Filene's Basement awaited across the parking lot, and there all my illusions of urbanity shattered. We seemed underdressed for the store. Our T-shirts and jeans stood out against the garb of customers and employees alike. The man who approached us noticed it, judging by the downward turn of his mouth, but Benjamin snapped, "Your boxed ties, please?" I realized the object of my objection occurred in a word that, bad punctuation aside, was also completely unnecessary. It's not as if there were a separate station for *women's* boxed ties.

The well-dressed employee escorted us down an aisle to a fixture that looked familiar. Benjamin gave our thanks with a sharp nod, letting the man know that his assistance was no longer required. Benjamin's whole manner seemed to suggest that he was often, in fact, *over*dressed for such a store, but that this was merely his Sunday off and no one had better question it. For the first time it occurred to me what an asset it was to have a retail employee on my side. He'd seen all the customer types often enough that he could mask himself with any attitude to match the moment, and so much of the typo-finding realm would overlap with his familiar turf. Benjamin was striding into the echoing ivory halls of typo-hunting with gusto. I took it as a promising omen for this leg of the trip.

"*Précisement,*" Jenny declared, channeling Hercule Poirot as she gestured toward the offending sign. She and Benjamin cuddled together, delighted at how they'd sleuthed the cause of one of my earliest finds. Not merely the same error, but the same sign. These errors had been run off en masse. I twisted around to check for another problem, sighted it, and this time snapped better photos of what I'd failed to adequately record a few hundred miles north. MENS' BOXED TIES. And above us, MENS CONTEMPORARY.

Adding to my sense of déjà vu, Benjamin said, "Since *men* is already plural, the *s* can only declare that it's possessive; therefore an apostrophe is strikingly absent."

Declare? Therefore? Strikingly? I wondered how much longer he'd be wearing his snootier-than-thou persona, as much as I'd appreciated it. "See, dude," he said, and I sighed with relief that I wouldn't

have to poke him in the coconut after all, "there's no use trying to correct this apostrophe here, and it wouldn't have helped to confront anyone in Boston either."

I stood shocked. They had casually removed the dark stain of cowardice from my first day's hunt and washed it clean so that, in hindsight, my deeds shone pure, giving off an aura of *discretion*. Jenny drove the point home: "We'd have to call their corporate office. See, the employees could even get in trouble for taking signs down or fixing a mistake if their district manager failed to understand. Their merch people are supposed to put up the signs they're told to, no questions asked."

Though Benjamin and I resolved to call the Filene's Basement corporate headquarters at the close of the trip, we never got the chance to do so, thanks to the interference of certain dire events. As it turns out, our efforts would not have been that productive in the long run anyway—as of this writing, the chain has been sold to a liquidator and has filed for bankruptcy, another victim of hard economic times. What was truly important about that day's adventures was that I had gained a valuable ally in the fight for better spelling and grammar.

TYPO TRIP TALLY

Total found: 16
Total corrected: 9

5 | Maladies

March 11-12. 2008 (Kill Devil Hills, NC, to Myrtle Beach, SC)

In which our Heroes suffer numerous Trials against their spirits, plans, and digestive abilities in their inexorable Quest across desolate beaches, cold woodlands, and ferryless harbors.

Another burst of cold wind blew across the beach in Kill Devil Hills, North Carolina. I recognized that the sand wasn't flying in our eyes, but that was about the sum of our blessings. The afternoon had yielded a fairly lousy hunt—not from hesitancy on our part, but because we didn't know where to go. As Benjamin tromped over to a far sign, the sole bit of text on the beach, I examined the magazine I'd picked up at the only place open for business this early in the season. The cover promised suggestions for outdoor "activites". Benjamin returned shaking his head. "Some notice about which parts of the beach are unsafe for swimming due to sewage." Disturbing, but grammatically clean.

Our nose for fertile typo ground was proving to be stuffy indeed. We had entertained thoughts of a thriving boardwalk along the beach. Instead we found ourselves plodding along frigid white sands, gazing in both directions down an empty shore.

Benjamin pointed out that we'd found a couple of fascinating historical typos earlier that day at the Wright Brothers National Memorial. The fathers of modern aviation had tried their hand at a newspaper, and one front page showed why their talents lay skyward instead—they'd spelled the name of their own paper wrong!

Another exhibit specifically called attention to a typo. A telegram about their initial flight success had misreported the duration as a mere fifty-seven seconds rather than the full fifty-nine (not to mention calling Orville "Orevelle"). While Benjamin found this intriguing, to me it meant the League had arrived a hundred years too late on the scene of a devastating offense.

"Sorry, man," I said. "I suck."

"It can't be helped. Nothing's open," he said as we wandered by the gray waters of the Atlantic.

Yet the typos were out there, somewhere. The town slumbered in seeming peace, but knowing what I knew, I could find no such respite. I had chosen to come here on the hunt, and I had gotten it wrong. A mere three typos had been found, and none corrected. Benjamin, a numbers guy at base, would be crushed once he realized we'd dropped under the fifty percent mark of mistakes corrected versus found. We headed to a campground, where a new problem would elicit his regret with mightier force.

It was a decent enough clearing in the woods, but it appeared deserted. We selected one of the little sites facing a pond, and then found no one to take our payment at the office, which stood as abandoned as the rest of the grounds. During the off-season, campers were on the honor system to drop an envelope with the proper amount into a slot. We didn't have cash, but we had to go grab some hot dogs to make over a fire anyway, so we could hit an ATM while we were out. First, though, Benjamin wanted to set the tent up. He was excited about the tent. He'd nabbed it for half off a price that he already considered low (and rejoiced when I went in for half of that). As he leaned into the trunk, where he'd stuffed the tent that very morning at his parents' house in Virginia Beach, he discoursed at length on all its marvelous features, such as how quick and easy it was to erect, and how well it held up against an insane wind during a trial setup. This last bit cheered me, since the wind here still kicked up an occasional rough gust. The dying sun spilled fantastic colors into the sky and the pond. I stood smiling in its glow until I realized that Benjamin was caroming between the tent he'd unrolled and the trunk.

"Something wrong?"

He didn't answer, muttering to himself as he shook the empty tent bag like Heracles throttling the Cretan Bull, but with a more distracted air. I looked over at the unrolled tent, which waited to be unfolded, hoisted onto poles, and staked into the—wait a minute. Where were the tent poles?

"I can't believe this. I can't believe it!" Benjamin shouted. He turned to me. His voice became perfectly calm, though the wildness of his eyes betrayed the tempest within. "This simply cannot be. I'm not the kind of person who *does* this. This is a rookie mistake. How could I have . . ."

He'd left the tent poles wrapped up in the tent's protective outer coat, the rain fly, back at his parents' house. The wind had turned so furious the day he'd done the test setup that he couldn't roll the fly up with the tent without the thing blowing away, so he'd spun the fly around the poles and then rolled up the heavier tent. He'd stashed the two bundles side by side in his closet, but the pole/fly bundle fell back into the dark recesses, and Benjamin had forgotten all about it this morning when he'd reached in and grabbed the tent.

I recognized in his apologies a note of my own glistening self-flagellation from the beach and resolved that tomorrow, by the light of a new day, we'd learn from our mistakes and charge forward, not allowing a defeatist attitude to get in our way. I did wonder, though, as I stared up at the moon that had risen during the search for the poles, where we would be lodging here in rural North Carolina with no notice. Then I remembered that my GPS had uses beyond simple navigation. I had it search for nearby hotels as we came back out onto the main road, now in full darkness. Six or seven places came up.

"Which of these sounds cheap to you?" I said.

"Uh." Benjamin scrolled through the list. "Probably anything with 'Econo' in its name."

The bolder future that I'd envisioned came true, in perverse fashion, the next morning after we set off from the Williamston Econo Lodge. We'd checked off lessons learned, with nary a glance at our mistakes in the rearview, but then everything else began to fall apart. Callie's troubles began that morning with a faint protest that would get worse over the coming days. I'd realized before I even began the trip, when I'd taken her to the shop for a full inspection and a mani/pedi, that I'd be putting some serious miles on her and that she was entering her elder years by automotive reckoning. Even so, Callie's grumbling took a backseat to the rebellion of another modern technological wonder.

During the first days of this journey, probably somewhere in New Jersey, as I listened to the tinny female voice squawking orders from my dash, I'd decided that my GPS needed a name, and that the only proper name would be Authority. I was being somewhat ironic at the time, but as the days went on, I slipped into placing more and more trust in the inerrancy of her dicta. O folly! How soon I forgot the motto of my parents' generation: *Question Authority*. Thus, Authority caught me off guard when she announced that the trip from Williamston to Beaufort would be nearly an hour shorter than the Google Maps route I'd looked at before nodding off to bed. Benjamin, too, thought the eastward heading strange. We looked ahead in the GPS route and saw that Authority had steered us toward a ferry. Oh, all right, so that solved it. Except that the ferry, like everything else along the North Carolina coast, wasn't running in early March. Our road ended at a chain blocking access to the dock, with a sign that said CLOSED FOR SEASON.

Benjamin shut Authority off and yanked my road atlas from the pile of stuff suffocating the backseats. "A chance to redeem myself," he announced, taking over the navigational duties. The trip to Beaufort would take an additional hour, thanks to the necessary backtracking.

We could at least take comfort in the fact that each of our trials carried with it a crucial lesson. For example, very few typos exist on beaches. And: Tents need something to hold them up. And above all, I now knew not to place blind trust in Authority again; I would always compare her routes against the maps. Though she'd mislead us a little here and there, never again would she send us so far astray. We paused for lunch along the way, making a shopping trip for supplies and eating peanut butter sandwiches in a grocery parking lot before heading onward. Beaufort was a little coastal town with a big heart and an exceptional Maritime Museum, wherein Benjamin scraped an errant apostrophe off the wall with his thumbnail.

Another spartan day for finds, but at least this time we went three for three, knocking us back over the fifty-percent correction mark. In retrospect, that day was also notable for our first run-in with an enemy whose name is Legion: CARS WILL BE TOWED AT OWNERS EXPENSE.

As I wrote my day's blog entry, I reflected on my continuing struggle to find the places in most dire need of our typo-hunting services. I needed more text-rich locales than I'd been able to find yet. Still, at least Benjamin was on board with my mission, we'd be picking up the tent poles tomorrow, and we could once again claim to have corrected a (slim) majority of our discovered nemeses. We went out to dinner thinking our troubles had mostly concluded, powerless to resist the grotesque "thickburgers" that Hardee's had been bombarding us with through highway advertisements for some time now. Alas, the worst was yet to be digested. For Benjamin, it turned out to be utterly indigestible. By morning he lay prone across his bed and skipped our second Econo Lodge's continental breakfast. He retched to try to force the fast food out of his tract, but to no avail.

I realized then that my poor friend wasn't used to consuming the mounds of terribly unhealthy food that an epic road trip requires. The Hardee's tera-burger had been his grim initiation into the lifestyle. This seemed the culmination of our woes of the last few days, as if an accumulated sludgeball of ill luck were what was actually troubling Benjamin's guts. If we could propel it from his system, I thought, we'd see an immediate change in our fortunes.

On the harrowing drive to Myrtle Beach, I thrice feared for Callie's interior, but the burger remained lodged in place. Each Hardee's billboard we passed made Benjamin's nausea swell, and there were many, but when we cranked up the latest album by his favorite jeans-clad bard, Springsteen, some eldritch Magic helped quell his troubled stomach's pains. We managed to arrive without the forcible ejection of any internal organs.

Once inside the city limits, we drove past lurid signs promising simulacra of whatever one desired. Dinosaur putt-putt! Medieval banquets (serfs and wenches included)! A rock-and-roll theme park! I hadn't visited this particular honky-tonk since my dad led a family expedition here many years ago. Time had not moved on here; apparently the place was still catering to my prepubescent self. Our first stop in Myrtle Beach was the FedEx office, where missing tent parts had arrived ahead of us. We put them to use right away at a KOA campsite in a modest wood not far from the beach. After Benjamin and I erected the tent, which proved at least as easy as he'd told me two nights prior, he crawled inside it to die. It was late afternoon at that point. I had to get the day's typo hunting done soon, and it looked like I'd be doing my rounds without a companion. I told him I'd be back in a little while. The pedestrian exit led me past a fundamentalist church and into the touristy main commercial district, separated from the beach by a bulwark of outsized chain hotels.

On my own again so soon! How vital was a partner in correction—how forlorn felt I without one. Benjamin's absence hobbled the League's gait. I visited a couple of souvenir and T-shirt shops and made rote fixes to a few typos here and there, but my orthographic heart was listless. Then I came upon the biggest typo I'd seen to date, on a giant marquee outside the "Pacific Superstore."

Suddenly vigor crested over me. I had to show Benjamin that I could do this alone. I strode into the store. The place was a cavernous repository of beach gear and trinkets, perhaps imported wholly from the other coast, as the name of the store implied. I saw one shopper present. I hung around for a moment until a short lady approached me. "Can I help you?"

"Hi there," I said. I gave her the heartiest grin that I could manufacture. Which may not have been all that convincing, I admit; I've always been a more adept scowler. I knew I'd have to work on my salesmanship, though, in this and future typo-related endeavors. "I noticed that your sign out there in front has two *t*s in SWEATTS, and I was wondering if there was a reason for it."

She gave me a puzzled look and accompanied me outside, where she looked up at the sign. She was unmoved. "Oh yes, but I thought that *sweatshirts* did have two *t*s when shortened . . ."

"Well," I stammered, "no. I actually have a strange request for you—can you take one of the *t*s out? I'd really appreciate it. You see, I—"

"I'm sorry, you'll have to ask the manager," said the lady, indicating a long-haired guy perched on a ladder while talking on a cell phone and making adjustments to surfboards on display along the wall.

"Hello," I said to the manager when he came over. I gained some more momentum, sensing that this was an essential trial of my mission. Its outcome would predict the success or failure of the many confrontations to come. "I couldn't help but notice that your sign out front has two *t*s in SWEATTS. Could I ask you to, uh, fix it?"

"Does it?" he said. Now it was our turn to promenade in front of the Superstore. He headed for the door. "Who would have done that?"

Certainly I had a suspect in mind, but since TEAL's mission focused on amending the error and not on finger-wagging, I shrugged, following behind him. "I'm actually traveling around the country correcting typos, and it'd be great if you could fix this one. Would you be able to do that?"

Strangely, my story did not faze him in the slightest. The guy was but the first of many supervisors, middle managers, and wage slaves who would take the tale of the League at face value with no visible reaction. Probably half of them didn't believe me, or didn't care.

"No, they don't care," Benjamin would explain some few hundred miles down the road when the topic of responses came up during our westward journey. "When you're a service manager, things break into two categories: typical and atypical." I had become atypical, and atypical was bad.

The manager peered up at the sign, squinting in the sun. "Yes, that's not right. Don't worry, I will make sure that it's fixed." Evidently he thought this would be enough of a response, as he started for the door.

"Oh, I'm sorry," I pressed, "but could you fix it now so I can take a picture of it? I'd really appreciate it. I'm keeping a blog, and I can write this in."

He hesitated, then glanced back into the echoing interior of the store, still nearly devoid of customers. "All right, I will do this for you, but you must hold the ladder."

I nodded, sensing a solemnity to the moment. "Sure."

He returned with a ladder a moment later. For some reason it was a different ladder from the one he'd been using to adjust the surfboards. Perhaps it was reserved for handling requests from meddling passersby. He set it up beneath the sign, and I held the legs while he climbed up. Keep it steady, I thought, wouldn't want to have this crucial encounter end in a sprained ankle. As I stared up at a rear end in board shorts, I realized the greater import behind my ostensibly simple duty. To come to this juncture, to hold that ladder, was why I had dreamed up the Typo Eradication Advancement League in the first place—so that I could aid in endeavors such as these, pointing the way for the managers of the nation to correct problems in their own territories. With my hands firmly grasping the ladder of attentiveness and care, who knew how high my countrymen could ascend? Perhaps to the very heavens of perfect spelling and grammar, where seraphim cry hosannas to the correctly deployed apostrophe and cherubim strike down subject-verb disagreements with their burning blades!

Above me, the manager popped a T out, then moved the rest of the letters closer together. "There, do you feel better?"

"Sure do," I said, taking the question at face value. "I can count this as a success story."

"Just don't include me in the picture, eh?"

I stood marveling at the small but visible improvement in the world that my ladder-holding had brought about. I won't say that it was a *rush*, because we're not talking about Xtreme snowboarding here, just a small and early step on the brambled road to righteousness. But I did feel a palpable lifting of the spirit, a realization that the landscape around me was more malleable than it seemed. All I had to do was ask. Though, as this episode had demonstrated, sometimes asking more than once would be necessary. Persistence was my most potent weapon against the black hordes of error. For the first time in my life I could see the panoply of possibilities opened up by merely engaging people. Imagine what else could be accomplished!

I returned to the campsite to share the happy news with my TEAL colleague. My tale of success lent him needed vitality. He struggled into a sitting position. "Let's go for a walk," he wheezed.

"Are you . . . sure that's a good idea?"

Benjamin grinned bravely. "Here's the thing, Deck. I need to puke, but I can't physically get it out. So let's walk, and that'll agitate my insides, and eventually—"

"Okay, I get it," I said. "You need a hand up?"

He waved his hand dismissively and heaved himself upward on shaking arms. He took a couple of tottering steps over to Callie and grabbed a water bottle from the backseat. Then we made our ponderous way out of the KOA camp and into the commercial district. Benjamin still grimaced like a hurting cowboy, but he persevered, taking liberal swigs from his water, which, he explained, was another facet of his vomit-inducing strategy.

We walked between two giant hotels and onto the cool sand of the beach. The sun sank into a brilliant slumber over the ocean. Mere days ago we'd hung our heads on another beach, one state north, but our mission itself had made progress far beyond geographic measure. I knew now that I could muster the courage to handle whatever orthographic challenge came my way. Perhaps all our recent tribulations had served to lead us to this consecrated moment. I turned to comment on the splendor of the sunset, and saw Benjamin jumping up and down on the sand. Between jumps, he gulped down more water. Something would shift in his internal tracts soon enough. The League, purged of its ill humours, could then commence its true work.

TYPO TRIP TALLY

Total found: 25
Total corrected: 14

6 | Beneath the Surface

March 15-16. 2008 (Atlanta, GA)

Wherein our oblivious yet infinitely amiable Heroes invite
contests for which they are ill-equipped, and an unforeseen
conversation riddled with deep and ominous subtext precedes
a mental maelstrom & literal hailstorm. Soaked through with
insight and precipitation, our Chief Arbiter of Grammatical
Justice recognizes that, like sewer-dwelling, nunchaku-wielding
amphibians, more lurks 'neath the roads our Heroes tread.

In 1861, Georgia and six other slaveholding states seceded from
the Union, protesting the election of Abraham Lincoln, that infernal
Northerner who plotted against the expansion of their chattel-based
business. Georgia, the railroad hub of the South, ferried supplies
to all corners of the newly hatched Confederacy, until the Union
shelled the heart of Atlanta. When the war ended, Atlantans rebuilt
their city center, creating a vibrant business district around their
new train station. Over the next hundred years the city grew over
that district, with bridges and viaducts turning the former street
level into subterranea. In 1968 the funeral procession of Dr. Mar-
tin Luther King Jr. clattered directly overhead; the following year,
the "city beneath the city" was reopened as Underground Atlanta, a
retail and entertainment destination. Its charming old architecture
helped the district to flourish as the Bourbon Street of Atlanta, but
eventually subway construction and crime shut down Underground
Atlanta. The cookfires of vagrants ravaged the old historical sites. In

1989 a revamped, mall-like Underground Atlanta reopened. Three years later, following the acquittal of the L.A. policemen who had beaten Rodney King, rioters smashed up the place. In 1996, Underground Atlanta opened its doors for a *third* time, now in time for the Atlanta Olympics. In 2008 two white boys wandered into Underground Atlanta, looking for typos.

We gazed down the little thoroughfare. Having come from the MARTA, Atlanta's mass transit, I felt that, strangely, we'd reentered the station we'd just left. With the pipes running along the ceiling, this place looked more like the subway than the subway did. A row of clothing stores, interspersed with dollar stores, ran along the wall, and the walkway was broken up with mid-mall kiosks peddling hats, sports jerseys, and your instant photo plastered on mugs or shirts. Light filtered through windows that ran below the ceiling. Perhaps owing to the threatening clouds outside, the lighting in here felt gloomy. Consumers moved along in no hurry, giving the impression that no one came here to find what they needed, but because there wasn't anywhere to *be*. Whatever its past glory, Underground Atlanta stood before us as testament to capitalism's slipperiest slope, junk for people willing to buy junk because it's there.

A whiteboard affixed to a metal railing contained some spelling issues. I pointed the sign out to Benjamin, who spotted the bright

pink PREGNANCY TEST immediately, but needed a second to see, in yellow block letters outlined with a black marker, the transposed vowels of SOUVINER (it's a tricky word, one we'd see botched again before we reached the Pacific). My Typo Correction Kit, a plastic shopping bag holding the tools of my amending trade, bulged heavy in my coat, though I found myself ill-equipped for our entry into this particular den of errata—I lacked dry-erase markers. Still, I felt the fervor of the mission coursing through my veins. It had carried me through sundry trials thus far, including road-acquired ailments: one of my eyes, at present, was welded half shut thanks to an unknown irritant.

The store that the sign advertised lived yet another level down, as if sent to a sub-subterranean time-out corner. Our soles squeaked down the staircase, bringing us into what turned out to be a dingy purveyor of everything from party favors (balloons and streamers) to random household items (clothespins, kitchen utensils, baby bibs). The clientele seemed mostly Latino and black. A woman reached out at us from an ill-defined enclosure at the front, a greeting that made me take a surprised step backward. She wanted our backpacks.

I replied that actually I'd come down to mention that there was an error on one of the store's dry-erase signs up the stairs.

She stared at me.

I could tell by her sour expression that I'd gotten this typo correction off to a rough start, effectively saying, *I don't trust you to take my bags or my money, much like you can't be trusted to spell, woman!*

"Oh, my cousin did those," she said. We waited like a couple of dolts for her to continue, then realized that she'd said all she had to say.

"Uh, so . . ." Benjamin stumbled. Was the cousin going to fix it? Was it an idiot cousin who always made a mess of whatever she touched? Had that been a buck-passing maneuver so subtle we'd completely missed it?

I decided it was best to ignore the response completely, treat it as a non sequitur, and begin again. "It's just there are a couple of words misspelled."

"Oh, that's okay," she said.

No, it wasn't. I didn't think I would be able to convince her of that, though. Of course, my customary line at this point in the conversation would have normally been that I could fix it no sweat Sally, but without the right kind of tool—a plague upon the permanence of mine markers!—I couldn't do anything without marring the sign. Benjamin looked toward me expectantly. "It'd be an easy fix, and if you've got a dry-erase marker . . ."

"Nope. My cousin did those signs. At home."

The one gap in their bountiful inventory! "Uh, if I came back with a dry-erase marker . . ."

Ha, now she was the one thrown off.

"Right," Benjamin added.

"Right," I said. "So we'll grab a dry-erase marker somewhere, and then we'll come back."

"Oh . . . kay?" she said as we spun toward the red rubber stairs.

Now we sought not only typos but a shop that might sell a dry-erase marker or two. We passed by groaning kiosks of purses and wallets, hats for every occasion (even pay-by-the-letter designer hats—I considered a TEAL hat, but they didn't have them in teal), and assortments of items labeled "gifts" since you wouldn't *need* any of those things yourself. We saw shirts and shoes and women's accessories (no glitter was spared) and art and more clothes, but in spite of the wide, wild assortment of everything you never knew you desired, we couldn't find the one thing we wanted to buy.

We halted at a mid-mall clothing stand that featured dozens of locally designed Barack Obama T-shirts. We might not have noticed the mistake therein had it not been for our unwavering support of Obama, who was currently squaring off against Senator Clinton in a drawn-out Democratic presidential primary. As we perused the homemade wares, a typo on one shirt knocked us out of shopping mode and back into typo-correction territory.

Speaking of territory. Typo correcting can be awkward enough, but this one offered an altogether new brand of discomfort. I read

He's Black
And Im
Proud

Barack Obama

it aloud: "He's black, and Im proud." We looked at each other, and then took another look at our surroundings. Not that we'd been oblivious of the absolute lack of other white people until this moment; it simply hadn't been a relevant factor in the equation until now.

I could see the question on Benjamin's face. Were we two white kids going to approach this nice black lady and criticize, in even a small way, this shirt that advocated pride in the most significant black public figure in decades?

Yes. We were. The whole point of typo correcting is that it's a subcategory of a larger goal to improve communication. Could we back down from typo correcting when the perceived communication obstacles grew too large? We couldn't, and we wouldn't—the ideals of the League demanded that we summon our courage. This typo of all typos, here in the epicenter of a hundred and fifty years' worth of racial clashes and tragedies, demanded redress. If we'd acted differently than usual, then that would have been, perhaps, racist. Our hesitation highlighted a crucial characteristic of racial tension within our generation: blacks and whites may not fear *each other* the way they once did, back when slavers owned Atlanta or bigots felled Dr. King, or even as recently as the Rodney King riots, but we do fear the awkwardness of failed communication attempts. The progress made by our parents' generation gave us necessary social proscriptions against racism. But now we have the tendency to self-censor, to be overly delicate with the words we're using. The irony here is that the fear of saying the wrong thing has focused us too much on *how* and not enough on *what* we're saying. Speaking correctly has become more important than the substance of communication between blacks and whites specifically, and among all races in general. Even as I pen this, I find myself wondering if I should go with *African-American* instead of *black*. Uh, "communication between African-Americans and whites"? No wonder racial progress is in low gear.

We approached the short, trim woman with graying hair who was attending the stand. She greeted us and asked if we were interested in anything, so I fell back on the reliable, more familiar awkwardness of explaining that I wasn't shopping so much as typo correcting. "The Obama shirts caught my attention, as we're both big Obama supporters. I noticed something about one I wanted to show you." She left her seat and followed me around the stand. "See, we're going around the country fixing typos, and . . ."

I pointed out the shirt and the missing apostrophe.

"You . . . probably don't want us adding it in with a marker," Benjamin said.

"No, that'd be a bit much," she agreed, pointing out a whole stack of them. With that many, I'd be afraid of making too big a marker blotch and ruining more than a few shirts. "But, now that I know about it, we can correct it on the next run."

For the most part, I'd wanted photographic proof of every typo corrected in order to count it as a correction, but since she'd come up with the solution and seemed thankful that we had mentioned the typo to her, I believed her. Benjamin's well-calibrated alarm for detecting liars didn't sound, either. We knew she wasn't telling us this as an effort to repel us from her stall, because she then struck up a conversation.

She told us how glad she was to talk with other Obama supporters and wondered what had drawn us to his campaign. Seeing as we were out of typo turf and into politics, I literally stepped back to give the expert proselytizer Benjamin room to gesticulate. Only then, as I became almost an outside observer of their conversation, did I feel the ponderous weight of subtext. She wasn't asking "fellow supporters" to tell their favorite thing about Obama; she wanted to know how we two white kids had come to vote for a black candidate. I felt the familiar sensation of wanting to reach for my editing pen and make corrections to a rough draft. Red pen to slash through "white kids" and "black candidate" as I scribbled notes in the margins like: "Define your terms. Is *black candidate* any candidate whose skin is dark, or someone like Al Sharpton who only speaks to black voters and issues?" I listened as if from far away as Benjamin explained his preference for pragmatic, bottom-up solutions to political problems. Yet even my TEAL colleague failed to directly address the conversation's thesis statement because he couldn't blurt out, "I honestly don't care that he's black. That's a bonus, I guess, for the future of American race relations, but the bonus isn't the reason." I wanted to cut whole sentences, redact phrases, and generally ask my authors for a more focused revision.

"What about this Reverend Wright thing?"

Benjamin explained that we'd been traveling and hadn't heard about this yet. She gave us the abbreviated version, telling us that Obama's pastor had spewed some anti-American rhetoric on clips that were now all over the news. Benjamin gave a dismissive wave of his hand. "They're going after him for what his preacher says? Oh man, that sounds desperate. I think it's a sign that he's winning."

"You don't think," she asked us, tentatively, "that it'll dissuade . . . *some people* from supporting him?"

Some people. Which people? Us people? White people.

What a treacherous verbal path we walked, black and white alike, and understandably so. Slavery had been abolished from the United States a bare hundred and fifty years ago; segregation, not even *fifty* years ago! In the mammoth scope of human history, this was basically yesterday. The scars were fresh, some of them still oozing. Factors like typos could only infect the wounds. In 2002, for instance, an African-American spokesman for the Congress of Racial Equality appeared on MSNBC. His name was Niger Innis. Picture the worst way you could misspell his first name onscreen. Yeah, that actually happened. Or, in 2008, how about the "Lunch and Learn" event for Black History Month at Des Moines Area Community College, advertised in a widely distributed handbook as a "Linch and Learn".

Both of these errors were, I'm sure, completely unintentional, but they—and the outrage that followed each incident—speak to the dangers of carelessness, and the fragility of the peace forged among diverse quarters of the American population. (Let's not even get into the seething cauldron of issues hinted at by the absentee ballots sent out in November 2008 to Rensselaer County, New York, voters, who had their choice between John McCain and . . . "Barack Osama".)

Anyway, would *some people* be scared away by Reverend Wright's gaffes? Benjamin said no way and then proceeded to explain what he *really* liked about Obama—the man's ability to take even the attacks against him, break them down, and analyze them. "He'll end up responding in some way that turns it to his advantage, because he's a great communicator." There I heard it again, like an insistent tympanum behind the conversation that had steadily gained force and tempo: communication. As he explained his lack of concern, Benjamin essentially predicted Obama's landmark speech on race that would come three days later, but I hardly noticed, caught in a revelation of my own.

What if the typos themselves weren't my real nemesis? Graver communication issues skulked in the shadows and back alleys of our conversations and relationships. What good would fixing spelling do if the message remained distorted? My mind reeled in the grip of these ideas. One typo—the absence of a tiny mark to contract "I am"—had triggered an illuminating conversation that I'd never have had otherwise. There was more to this than the mere hunting of typos. Without being able to express the true extent of my gratitude, I thanked our fellow Obama booster for her promised contribution to orthography, and we took our leave.

I didn't know how to explain my thoughts to Benjamin about communication troubles, my mission, and the dance of subtext I'd witnessed, so I didn't bring them up. Instead we went on through Underground Atlanta, ate some subs, and caught a couple of spelling goofs topside that were encased in thick plastic: "entertainmvent", a typo in the strictest sense of the word, and double-letter confusion with "pavillion". Benjamin noted the phonetic logic of the latter, as double letters usually signal that the vowel preceding them is short.

I wanted to reflect more on the discoveries I'd stumbled onto underground with the Obama correction, but first we had to complete the day's initial objective: to find some dry-erase markers. Unfortunately, as we wandered around the downtown avenues, the clouds carried out their threat and let loose. At first we trudged on through the instant soaking, but as the intensity of falling rain increased and I noted the sky's odd glow, some primal alarm went off in my brain. I saw a bus-stop shelter, shouted to Benjamin, and we dashed in and huddled in the corner with a woman who wouldn't quite reach that baby shower on time. Two gigantic, gift-filled pink bags sat on the bench beside her.

The three of us watched the sky falling. The rain now plunged down not as individual drops but as thick, heavy sheets, slapping the streets with layers of water that overwhelmed the drainage system. Half the street flooded. I was regretting that I'd parked my pollen-covered Callie in a garage, since she could've used a bath, when we heard the first of a series of raps on the shelter that rang out above the sound of the slamming rain. Hail. I changed my mind about my car's current crash pad, glad to have her safeguarded. Soon our ankles were being pelted with chunks of ice that ricocheted off the sidewalk. The shelter took a hard beating, and we watched cars crawling by, the water level halfway up their tires, their windshield wipers swinging like wild swords to fend off the attack of a thousand hailstones.

Apparently a tornado had blown through here yesterday. Atlanta's mayor, we later heard, had asked everyone to stay out of the city today. I'd never imagined that typo hunting could be fraught with such peril.

When finally the storm had spent itself, returning to a hearty rain, we saw our shelter companion safely onto her bus and sloshed

onward. Within minutes we found a CVS where I picked up an assortment of dry-erase markers. With a new appreciation for underground
shopping, we returned, as promised, to the supposed cousin-rendered
sign. Our work couldn't be up to its usual standard. Despite the eras-
ability of whiteboards, the text was meant to be permanent, and the
letters were crammed too closely together to allow a natural insertion
of the second *n* into PREGNACY, so I had to use the proofreader's caret
to do so. Having already marred this sign somewhat, I went ahead and
crossed out the offending letters in SOUVINER and wrote in the correct
ones above, considering after I finished that a quick arrow would have
done the trick. Benjamin and I glared in mutual dissatisfaction at the
sign, but we felt we'd met our daily obligation to humanity.

The next day, my good fortune continued as our Atlanta hosts,
Abby and Eli, brought me to the Emory University Hospital ER
(the one option for medical care on a Sunday) to get my ailing eye
treated. Then, while Benjamin headed off for a necessary haircut, I
strolled down to another drugstore for a transparent makeup bag
that would serve as a container for my ever-burgeoning collection
of typo-correcting tools. My Typo Correction Kit was finally an
actual kit.

Still, one thing nagged at me that morning as Abby loaded us up
with her savory, buttery scones. The whole purpose of this quest,
to rid the world of the scourge of typos, could be viewed in a different way: I was attending to public communication in its written
form, attempting to enhance the clarity of the message. If typos
were a communication issue, I wondered what other barriers existed
among my countrymen that frustrated attempts at open and honest
interchange.

Maybe my mission itself should be broadened to include all forms
of communication troubles. Unfortunately, I didn't know how to do
that. I wasn't even sure what I meant. For the time being, I decided to
make a mental note of how broader communication issues surfaced
during our labors. Benjamin and I said our farewells to our exceed-

ingly gracious hosts and climbed into Callie to continue on our way westward, unaware that the Underground Atlanta episode was only the first that would complicate our seemingly straightforward quest. Like physics in the late twentieth century, my mission had begun to gain extra dimensions.

TYPO TRIP TALLY

Total found: 38
Total corrected: 21

7 | Fear and Retail

Chronicling a tale of two cities' reactions toward our heroes'
fateful Endeavors: It was the best of typos. It was the worst
of typos. From Mobile to New Orleans, the battle betwixt
Automatons and Autonomy blazes.

I awoke to a joyous morning in an Alabama hotel room, finding that
my battered eye had convalesced enough to actually permit vision.
Markers and pens and elixir of correction are important, but oh how
vital to have the most basic of typo-hunting tools, the ones physically yoked to your head, in good working order. Now I could tend
to my most faithful companion, Callie, who had expressed greater
distress with each turn of her engine. Before leaving Montgomery,
we took her in for a new battery, and for part of the wait, Benjamin
and I explored the dark caverns of a nearby mall. A deserted mall, it
turned out, with more space open for rent than for business; they'd
decided to save money by leaving most of the lights off. Surely this
was not what Victor Gruen, architect of the fully enclosed shopping
complex, had envisioned. Our footsteps echoed with eerie clacks.

From my first blunderings around in Boston to more recent
stumbles in Montgomery, I'd discovered that to find more typos, I
needed to find more text. A grocery store in Philadelphia proved as
fertile a breeding ground for typos as is a stagnant pond for mosqui-
toes. Other venues had offered mixed results: restaurants in Maryland and Virginia, museums in North Carolina, tourist traps and

upscale promenades in South Carolina, and of course Underground Atlanta. That's when it occurred to me that the League had failed to scrutinize American capitalism's most sacred territory. Montgomery's ghost mall wasn't the proper place to begin, but I had yet to call any mall to account.

I had great hopes of seeing more significantly historical—and fun—things when we got to Mobile on that St. Paddy's afternoon. My guidebook mentioned the World War II battleship USS *Alabama* and submarine USS *Drum*, as well as other tourism focused around instruments of war. Yet the need to visit a mall lay heavy upon me. Immediately after checking in at our latest Econo Lodge, we struck out for the nearest shopping behemoth. There we viewed a familiar roster, the exact same stores we could find in our own home cities—and anywhere else one happened to roam.

"I hope they have Dippin' Dots," Benjamin said as we entered through Dillards. "I have a hankerin'."

We hadn't trodden far into the mall when we came upon an *autonomous unit for mid-mall snacking,** and though this concession stand held no dots for dippin', we stopped to look over the assorted snacks. There, on a candy cooker, I found a sign that stirred only my hunger for grammatical clarity: CAUTION: DO NOT TOUCH VERY HOT!

---

* *Mallrats* (1995).

What's the sound you make that indicates a period? Or a semicolon? Whereas the rest of written language is supposed to correspond to the oral form directly;* punctuation doesn't seem to fill in for any sound at all. No, it indicates the spaces in between, and that's a relatively new invention, but one that we've stuck with since the mass production of books became possible. Printer Aldus Manutius is credited with creating our modern system of punctuation, though his marks have migrated downward on the line and gotten smaller and subtler (the way the indicator of a pause should be). He created them for the very reason you originally learned to use the comma wherever you'd pause: to give writing speech effects. A period's utility is immediately obvious it marks the completion of each thought think how difficult it would be if we didn't have those to tell us where one ended and the next began that would make reading a much more stressful task. The comma's helpfulness is more understated, but it has the same effect of aiding the reader in breaking a full thought up into pieces, offering us pause-points between each segment.

In this case (CAUTION: DO NOT TOUCH VERY HOT!), any one of several different marks after TOUCH would fill the bill. Traditional grammar might favor a colon: the directive DO NOT TOUCH is followed by a clarification of why touching is not desirable, much as this very clause clarifies why a colon would work in the sign. Given that there's already a colon after CAUTION, though, a dash might be better—to emphasize the very hotness! A period or exclamation point would break the two parts into separate sentences, though VERY HOT doesn't make for much of a sentence, lacking both a subject and verb. Personally, I could find room in my heart for a semicolon, that old benchwarmer of the punctuative ball club, or even a comma. Just to have *something* there, to plug the yawning absence that currently confused the warning. The girl behind the counter—or rather, enclosed within it—had been cavorting with

---

* Granted, a good number of words stray from pure phonetic representation, but we'll get to that in Chapter 13 and beyond.

a young suitor and only took notice of us when we'd remained stationary for a long moment.

"Oh, don't mind us," Benjamin said. "We're crossing the country correcting typos."

She laughed. "All right."

"See, it says 'DO NOT TOUCH VERY HOT!' " I said. "But without a dash or colon or anything, the meaning is confused."

"Like, they don't know what not to touch," said Benjamin.

"They're looking for the Very Hot. And they can't find it."

"They say, 'Yeah, I can't touch the Very Hot, but I can touch everything else.' "

"It's like a 'Don't tease the snake' pet-store sign."

"Right, yeah," said the girl, still laughing, "I see what you're saying."

"So we'll just fix this, then," I said. "We'll draw in the comma. I have a black marker."

Immediately our standing in her view changed from that of jocular pals to troublesome customers. The candy seller's eyes narrowed ever so slightly. "Ha, ha, no, that's okay."

"Seriously, we can just fix it for you," said Benjamin.

"No . . . ," the girl said. "I'd get in trouble with my boss."

I couldn't help but glance at her suitor as she said this. What would she get in trouble for, exactly? "Aww, you can look the other way, right?" I said. Benjamin cracked up at that, having heard the same phrase innumerable times at the bookstore, though in more earnest tones, as someone attempted coupon abuse or truffle-pocketing at the register. I was no natural wheedler, but I pressed on anyway. "We'll make it quick."

She pointed at the ceiling. "The cameras are always watching."

Now nobody was laughing anymore. I gestured at the sign, the barest hint of frustration creeping into my voice. "So you're saying that if we put one little comma in here, to correct this, we will get you in trouble. That is really what you're saying."

That was really what she was saying. Sensing that we could reason no further with her, Benjamin and I left the candy stand to resume our course through the mall. I wondered if the hidden supervisor had been watching us through his ceiling-mounted camera, cackling softly in some darkened control room. "You can talk with your little boyfriend all you like," I could hear him wheezing at his charge, "but even he can't save you if you let them touch my caution sign!"

Though the concession confrontation had disheartened us, our next encounter ripped the cardiac muscle from our chests with even greater force. We strolled into a Hallmark store, and Benjamin blinked, then darted for a sign on the wall. I confess that I'd passed it without noticing anything amiss, but Benjamin has a special mental tuner for errors that slip the bonds of logic and travel into a madder space. NO REFUND OR NO EXCHANGE ON ANY SEASONAL OR SALE ITEM.

As ever, our examination of a sign did not go without someone examining us, in this case a young guy at the store's register. He leaned over the counter. "Can I help you, sir?"

"Hello, yes," I said. "I had a question about your store policy on seasonal or sale items. Do you offer no refunds, or no exchanges?"

"Yes, that's correct," he said. "No refunds and no exchanges."

"Right, but the sign says no refund *or* no exchange," Benjamin pointed out.

"Yes, that's what I said," the young man replied.

"No, there's a difference," said Benjamin. "See, your sign says no refunds, or no exchanges, implying that only one of the two can be true at any given time. If we make a simple change, making the 'or' an 'and,' the sign will forbid both refunds and exchanges on seasonal and sale items."

"I have some Wite-Out and a pen, right here," I said. Before I could suggest, alternatively, eliminating the second "no," I noted another sales clerk moving over from an endcap display she'd been working on. She stepped forward like an actor with no speaking lines who's been told to act intimidating. The universal "you wanna *go*?" gesture, implying a willing readiness for violence as a gambit to prevent it. Benjamin had made the same aggressive forward-step once at work, after a crazy homeless guy had thrown a bag of food past one of his café employees. In character, the woman said nothing. After a moment of cold silence, the young man behind the counter said, "Okay, we will make the change later. Thank you."

"We could do it right—"

"No. Thank you. We will make the change later."

"Now *they* are lying," Benjamin said as soon as we'd reentered the tiled floor of the mall proper. "If they didn't understand the problem, there's no way they would be able to fix it, and they definitely didn't understand what we were saying."

"They didn't want to listen," I replied, wondering about that immediate resistance. Once I turned from the return policy to the subject of the sign itself, a wall had gone up, hindering them from processing anything I said. That clerk's eyes had remained so *blank*.

Benjamin muttered, *"Future Shock."* I could see him jerk perfectly upright, as if inspiration had tugged on his marionette strings. "This is what Alvin Toffler pointed out almost forty years ago." He tried to articulate how we'd witnessed the consequence and conundrum of the Industrial Revolution and the throwaway society. We've got Model-T employees in Eli Whitney's cotton-gin workplace, he explained—interchangeable workers, did I dig?

I dug. The Hallmark clerk had not required an apprenticeship to learn his job; it was largely mechanical. Even an employee who excelled could only do so much good here. Both the employer and the employee saw the relationship as temporary. The employer saw no benefit in the relationship's being permanent, and the employee recognized that and acted accordingly. Employees in a retail setting lacked any vested interest in the company's success or failure; they got paid the same whether the store reached its sales goals or not. Making a decision could only offer repercussions for the wrong choice, and no reward for the right one.

Switching gears before his comments had caught up to each other, Benjamin almost offhandedly added, "I'd never thought about it before, but a typo that everyone walks past and no one ever corrects signifies a much deeper communication breakdown." He started singing Zeppelin to work off his frustrations. I wondered if Benjamin meant that a typo no one noticed signified a breakdown in grammatical awareness or if he'd meant that a typo people *did* notice and didn't comment on suggested that the employees weren't talking to one another. When he attempted a screechy high note, I interrupted. He clarified that he'd meant the latter. "No one cares about their work environment enough to deal with the drudgery of actually talking to each other. What a drag that can be."

I nodded, then backed up to what had bothered me most about that *hallmark* of grammatical obstruction. "So I get that retail sales positions are as replaceable—and disposable?—as the clothing we buy rather than mend, but I'm a customer making a request. Aren't they supposed to listen to *my* feedback?"

"From my own experience, no." He then launched into a jeremiad about handling customer complaints. He would go out of his way to fix the problems most relevant to service. Someone's order hadn't arrived? He'd track it down. Someone ripped the soap dispenser off the wall in the men's restroom . . . *again*? Okay, he'd arrange to get a bottle of soap in there and then survey the damage. But when someone wanted to complain about something that came down from the corporate office, well, Benjamin would have no control over the policy-making of higher-ups. When people brought up *noncontrollables* such as this, he couldn't do much about them, so he'd work to end the conversation quickly rather than attempt to resolve the issue—because he couldn't. And an author coming in with her self-published opus and wanting to do a book signing, or someone wanting to put up flyers for their half-marathon downtown, would fall into an even more unfortunate category: stuff Benjamin doesn't care about that is interfering with his focus on actual customer service. It wasn't his job to help a writer who'd photocopied her self-help ramblings and expected people to pay for them. Nor was it his job to run a community bulletin board, as much as he likes those. His sole purpose at that store boiled down to helping customers obtain their next awesome read, and to make that process as smooth as possible. Anyone coming to him about anything else was in his way.

He stopped to reflect. "The typo hunting is an interesting case, because I would group this in the same category as the bathroom thing. It's a controllable thing that reflects on the store, so while I might not want to hear it, I'd still want to act on it. Also, the Hallmark store had no customers. The other lady was using the time to do a merch display, but we didn't interrupt her. We went for the bored clerk."

Benjamin's observations sang true to my open ears, but I sensed that the melody of the modern retail worker contained still richer timbres. He had described the perspective of an employee making thoughtful decisions that ultimately served the greater welfare of the store, but the Hallmark guy had been acting via instinct, not his gray matter. Why did he respond differently than Benjamin would have?

The journalist Art Kleiner offers one rather dismal answer in his book *Who Really Matters?* The Hallmark clerk struck a deal with his supervisors that effectively sells off his brain for each eight-hour shift behind the register. We tend to automatically bestow the mantle of legitimacy upon the shoulders of our bosses; we do what they want us to do. Eventually, says Kleiner, this transforms into us doing what we *think* they'd want us to do. We create a miniature, mental version of our supervisors, and then consult this imaginary stand-in whenever an issue arises. Frank the real-life boss might have once said in passing, "Could you order me some more blue pens?"; henceforth, the mental Frank will decree, "At this company we use blue pens, so don't you dare use a black one on any official forms!" Thus our decisions are easier, faster. Now you're using blue ink on all your paperwork, even if it doesn't show up very well on corporate's new green forms. Our gift to those above us in the company hierarchy is legitimacy, and their dubious gift to *us* is simplified cognition. Such a trade-off perfectly explains not only the dead-eyed Hallmark guy, but also the girl at the candy counter, who imagined her boss as literally peering down at her from the ceiling, like some adjudicating god.

In an infamous experiment on obedience, the psychologist Stanley Milgram led test subjects to believe they were administering electrical shocks to individuals in another room. The troubling results showed that as long as an official-looking representative stood nearby and nodded for them to continue, a majority of people would administer continually greater shocks, some going all the way to the highest voltage even when the supposed victim had become nonresponsive. Having an authority figure to look toward releases us from *feeling* personally responsible for our decisions and actions. *Not my problem; I just work here.* Milgram also carried out many variations on this experiment. In one, he played with the physical presence of the authority figure, removing him from the room and having him give the subject instructions over the phone. Subjects complied far less readily without the authority figure looming over them in person.

The disquieting implication of Kleiner's argument is that the work environment is short-circuiting this last effect, bending the employee's will permanently toward following the instructions of a boss-avatar perched on her shoulder.

Rather than pursue these dour reflections further, I suggested we shelve the typo hunting for now and head for RadioShack. We hoped to find a new battery for the video camera my cousin had mailed us in South Carolina, but they'd apparently stopped manufacturing batteries for this model right around the time that *Murphy Brown* went off the air. I passed by a whiteboard on our way out, then spun around and headed back inside. A different clerk greeted us, and I said, "Sorry. I noticed something on the whiteboard out there that I don't think is quite right. Isn't there a double *s* in 'Sony Ericsson'?"

"I think so," she said, and followed me out to the very edge of her jurisdiction. I'd been reaching for my camera to take a quick photo, but she took one look and, while saying, "Yeah, that's wrong," swiped a hand across the last two letters of the original rendering, ERICSON.

Wow! Immediate action! So immediate that I swore that, from this day forward, I would be certain to snap a photo before mentioning a given typo to anyone. As it happened, I now had a dry-erase marker, albeit not in exactly the right color, that could aid in the correction. We thanked her, and she thanked us, and we thanked her for thanking us. After an awkward pause during which Benjamin and I separately considered that we already had beautiful girlfriends waiting for us back at our respective homes, we parted company from our fetching, forthright ally.

When I wondered aloud about the difference between RadioShack and our other two encounters, Benjamin burst into hearty laughter. "RadioShack! Of course!"*

Our last stop was to roam Target for a strap for my Typo Correction Kit, like the one I used for my camera bag. I'd envisioned crossing the straps like bandoliers over my chest, a badass gesture that would send the message to grammatical vandals, defilers of language, and other itinerant evildoers that trifling with Jeff Deck

---

* When I asked Benjamin what had induced his hysterics, he offered a story about autonomous action, RadioShack, and one of his favorite bands. Matthew Good Band, a Canadian rock group, had shot a video featuring a RadioShack logo and a scene inside the store. The general manager of that store—and fan of the band—even got a cameo in the video. The band had gotten permission, presumably via the GM, from the regional office. When the video came out, and people at the national level heard the lyric "Down at the RadioShack / We're turnin' sh*t into solid gold," they attempted to sue the band for using the storefront in the video. The suit didn't go far, of course, as the band had approving signatures from the regional office.

would be one's final trifle. Failing to find something appropriate, Benjamin grabbed a carabiner clip from the camping equipment section, and I simply linked the Kit to my camera strap. Now I felt like an authentic typo hunter, wearing the weapons of my trade. We exited the mall through the nearest department store and breathed the carbon-monoxide-tinged air of the parking lot with gratitude. Our mall adventure had yielded dispiriting results, but at least we'd broken new territory.

The following morning we hit the road for New Orleans, stopping in Biloxi, Mississippi, on the way (an adventure outside the bailiwick of our tale; suffice it to say that if you ever blow a tire in the South, look for Jerry, repairer of rubber and mender of dreams). By the time we arrived in the French Quarter, afternoon had already begun, and with it a hearty wind. The wind didn't prevent us from consuming some beignets at Café du Monde, but it did send the powder from those beignets all across Benjamin's jeans and T-shirt. My white-speckled companion and I proceeded to tramp down Decatur Street. Despite the ravages of Hurricane Katrina, this neighborhood stood pretty much intact.

After our troubles of the previous day, I confess we started out our typo correcting in stealth. Benjamin had been raving for some time now about the ratio of corrected typos versus total found. The percentage had dipped a hair below fifty percent in his first days on board, but we'd gotten it back on track by Beaufort, North Carolina. Since then it had wavered barely above that mark, ever threatening to fall again. With a horde of uncorrected Mobile typos, we'd begun the day at twenty-two of forty-two corrected, only one ahead of the zone of shame. Thus goaded, I consented to his nefarious strategy without much reluctance. We took down several typos via covert assassination, including a Styrofoam sign in a shop window and a cardboard sign for plastic reptiles at a tented bazaar. While fixing the latter, I wondered if many new speakers of the English language made New Orleans their home. We'd set a hard rule for the League to never go after non-native speakers. Those new to our language deserved to be cut some extra slack; English can still get difficult on me, and I've been using it my whole life. The spirit of TEAL focused on catching errors made by lifelong speakers, not by those who were still learning the basics.* In practice, this meant bypassing ethnic restaurants, stores, and sometimes even whole neighborhoods. Occasionally, though, we couldn't even tell whether we'd run into a second-language situation. People don't always fit into obvious categories. In those cases, more often than not, we stayed our pens.

Our clandestine campaign came to an end when I spied a blackboard typo that we had to bring to someone's attention. We went inside Jimmy Buffett's Margaritaville, where the lifestyle embodied by the song could be supplemented by the purchase of faux-tropical tchotchkes. The store seethed with employees lacking an immediate purpose, so we figured that we could peel at least one off to grant the permission we desired.

A friendly guy in a festive shirt came over. "What can I do for you?"

"Hi," I said, "we couldn't help but notice that Thursday was spelled wrong on your blackboard outside. With your permission, we'd like to fix it."

He said, "Sure, if it's wrong, we can fix it. Lemme see." We stepped back outside to look at the blackboard. Then something astonishing happened—the man laughed. "Oh no, we close at seven Monday to *Thrusday*? And it's all flowery and everything. I know who did this. Hold on, don't fix it yet, I got to show Jerome this."

He retrieved one of his co-workers, who, once shown the mistake on the blackboard, also had a titter over it. Then both of them reentered the store and came out a few seconds later with the employee who had probably made the error in the first place. She, too, was gracious enough not to get annoyed, even though her co-workers kidded her about it. *Thrusday!* We'd finally found some people who got it. They laughed again when we told them about our mission.

---

* There already exists a cottage industry for this in websites such as Engrish
  .com.

Benjamin mentioned how little errors like this popped up everywhere, mitigating the sign writer's embarrassment. Mimicking her flowery style as best I could, I swapped the letters and we made to depart, but the first guy told us to hold on for a moment longer, as he had a final errand back inside Margaritaville. Within two shakes of a tumbler, he emerged with a prize for us—a *prize,* for pointing out the mistake! We were now the beaming owners of a TIME FLIES WHEN YOU'RE HAVING RUM bumper sticker.

What a pleasant shift, we thought, from the latent hostility we had suffered yesterday in the Mobile mall. Here were employees who weren't afraid of acknowledging mistakes. Granted, an alteration in chalk carried less grave potential consequences than fixing permanent signs, but the gratis token of appreciation had helped to make the distinction plain. This was what I'd hoped for, a friendly reaction to our quest, displaying humor and gratitude. Sure, I'd expected that many wouldn't like being told they'd made a mistake, but I saw my efforts as a clear boon for humankind. Reactions like Margaritaville should thus have been more common, but they weren't, making this one all the sweeter.

Benjamin checked his cell phone. "If you want to head back to the car so we don't have to pay for another hour, now's the time."

I nodded, and we sped up, until one last typo blazed out at me from the window of a tourist center. "Dear God, that thing's huge," I said.

"Another hour it is, then," Benjamin replied, following me into the place.

Inside, a middle-aged woman surrounded by pamphlets on various attractions and arcana of New Orleans ruled over a surprisingly large amount of office space. I deduced why the room was so big when I spotted a couple of Segways parked over in the corner—tourists would be able to fumble around open floor for a while before taking to the narrow streets. I went up to the woman and smiled. "Hello! We noticed that the word *cemetery* was spelled wrong on your sign in the window."

She seemed dazed by this pronouncement, and her gaze didn't follow my finger to the window. Instead, she gave both of us an uncertain stare. Pranksters? Miscreants? Even worse?

"It should have an *e* instead of an *a*," said Benjamin, pointing at the reverse of the sign through the window. "See?" He helpfully plucked up a flyer that rendered the word with all three of its *es*.

"We'd like to fix it," I said. "If that's okay."

She eventually looked at the sign. "Oh, you're right." Immediately she switched from wariness to staunchly supporting our cause. "Hey, we hired somebody to do those signs." Ah, I hadn't even spotted the second copy of the sign in another window. Double the error and potential shame brought upon the tour office. "We didn't do those ourselves. We paid a lot to get them done, and hell, they didn't do it right, did they?"

"We're actually traveling the country correcting typos," Benjamin said.

"It'd be nice to have this as another success story," I said.

"Well, hold on," said the woman. "I'm going to call someone right now to complain about this." She picked up the phone and spoke to her supervisor without preamble. "Hey, you know those big signs we paid two hundred and fifty bucks each for? They've got a mistake. Two guys came in and pointed it out. Cemetery with an *a*. Yeah. These guys are going around the country fixing typos, and they want to fix these, make this a success story. Uh-huh. All right."

She hung up. "Well, you are welcome to fix them, but I'm not sure how you're going to be able to do that. I mean, we still want them to look professional . . ."

"Got it. Do you have a red pen or red marker?" I asked.

"No . . ." She searched around the pamphlet stands. "No, I don't believe I do. I can bring something in tomorrow from home, though. Just come back tomorrow and you can fix these."

An earnest offer, not an attempt to get rid of us. But tomorrow night happened to be the first night I'd actually booked ahead, at a hostel in Lafayette. We said we'd hunt down a marker, a familiar mission that we hoped this time wouldn't invite hailstorms.

"Okay, you can check the Walgreen's up the street. You know, if you boys are looking for typos, you came to the right place. You'll find them all over this town. Why, the other day I saw a big pink building with a yellow and blue sign, said WE SALE FISH. Now, what kind of sense does that make?" She proceeded to regale us with stories on every typo she had ever found throughout the watchful course of her life. I found it interesting that our mission would trigger such a monologue. Indeed, in other stops we made around the country, many people we met had typo tales of their own to share, usually unbidden. I think most of us must carry a kind of repository of errors noticed and internalized during a lifetime of bombardment by signs and ads and billboards and flyers. We may not even be aware of the repository until it is unlocked by the right stimulus—say, for example, a couple of yahoos walking around with elixir of correction.

Having a destination and directions for our marker-finding mission turned out to be helpful. I debated whether a red marker alone would be a sufficient enrichment of the Typo Correction Kit. Who knew what other hues a typo might choose to garb itself in? I ended up adding a whole rainbow's array of Sharpies to my arsenal.

When we came back, we saw that the woman had some actual customers to attend to, sweaty Midwesterners manhandling the Segways. So we just went about our business. Benjamin and I pried the signs from the windows and laid them out on the flattest surfaces available. As I uncapped my elixir and red marker, the tour office manager paused in giving instructions to the tourists, as if she could *smell* fresh corrective fluid. She stared us down and said, "It better look good."

Benjamin looked apprehensive at this sterner shade to the woman's tone, but I felt confident in my altering abilities. I worked at the *a* first, blotting out the offending portions, then used marker to shade in areas that would complete the letter's transformation to an *e*. I repeated vowel surgery on the other sign, and then we erected the beneficiaries of our handiwork, Benjamin climbing up on the windowsill to affix the higher copy. Once they'd been put back in place, the proprietor thanked us, noting that the signs looked great. A success story indeed, and one of my overall favorite typo corrections.

All in all, New Orleans was one of the most receptive cities to typo correcting that the League found during its entire journey. The employees we'd happened upon had demonstrated the most autonomy. A little faith in basic human judgment can do wonders.

TYPO TRIP TALLY

Total found: 50
Total corrected: 28

8 | Davy Jones Isn't a Biblical Figure

March 20, 2008 (Lafayette, LA, to Galveston, TX)

Plans cast aside like naughty apostrophes plucked from plural nouns, our Young Adventurers tack southward. Controversy, FLAME, and government regulations abound; truly, everything is Bigger in Texas.

"Those drivers'll kill you," the hostel clerk had said. "They will run you right off the road in Houston, swear to God."

Benjamin and I had shivered, as if we were huddled by a campfire listening to the grisly tale of the Halberd-Wielding Hitchhiker instead of baking in the midmorning Louisiana heat. The clerk shed her identity as front-desk guardian of the Blue Moon, Lafayette's preeminent hostel-slash-honky-tonk, and embraced her camp-counselor role, leaning toward us with a darkening brow. She described to us six lanes' worth of unadulterated fear, populated exclusively by motorists whose driving education had been paid for by the blood of pedestrians. "So when you see that Houston skyline in the distance, *watch out.*" Her eyes grew dim with remembered horrors.

We checked out and did not look back at the Ancient Mariner of the bayou. As we approached the Texas border, the de facto boundary in my mind between familiar East and the alien territories of the West, we considered heeding the warning of the desk clerk and bypassing Houston. My U.S. guidebook confirmed her dire words about the city: "Visitors should be prepared . . . to get lost more than once." I pictured a frenzy of glittering windshields in the heat, death-machines caroming at my poor girl with a conscious intent to murder. Benjamin recalled hearing a tale once of Houston drivers moving bumper to bumper on the highway—at seventy miles per hour.

When we pulled over to investigate one of the Waffle Houses, which had become a regular fixture of the Southern terrain, we discussed it over hash browns. Did we dare veer from my carefully prepared itinerary to avoid down-home Southern vehicular manslaughter? Benjamin unfurled his trusty map, and our eyes simultaneously landed on an alternative destination: Galveston. He confessed to a fascination with the town. I agreed, remembering details from my hostel guide. "A beach resort," I said brightly, "an *island* beach resort . . . in Texas! Imagine that! We could even go for a swim."

He fixed me with a peculiar glance. That hadn't been what he'd meant. Having read *Isaac's Storm* by Erik Larson, about the deadly hurricane that struck Galveston in 1900, Benjamin couldn't understand its continued existence as a city. "Larson explains in the book that Galveston Bay's features serve to effectively *maximize* the damage of hurricanes' storm surges. I sort of assumed, when I finished reading the book, that everyone had given up on it. Packed up and left."

Apparently not. Two weeks into the trek around the country, we strayed from my original course thanks to Benjamin's curiosity, my desire for an ocean dip, and the clerk's terror-inducing warnings. We parted ways with I-10, taking a jaunt south to the lustrous Gulf of Mexico, which we would hug for almost thirty miles until eventually confronting a pier. Partway through this stretch of sunny, quiet coast, we made an heinous discovery. I immediately pulled over to the side of the road and Benjamin and I walked back to examine the object that had so affronted us—not through its existence alone, but also the fell undercurrents that, at least to Benjamin, it implied.

Thus Canal City becomes ANAL CITY.

"Well!" Benjamin said, his eyes popping even more than was customary. "We are in trouble."

I frowned. "It's too bad that the juvenile delinquents of the Bolivar Peninsula don't have anything better to do, but I don't see how that means trouble for *us*."

He responded with a knowing laugh that I didn't like.

"What?" I demanded.

"Oh, what refreshing naïveté to think that this is the isolated work of a couple of Dos Equis–swilling punks with Freudian hangups," said Benjamin.

"Er . . . what else would it be?"

He looked out across the sea, a troubled cast settling over his bewhiskered face. "I've long suspected their existence. But I never thought I'd see evidence like *this*."

"Evidence of what?!"

Benjamin paused before answering, his eyes narrowing and his fists curling. "*FLAME*," he finally intoned. "Our dark inverse."

I looked to the sign again, but I found no guidance there. "All right," I said, "I give up. I'll bite. What does FLAME mean?"

"The Fiendish League for Advancing Mistakes in English," he replied, shaking his head at my astonishing ignorance. "Or, as they would have it, Feindish Leege 4 Addvancen Missteaks n Englesh. Even as we roam the nation performing good grammatical deeds, my dear Deck, I fear these villains are doing the same with acts of absolute evil."

After a significant pause, he added, "And . . . *Great Scott,* I just realized . . ." I sighed in exasperation as I waited for him to continue. "I didn't pack any swim trunks," he said. "I can't go for a swim when we get there."

Leaving the perverse (and probably wholly imaginary) world of FLAME behind for the time being, we returned to the drive, watching the stilt houses go by. Eventually we came to the end of the road, or at least the end for cars lacking amphibian outfitting. I had seen the (belated) warning from Authority several miles back that there would be a ferry involved. I hadn't forgotten the off-season ferry debacle back in North Carolina, but I figured this time, since we were headed for an island, and a touristy one at that, the ferry had to be running. To my delight, we saw a queue of cars, and a boat hove into view on distant waters. Here the ferry ran year-round, and was free, what a bonus!

We drove Callie onto the ferry and then stood at the rail, watching the Gulf, as the vessel chugged on toward the island. Earlier in the day, I had booked us a room at a hostel that promised easy access to the beach. When we arrived at the place, we saw that they hadn't been kidding; we were steps away from white sands. It was a dive hotel with a few rooms converted to hostel space, somewhat dingy, but hey, we were men of humble tastes. We gulped down the last of Abby's scones and then pulled on our trunks (or, in Benjamin's case, changed from jeans into shorts) for a late-afternoon dip in the ocean and some relaxation—er, I mean, a trip to ensure that the beach was free of typos. Though we *did* find and fix an error on the entrance sign, the excursion was more for a moment of rest for these weary travelers. I called Jane, stuck in frozen and miserable New England, from my beach towel. Benjamin, absorbed in his Frank Herbert book, didn't even go into the water.

Evening fell, and we realized that we still needed to do more typo hunting to justify our earlier lounging. We took off on foot and found a couple of typos in touristy locales reminiscent of Myrtle Beach, but the most memorable (and notorious) discovery of the night took place in an abandoned miniature golf course off Seawall Boulevard. We were walking back to the hostel, since Benjamin and I had thought our search to be over, but then I spied the shack with its dubious legend. From the look I caught on Benjamin's face, he must have seen it at the same time. Together we clambered down the incline and walked over turf and concrete.

"Arr," I mused at the sight of the little wooden structure astride the green. DAVY JONES LOCKER, it said in painted white letters. Surely someone *possessed* this locker, and it was not merely *named* Davy Jones. A crucial mark was missing. Benjamin inquired, Watson-like, as to my implement of correction. We didn't have a white marker of any sort. I had already fumbled for the elixir that would grant Davy Jones the soundest sleep, and I held it up for my friend.

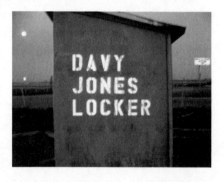

"Could be a lot of Wite-Out," he said, hesitating, then asked the question that was really on his mind. "Is it also going to need . . . ?"

"Yes," I replied, "Davy Jones isn't a biblical figure."

"Could be a lot of Wite-Out," Benjamin repeated. "You sure about this one?"

It occurred to me that while the path of correction had seemed obvious to me, given the style book that the League had more or less chosen to follow, Benjamin was not lugging around the *Chicago Manual of Style, 15th Edition,* in his brain like a mental brick. I had internalized its tenets only through the years of my academic publishing job in D.C. I couldn't expect my companion, adept hunter though he was, to have absorbed the book's contents purely by walking through the reference section every day.

There is widespread confusion over what to do with these s-possessives, partly because no absolute rule exists. Different style manuals diverge where Davy Jones possesses his locker. Each style guide aligns its rules with its overall purpose. Associated Press style has the mission of eliminating anything deemed unnecessary for communicating an idea, such as the serial comma (e.g., the second comma in "Benjamin, Jeff, and Josh"). They see that same redundancy in an s following an s-apostrophe. *You're already ending on an* s*-sound, why add another* s*?* The style I'd learned to use, *Chicago,* which is favored by the publishing industry, aimed to simplify the rules themselves; thus, *Chicago* would prefer to keep things consistent, adding an s after the apostrophe and thereby treating s-ending possessives like any others. (*Chicago* does make an exception for names from the Bible and antiquity that end in s, like Jesus or Xerxes.) The Modern Language Association (MLA) style, employed by academic writers, prefers this route as well. Though it helped that at least a couple of style guides backed my desire to use the s after the apostrophe, I knew deep down that my preference did not spring entirely from reason: I simply liked the way that JONES's would look better than JONES'. Perhaps this was how style guide variances happened in the first place.

After I'd explained the competing views about the s-apostrophe situation, Benjamin suggested that we *could* go with whichever best preserved our supplies. That, of course, would be AP style. Denied the wholehearted support I had sought, I grew defensive. "Are you at heart a spelling *minimalist,* old friend? Do we part ideological ways here? Is that it?"

"Hey . . . I only want the simplest means to the end of correcting this typo, yo."

I reflected a moment more. "This could be the first time we've come across something with two possible corrections. For the sake of consistency—even if that's a silly consideration for different signs in different contexts across different *states*—we ought to correct with *Chicago*. That's what I've been using, more or less, so far."

"Okay, I'm cool with that," he replied. We couldn't very well switch typo-correcting parameters mid-journey, any more than a grad student could swap MLA for APA mid-thesis. I turned back to my plywood canvas and went to work. We would have to hope that the cop stationed a block away wouldn't look over and take us for vandals. The bad kind of vandals, I mean.

Perhaps I should have considered Benjamin's words as a harbinger of comments soon to befall the League. I'd been proud of my handiwork afterward, the painted-on *s* making a respectable attempt at fitting in with its stenciled brethren. Some folks in the wider world later scrutinizing our adventures expressed their disapproval with the correction, however, especially when the *Boston Globe* article on us ran a week later and used the 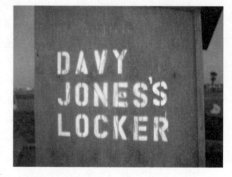 Davy Jones pictures as an example of our typo-fixing. The entry on the TEAL blog filled with comments such as these:

> *You could have saved some white paint by adding only the apostrophe and not the (extra) "S"*

> *I too had always been taught that words ending in "s" did not receive an additional "s" when they become possessive. A little controversy with your morning coffee?*

> *I can state with confidence that AP style does not put the extra S on anybody, Biblical or contemporary. I think you could have saved the Wite-Out on Davy's name.*

*Associated Press Stylebook says—you need to go back to
Galveston and remove the superlative* [sic . . . did they mean
superfluous?] *S.*

I was perplexed at first by the criticism. I had expected everyone
to agree that we'd left the Locker in a better state than we'd found it.
But many of these people were acting as if we had done something
wrong.* Why was everyone talking about AP? Had they confused me
for a journalist? I realized, finally, that a couple of threads of misun-
derstanding were unspooling here.

I had been assuming that everyone was at least aware that stylistic rules of the language could vary depending on who was using
them. But now it hit me—some people, like the writers of the first
two comments above, were unaware that different style guides even
existed. They thought that long ago, an overlord of the English language had, with a slam of his mailed fist upon some oaken table,
definitively put all grammatical questions to rest. "Never end a sentence with a preposition," quoth he, "and that is bloody *that.*"

How much I had taken for granted! Of course there'd be loads of
people out there who had stopped thinking critically about grammar
the day they escaped their last English teacher (the stand-in for that
overlord from the misty past). Forget this, they said to themselves, I'm
going to be a biochem major. If they were not bound for editorship,
as I had been, they might never have had the occasion to consider the
existence of—the necessity for—different approaches to the language.
A journalist trying to squeeze a story into a newspaper column would
naturally have different grammatical priorities from, say, a scholar
writing up a journal article on the significance of the color green in
Proust. The former will want her punctuation, abbreviation, and so
forth to be as economical as possible. The latter will use his comma and
quotation placement to elucidate his close textual analysis. So you give

---

* See also chapter 10.

the journalist an *AP Style Guide* to inform her work, and you advise the scholar to use the *MLA Handbook*. Medical writers have still different needs, so they'll find the *APA Guide* helpful, and so forth. Fiction and mainstream nonfiction writers will mostly turn to the *Chicago Manual*. In fact, the vast majority of books on the North American market are edited according to *Chicago* rules. A bibliophilic fellow such as myself would naturally gravitate toward such a style.

Which brings me to the other type of comments left in regard to the Davy Jones correction, the ones that chided me for not using AP style, of all things. This mentality is, in a way, more pernicious than simply not knowing about the plurality of style guides. Its proponents *are* aware that different rulebooks exist, but for whatever reason, they insist that one particular guide is king of all, and any others should be discarded. Consider this argument another wedge served from the malodorous pie known as "My Way Is Right," the dessert of choice for politicians, religious leaders, and warring pastry chefs.

If some other marauder had gotten to the Locker first, and had chosen to make Davy Jones possessive per AP style, I would have no problem with that. TEAL is not about elevating one style guide over the other. The point is that any *correction*, regardless of the stylebook, is better than leaving the thing *wrong*. Whether it's Davy Jones's Locker or Davy Jones' Locker, kindly acknowledge the fact that we have improved on "Davy Jones Locker."

The one argument that I will consider was offered by someone claiming that *Chicago* also calls for withholding the extra *s* in the case of mythical figures (which probably pertains more to classical heroes like Achilles and Odysseus, but who knows, may extend to folk legends).*

---

* Copyeditor's note: *Chicago* doesn't specify omitting the extra *s* in names of mythical figures per se, but only those ending with an *eez* sound, or in cases where it would make the result look and sound odd. (*Chicago* considers the way a thing would sound when read aloud; see its section on handling of inclusive numbers.) It also takes into account customary usage; thus Achilles', Euripedes', Rameses', but also Isis', Moses', Odysseus', Jesus'. Davy Jones's would not qualify for this exception.

The rest of the angry commenters must clomp back to the Barony of the Trolls, where the Internet's full-time instigators dwell.

In the morning we decided to make a stop or two in the little downtown of the island. Benjamin had discovered a flyer in our room for a used-book store that sounded enticing. We stopped in and bought a few more books for the road from their enviable sci-fi and fantasy collection. Other genres were, shall we say, less well represented. Namely, their "Horor" and "Tecno-Spy" genres. When we came down to the desk with our respective stacks of great finds, I asked if we could do something about the typos. A resounding "Definitely!" came from the woman behind the desk as she handed me her marker, cementing the place's status as my new favorite bookstore. Last night we'd started our hunt as the sun dropped out of sight, but today we'd already scored a hit well before high noon.

After stowing our book haul, we headed for the post office, housed in the lobby of a federal courthouse of impressive proportions. On the courthouse lawn I found an engraved sign with a small problem. They'd spelled METEOROLOGICAL wrong, leaving out the first *o*. While Benjamin got in line to mail a present back to Jenny, I went off to see if I could alert the town fathers to the error. I walked alone down the vast and echoing hall and came to a security gate manned by a white-haired guard. I said, through the gate, "Hello there. I noticed a typo on the sign on the lawn outside, and I was wondering who I should talk to about having it fixed?"

I turned my camera on and found the appropriate picture in its memory, then handed it over to show him. He accepted the camera through the gate, which began beeping at the intrusion of a metal object. I said, "See how *meteorological* is missing an *o*?"

He nodded. "Yep. But they'd need an engraver to fix that, and the way this town spends money, I don't think it's likely to happen."

Well, he'd know best. Though disappointed, I could not have even feigned surprise that this one had gotten by us. "All right, thanks for your time."

"One other thing," the old sentinel added, as he handed me back my camera, this time around the gate. "You want to be more careful with this camera. Taking pictures of the inside or outside of a courthouse is a federal offense."

"But my picture was of a sign on the *lawn* of the courthouse," I said. "Not of the courthouse itself."

He shook his head. "They . . . ," and he let the word linger, either considering his next words or making a thoughtful distinction, ". . . could still construe it as the courthouse, and confiscate your camera. So don't take any pictures around here. Especially not of the inside!"

Thanks for the tip, I thought. Maybe such a policy existed, and he was showing me mercy, this man bound by the iron fetters of bureaucracy. Or maybe he was feeding me an extra helping of tripe. At the time, I just didn't know. I said, "Thanks," and scurried back outside.

Both this incident and the affair of the Locker struck me as examples of a peculiar kind of blindness or, perhaps more accurately, nearsightedness: fixating upon one stately elm while missing the proverbial forest behind it. For the style-guide naifs, and the AP-style devotees, their tree was assumptions about language convention that they had never thought to question. For the federal overseers, it was security at all costs, laying down rules with a rational premise and then enforcing them to the point of paranoia. Galveston boasts a beautiful courthouse, and I'm guessing that not everyone who wants to take pictures of it is a terrorist. Though, in fairness, at least I still have my camera, which the guard *could* have confiscated.

Ahh, but all hunters must take care not to fall victim to their own weapons. Visual impediment is a hazard of typo hunting itself, since the sport is about zooming in on the little details of our surroundings, focusing on elements that are oft taken for granted while ignoring the broader purposes of their existence. Woe to any who entered that bookstore and saw only the "horor" of misspelled words, but missed that glorious fantasy and sci-fi selection! I vowed that in my quest, I would never lose sight of the *spirit* of whatever text I came across, or whatever institution fate brought my way.

I wish that there weren't an unhappy postscript to the tale of Galveston, but there is, as Erik Larson perhaps foresaw. Add this doomed island to New Orleans and Biloxi as victims of Hurricane Alley. Some six months after our visit, Ike would tear through the Texas coast and leave behind stacks of kindling and bare patches where houses used to be. Anything on the Bolivar Peninsula was pretty much flattened, so say farewell to Anal City. Our beachside hostel-in-a-motel, a grubby Galveston icon for almost fifty years, met ruin. Davy Jones'(s) Locker, subject of so much impassioned debate, is now purely a symbol, as the hurricane obliterated the actual plywood structure, along with the rest of the abandoned putt-putt course. Storms and tides hammered that wonderful bookstore (though it has since been remodeled and reopened, thankfully).

The courthouse, however, remains intact. You'll have to stop by and see its engraved sign, on the lawn at 25th and F. Leave your camera at home.

There is not much I can say about the ravages of nature that would not also, necessarily, apply to the impermanence of all things. The city is rebuilding itself, but a fair portion of what we saw and touched there is gone forever. That casual annihilation may make our efforts seem especially futile, but the bare fact is this: *any* sign that we noted along the entire trip could be gone tomorrow. Maybe the actual moment of noticing, of caring, is itself the important part, regardless of what may come after.

Typo Trip Tally

Total found: 61
Total corrected: 34

9 | Typos Aren't Charming

March 26-27. 2008 (Santa Fe, NM, to Flagstaff, AZ)

Discloses how the Mission, too long masticated, began losing
its flavor. Happily for the palate, vibrant Southwestern towns
offer a distinct savor all their own. Conflict arises between
the Grammatical Champion, wavering with contradictory feelings,
and his Faithful Dawg, obstinate to the last.

As I stepped out of the hostel bunk room and onto the back
porch, a couple of the donkeys raised their heads to acknowledge
me. They ambled about on the sandy ground, munching at whatever
lay conveniently nearby: a leafy branch, a stray shoot of grass,
the wooden railing behind which I stood. It took a moment to rec-
oncile the sudden appearance of five donkeys with the fact that I
was awake—not that I dream about donkeys often. I considered
the possibility that they were a missive from the divine lords of language, a reminder to stubbornly stick to my mission. I'd faltered
in Albuquerque last night upon spotting a typo beyond reach, but
Benjamin had swiftly identified a supervisor to assist us. Kelly's
Brew Pub need no longer endure the city's ridiculing them with
an extra *e,* as "Kelley's" had appeared in a municipal sign directly
beneath their own sign. Once I saw how we had helped a thin ray
of brilliance to shine down on the pub's dark night of orthography, I wondered why I had hesitated at all. As I reflected, one bull
attempted to mount a less-than-enthusiastic partner. No, best not
to look for directives here.

Benjamin joined me on the porch. He shook off his initial surprise and broke into an excited smile. "All right! We can do this in style! Let's saddle up for Santa Fe," he said, reaching over the rail to pet the nearest donkey on the head.

"Uh . . . ," I said, glancing uncertainly at the animals.

"Fine, fine. Callie it is."

Our hostel lay in the green hills of Cibola National Forest, between Albuquerque and Santa Fe. Cedar Crest had proved to be an authentically rustic experience. The little cabin that was our shelter barely had running water, and the proprietor thought "Wi-Fi" to be an arcane cussword, but what do you want for twenty bucks a night?

Since we'd covered Albuquerque last night, Santa Fe would be the site of our hunt today. After a gorgeous drive between the sibling cities, we came upon a town plaza with a row of shops leading to a central square, which boasted America's "oldest continuously used public building" and the towering Cathedral of St. Francis of Assisi. A stroll along the shops seemed in order. Continuing on the morning's theme, we made a turn down Burro Alley, where we spotted our first ill-begotten sign. In the window of an otherwise friendly little French café, a sign commanded, NO SMOKING ARE DOGS ALLOWED.

This amused Benjamin to no end. He'd spend the rest of the day playing with equally inappropriate word substitutions. "Dude, how about 'No smoking *our* dogs allowed.'" His mood crashed, however, when I declared that we weren't going to fix it. I pointed to my explanation before he could burst into a demand for one: the next three windows sported the same sign, but in those three the word ARE had been replaced with an even bolder OR in marker thick enough to make the two letters cover the three. Crude, but effective. Someone had already recognized the error and corrected most of the signs, so it seemed pointless to bother, at least to me.

Benjamin growled, then replied in staccato, "But. They. Still. Missed. One."

I resisted further, but this was mutiny, and Mr. Christian demanded I surrender to him my marker and elixir. Then he went into the café, somehow slipped past the host, and ducked into the room with the window that the original corrector hadn't remembered to visit. The fix happened fast, and after making sure the elixir had dried enough to not stick to the window, he reattached the sign and swung back out of there before any-one could comment. As we walked back the way we'd come, Benjamin broke the silence by offering, with a nod at the street marker, "What can I say? I'm just that stubborn." The sign of the donkey. Or was I the ass? "And Jeff—no smoking dogs allowed!"

I tried to make up for my malaise with the next one, sticking to my Sharpies over the initial irritation of the local bookstore employees. Feeling like an adventurer who'd recovered a stolen artifact thought lost for good, I returned the apostrophe to its rightful place in a sign for *Barron's* magazine. Strangely, something about the scene shifted. Happy as I'd been at my restored treasure of an apostrophe, I found myself caught off guard as a shadowy fig-ure began to prowl the corners of my consciousness—not the apos-trophe thief, but a similar, internal scoundrel with the potential for greater mayhem. I couldn't get a clear view, but I sensed its identity: doubt. Quiet, tentative, but nevertheless substantial doubt. If I tried to ignore it, the troublesome notion would sneak into backstabbing distance, dealing a critical hit to my confidence in the mission. Yet I couldn't catch it, the rogue dancing out of reach when I spun and lunged.

I stood outside staring back at the storefront for a moment, making the employees within fear that this mooncalf would be bothering them with oddball requests all day. Despite the rudeness I'd encountered, first by the younger clerk who thought I'd wanted an issue of *Barron's* and then by the older one, who'd given me the go-ahead to fix their sign with a hearty "whatever" to get rid of me, the place had an honest feel to it. A local little bookshop for people who actually read.

Benjamin nearly walked on without me before he noticed how I'd gotten stuck. "I liked that bookstore," I said.

He agreed. Nice place. Moving along . . .

But I couldn't. Something felt wrong about me or my mission, or both. Some contradiction between my feelings and actions. As we explored further, the thief at my heels continued to harry me with light fingers, challenging the preconceived notions I'd held when I saddled up for this adventure. Oh, but if I could stand here a moment more, I'd have it figured out!

Alas, not yet. We continued wandering down the street and made our way over to the Mineral & Fossil Gallery, where Benjamin decided to pick something up for Jenny. I began examining exhibits and felt my internal radio tune to a familiar frequency. I *knew* these words. I'd had to spell-check some of them before. I began to enjoy seeing in person some of the minerals featured in articles during my time at *Rocks & Minerals*. Then I spotted a specimen with a label locality that rankled. I waved Benjamin over, and he and a tiny carving of a turtle joined me at the case. "Minas Gerais, but they've got the *i* before the *a* here, and I'm pretty sure that's wrong."

"And *I'm* pretty sure it's too obscure for me," Benjamin said, a strange testing look in his eye. "It's all you."

Yeah. I approached a clerk for help, explaining my purpose immediately so as not to offend her as I had the bookstore fellows.

She came over to the case and examined the error. She'd obviously had more experience with minerals than I'd had in my short tenure at the magazine, and she immediately recognized the problem. It didn't *look* right to her, she said. Ah, surely she possessed the very spirit of the League! I almost invited her to join our mission; her able eye could fix upon the most difficult quarry wherever TEAL might boldly spelunk. We conferenced on the correct spelling, and she opened the case so I could correct the error myself, even thanking me. Benjamin gave a silent nod of approval from the other side of the store.

Then we bought some gifts for our girls, and oh, I'd hate to impose any further, but my receipt had a problem. So did Benjamin's. So had every receipt they'd ever printed from this cash register from the day the store had opened. At the top, under the store's name, lay the address: 127 W. San Francesco St. A simple glance at the street sign outside, West San Francisco, proved the receipts in error. Benjamin hung his head as I pointed it out, but when the kind woman ringing me up said she didn't know how to fix it, Benjamin ended the episode by requesting they "pass it along" and thanking them for everything. He figured that only the GM of the store would have access to what got printed on the receipts. They honestly could not change it then and there. "Not even the other store managers had access to the store personalization function." I nodded as if I knew what that meant as we headed into another store.

After we'd admired some local artwork for sale, we struck up a conversation with a friendly young woman named Hailey near the shoe section. As she chatted about the city's virtues, I began to realize how much I was enjoying myself here. Santa Fe would be added to the list of our favorite places, like Austin, that possessed their own character and felt *real*. Inevitably, though, a national franchise had infiltrated the town square, and Benjamin and I had watched, fascinated, as people dove into it, crowding the place as if afraid to venture from the haven manufactured for them by corporate America. I recognized that, yes, this street itself had probably been crafted as a capitalist simulacrum of a small town that had never quite been, yet it still had a sense of individuality brought to it by the independent businesses.

Hailey helped me pick out a cowboy hat and showed me how to set it properly 'pon my melon. When we left the store, I wanted to blurt out an observation about how much nicer these kinds of places were than the Walmart-ized communities or the strip malls featuring the same store names over and over again, some names so ubiquitous as to confuse any sense of navigating through a country. Which were you to believe? The odometer that said you'd come a thousand miles, or the storefronts before you with the same names you thought you'd left behind? Each new iteration would reveal unto you the exact same floorplan as its brethren back home, and you'd navigate flawlessly, as if you'd once visited this store in a dream. Before I spoke, though, Benjamin sighed and offered a thought of his own. "Not much text in that one. Too bad, we'd caught one in every single store we checked until there."

My new cowboy hat became the only thing keeping my skull intact as my mind exploded outward with the force of the revelations. I rewound myself back to the bookstore, understood what I'd missed there, and kept going. Back to Austin and New Orleans, back again to Alabama and the Carolinas, all the way to my first miserable typo-hunting excursion in Boston. Then I snapped back into the present moment like a rubber band. I'd apparently gotten in line with Benjamin at a humble fajita stand at the corner of the main square. The line moved fast, and we scored ourselves some sizzling food and lemonade, found a park bench, and enjoyed our repast. As if mirroring my mental overload, my taste buds bloomed in full thanks to a sensational rain of flavors. Benjamin handed over half of the ample stack of napkins we'd been given, tons of extras for the nose-blowing that unacclimated consumers would require; the well-spiced fajitas had opened our sinuses to breathe in the world. We kept pausing between bites to mutter our astonishment before blowing our noses and resuming stuffing ourselves with the food.

Benjamin leaned back on the bench. "Dude, I don't think I'm ever eating at a Taco Bell again. Fast food seems somehow offensive now."

I took a deep breath, putting down my empty wrapper. "Um. I have to tell you something."

We'd had trouble from the start finding the most fertile typo-hunting ground, but a pattern had emerged, and here in Santa Fe, it crystallized for me. The more homogenized a place became, the less likely we'd be to find typos. "Filene's Basement was a fluke," I explained, and Benjamin agreed. Most signs coming from corporate would have been checked for problems before thousands of copies were made. The bigger the company, the more widespread would be the single error that got through and thus the more they'd want to avoid that. "Owners expense" aside—and that didn't belong to corporate America anyhow—we'd found many more typos on individually made signs, the ones run off quickly in the store's back office.

Benjamin summed things up. "Okay, so the more independently owned shops you have, the more typos we're likely to find. So now we know where to go."

Yes, but no—he didn't get it. He didn't see the *significance*. "But I like these places better!"

"So do I. The whole *real America* thing isn't about urban versus rural; it's identity versus . . . Walmart."

I stood up, clenching my fists. Yes, yes, valid point, but *still*. "Benjamin, I—" I didn't know what I meant, or maybe I didn't want to vocalize it, but I flailed in a mental whirlpool, and I had to face the fact that my mission could be a mistake. It'd been impossible to know it when I started out, but the standards I graded on were flunking the wrong people. The soulless, concrete wastelands of strip malls and big-box stores that all sold the same stuff, I gave a clean bill of grammatical health, and then I came to these places, these living last bastions of independent thought and color and energy, and I *corrected* them. "Are we—am I—Look. What if typos are an element of this kind of setting?" I spread my hands out wide, as if to encompass all of Santa Fe, offering it a ride upon my shoulders like Atlas's burden. "Am I destroying a part of its character? What if I'm an agent of the very homogenization I despise, waltzing into town and demanding that everyone stick to our rigid grammatical standard, helping corporate agents claim these idylls by 'cleaning up' the language like a new high-rise 'cleans up' the area by evicting the poorer tenants?"

"Whoa!" Benjamin cut me short. "Dude, no smoking our dogs aloud. Calm down."

He had a point. I took a deep breath. Then he suggested that while it wasn't a bad idea to ask these hard questions, I didn't have to give up immediately. I hadn't explicitly suggested that, but he was right that I'd considered stopping the typo hunt right there on that square. It seemed like a perfect moment for true reckoning, that I could look back and say, "A fajita opened my sinuses and then Santa Fe opened my eyes to the evil I'd wrought!" Benjamin asked if I wanted to head anywhere else, offering that we could play tourists since we'd found a sizable chunk of typos already. I did want to see that cathedral, so we headed that way, after one last thorough nose-blowing.

As we left the park Benjamin reiterated that bringing these questions to the forefront could be healthy. "Everything we do raises contradictions. It's the people who examine them and work to resolve them who'll succeed every time. I have to say, you've hit some valid points, and I don't know what to tell you, but let's enjoy the beautiful day and not worry about it for now." Thus we moved from questions toward a destination many chose for answers.

We entered the enormous barrel-vaulted nave of the cathedral. We passed the eight-sided baptismal font in silence and admired the wall of saints and sainthood candidates on the far wall. A display showed that artwork in miniature, with the addition of names. We leaned down to see who was who, and what I saw rattled my heathen bones. They'd identified Saint Francis of "Assissi" in the very Cathedral of St. Francis of Assisi. The extra *s* didn't jump out at me like usual typos, didn't merely offend my delicate sensibilities. No, this spawn of the Evil One screamed with a thousand banshee wails, for it knew I wouldn't dare correct this error sitting on an ancient-looking placard on church property. Some things were sacred, and though I might be the only typo hunter around, I dared not presume to be a skilled enough artisan to exorcise this thing that transfigured a venerated saint into a paragon of error (not to mention what the extra *s* does to the pronunciation of the word; the Catholic Church would not approve).

Perhaps because I seemed so enraptured by the exhibit, Juan, one of the tour guides for the cathedral, approached us. Benjamin thought that he shattered the quiet and general sense of peace, but for me that peace had already been slain by a single *s*. A friendly older gent, Juan didn't hesitate to fill us in on any cathedral trivia we had questions about, as well as things we had not yet thought to question, so Benjamin eventually warmed to the garrulous chaperone. I also sensed that with Juan lay my best chance for seeing the error corrected. After we'd chatted long enough to confirm that he sincerely cared about the place and about educating its visitors, I gestured back toward the exhibit that named the people on the far wall. Immediately he began telling us stories explaining why these individuals had been chosen for the cathedral's coveted Top 15. By taking a backward step after every new anecdote of Juan's, I managed to get him to follow me.

Now I'd gotten him close to the exhibit, and then I stopped and stared at his name tag again. No! Betrayed at every turn in this my Gethsemane. By some inconceivable oversight, his name tag listed him as an official tour guide for the St. "Frances" Cathedral. The venerable saint's sister? The typos had now gone mobile on us.* "I'm sorry to interrupt," I lied. "But this is St. Francis Cathedral, right?"

---

* A phenomenon that had occurred only once before, in a Subway in remote western Texas. Benjamin and I had physically pursued a fellow whose name tag proclaimed him the "Restaraunt" Manager.

He confirmed that it was, giving me a funny look, perhaps wondering what he'd said that had made me so incredulous. I explained by indicating his name tag, which had swapped its *i* for an *e*. "Well, you know, the Spanish have their own way of spelling things," he replied with a dismissive wave of his hand, a slight eye roll, as if to add "those crazy Spanish." A quick glance at Benjamin's wide eyes confirmed my own reaction. The Spanish version was, in fact, *Francisco*. If we'd been talking about Saint Francis's original *Italian* name, Giovanni Francesco Bernardone, that argument would have held more water. But no, the church took its name from old Giovanni's Latinized name. It was a goof, a flub, and no cross-cultural shrug could deny it—or the exhibit error. I had now caught misspellings of both Francis and Assisi in the Cathedral Basilica of St. Francis of Assisi!

Juan had wandered off on another story, and as soon as I sensed the end of it, I pointed down at Assissi. How would he defend this one? He fed me the same line. "I believe that's the *Spanish* way of spelling it."

His repeated calumnies revealed his allegiance once and for all: this guide served a dark idol. No powers of mine could stand against the unholy agency of Juan's denial. I don't remember leaving the cathedral, but the next thing I knew I was standing on the terrace out front. "You okay?" Benjamin asked me.

I nodded, though I still felt dizzy.

He smirked at me. "Still want to give up your mission?"

I shook my head firmly. The questions and doubts plaguing my mind when I'd entered that building had been scrubbed away by the vinegary solution of St. Frances of Assissi. Ask, and ye shall receive—but be careful what you ask for. I squinted in the sunlight, still feeling unsteady. I decided I'd had enough for one day, and we retired to our dwelling among the donkeys.

"Frances," it turned out, had been our nineteenth typo found. Benjamin suggested we press for an unprecedented ten typos the next day. "If we hit one hundred tomorrow with a big day like that," he argued, "we could take the day off at the Grand Canyon, since there won't exactly be a lot of text scrawled on the canyon walls anyway. You could use a day off, Deck. It'd be good for you." I agreed. One day off for actual tourism wouldn't be bad. We'd be seeing the Grand Goldang Canyon, after all. Benjamin wasn't telling me something, but I let that pass, too.

We stared up for a while at the clear night skies, which allowed for extraordinary stargazing, and then headed back inside the cabin. I admired my new cowboy hat one last time in the bathroom's streaked mirror. Let this be a symbol, I thought, of the inarguable importance of the mission, a continual reminder to me of my realizations in Santa Fe. Henceforth, when I put the hat on, I would assume my League identity—the righteous marker-slinger.

"No smoking for donkeys allowed," Benjamin muttered as he drifted to sleep in the lower bunk. I relaxed in my own bed, relieved and grateful that this day had ended, but also drawing a renewed sense of purpose over myself like a Pueblo blanket. The next day, everything would change.

As we crossed the Arizona border the next morning, Benjamin literally cried out. I'd occasionally exaggerated our reactions when scribing the blog, but in this case it was absolutely true. Mid-sentence, Benjamin interrupted himself with a Charlie Brown–like "Argghugghhhh!" The first thing we saw in Arizona was an errant apostrophe the size of my companion's head.

A massive billboard beckoned us to a local tourist trap with BRING YOUR CAMERA'S.

Bring my camera's what? My camera's lens cap? We got off at the exit and circled back, parked close, and walked toward the billboard. A low barbed-wire fence stood between us and the field from which this mon-

strosity taunted us. We found where the ground rose the highest, and hopped over the fence. Then we crossed the brush, dodging cacti and tromping through stubby, thirsty grass, a sign that it hadn't rained here in a while. That was agreeable for my purposes, since the only way I could figure to correct this was to cover the black paint with yellow chalk. It'd disappear once the rains came, but for now it would look swell. As I applied the chalk, the apostrophe began to flake away, so I could at least shrink the readability of the gigantic blotch that greeted travelers to Arizona. Satisfied that we'd done some good, we pressed on, and more than a mile *up*, to Flagstaff.

Including the grandiose start back on the border, we'd manage to go six for nine for the day, breaking a personal best for typo finds (topping the eight we'd caught in New Orleans). As I moved through Flagstaff's intimate, frontier-town-like streets, I began to reexamine my ideas from the day before. Here again a town thrived with independent businesses and approachable people who for the most part appreciated our efforts.

We hit an obstacle or two along the way, of course, like when we caught a typo in neon and I didn't have any spare glass tubing handy for the rechanneling of inert gases. Flagstaff's true spirit came out, however, when we spotted mistakes in a sign propped up in the plate-glass window of a greasy-spoon diner. When we brought them up to the server, she thanked us for noticing the errors and seemed grateful that we wanted to fix them ourselves. Her only hesitation was wondering how much we charged for our "service." I replied that we worked for free, so she happily allowed us to attend to the "strawbery", "lemonaide", and "decafinated coffee" on the sign in the window.

At Benjamin's urging, I again put my *Rocks & Minerals* experience to the test at a gem shop. As in Santa Fe, I ended up catching a vowel in distress ("hemitite" rather than *hematite*, wouldn't you know), and again I couldn't keep myself from purchasing something nifty. Benjamin practically bounced as we caught the typos offhandedly, periodic discoveries during our exploration of an authentic community of artists and artisans. "I could live here! I've gotta come back with Jenny."

We treated ourselves to a nice Italian restaurant, where a kid's (not kids'!) birthday party sent the sole waiter scurrying to keep up. I, of course, found our ninth error for the day on the menu. When I showed it to Benjamin, he shrugged and said, "We're eating here. Maybe . . . we should forget it. I mean," and here he indicated the table filled with shouting children, "he's got a lot on his mind already."

"No, we've got to at least tell him," I argued, and Benjamin smiled. He'd been testing me. "You're *back*."

I thought he meant my frustration the day before, but he traced its roots back even further. "You went up an employee-only ladder in Austin. I stood on your *car* to get one in Fort Stockton, right after you made a big *X* on the side of a building. We've gotten bolder, taking on big errors."

I saw it immediately. I'd gotten bored with small-fry typos. El Paso hadn't featured anything big enough to stack up. The constant, lengthy driving and blogging had added to it all, and I'd begun to burn out. Benjamin had noticed it in Albuquerque, of course. We'd stumbled on the Kelly's/Kelley's sign, an error a bit too high to correct, and I'd shut down and said forget it. But Benjamin, donkeylike to the end, hadn't been dragged along on this crazy adventure only to let me abandon it. He'd committed to it somewhere along the line, and he'd charged forward, perhaps fueled by his anger at me for giving up. "Your whole thing yesterday," he said now, "that would have been an excuse."

"But it was a valid point."

"That typos are part of small-town character? That's conde-scending. Typos aren't charming. Misspellings are *not* the source of their independent spirit. These guys are fighting for their lives in a bankroll-obsessed, corporate-leaning America that's eight years into an administration that gives handouts to the big guys for successfully crushing anything in their paths. You're not hurt-ing the little guys; you're helping them by leveling the grammati-cal playing field."

How could I have forgotten that? I'd been trying to define the *why*s of my mission ever since Jane had asked me at my going-away party. Somewhere along the line I realized that—unfairly or not—stores and their products would be judged by their presentation. That included grammatical correctness. The big-box stores used profes-sionally made (and edited) signs to enhance the visual appeal of their stores. The little guy printed something out and taped it to the tables, walls, or windows. They started out at a disadvantage, but a grammatical error could set them even further behind. No matter how many clichés warn us against it, we are visually oriented crea-tures, and we do judge the books by their covers. By checking over their signage, we could help the independents ward against nega-tive judgments, perhaps adding a small measure to their perceived legitimacy.

Meanwhile, even amid my crisis of faith, we'd been getting bet-ter at this. The lesson here wasn't merely about whom to help, but where we could get better hunting done as well. Today we'd found an all-time high. Looking back over the last three and a half weeks, I noticed that our typo finds had been gradually increasing. Before Benjamin had come along, the best I'd managed was three finds in a single day. He'd immediately triggered a four-typo day, and we'd had only one day *under* three finds since he'd been along. Together we'd redefined what a successful day looked like. During the past four days we'd found twenty-eight typos. So I could stand for a day of refocusing, and what better place than out in the text-free wilds of the Grand Canyon. Thus we decreed we'd attempt a day off. Then I'd return refreshed, and kick off the new hunt with my hundredth typo found.

Typo Trip Tally

Total found: 99
Total corrected: 61

10 | Over the Edge

March 28. 2008 (Grand Canyon, AZ)

Into the House of Stone & Light our undaunted Heroes tread, and in the midst of consumerist pollution at the edge of all things Grand, discover the fabled One Hundredth Typo, one with the power to determine the Leaguers' fate forevermore.

Train horns took on an ethereal quality throughout the night, intruding into dreams as a forlorn wail of angels or oceans boiling in an apocalyptic vision. At other times the sharp call of warning jerked me from the absolute blankness—the depths of that well from which we draw the vital energies. A lady at the shops downtown had estimated that five trains pass through Flagstaff per hour, every hour, so figure on at least thirty whistles for the night entire. As a faint glimmer signaled the end of the long darkness, we both sat up. Benjamin mumbled, "The last time I had that much trouble sleeping, my parents were still burping me." Of course, he'd had the added fun of unrolling his sleeping bag on the hardwood floor. I'd reserved a two-bed hostel room, but I had not, well, *gotten* one. Benjamin had shrugged it off, saying that he needed to stay tough for the Appalachian Trail. He thought that all the Econo Lodges, along with a few friends' couches, might be making him soft.

I rubbed bleary eyes. The dawn cast its roseate light on my camera bag, hanging from a nearby chair. My Typo Correction Kit, still clipped to the camera bag, seemed luminous. One hundred typos, so near at hand. Today would—no! Benjamin had convinced me that I needed a day off, that I'd be a stronger typo hunter for it. My wave of fatigue and doubt had mostly reached its shore, but I should take this day to enjoy the glorious dimensions of the Grand Canyon, be a true tourist, committed to self-indulgence. I could be like everyone else, right? As I fumbled for a towel and my toiletries bag, I hoped Benjamin had guessed right about the Grand Canyon's absolute lack of text. It'd be like the Carolina beaches. What text could there be when the splendor of nature spoke in a language free of prepositions and apostrophes? I looked back at the camera bag, which lay innocently where I'd placed it last night, and again felt my eyes drawn toward the Kit. I could *separate* them. Take the camera but leave the Typo Correction Kit upon the chair. Yet that felt so wrong, and if we stopped in a diner after working up an appetite hiking around and *then* spotted the One Hundredth Typo, only to be without any tools of the League's trade . . .

The resolution was simple enough. I'd detach the Kit in the car, leaving it handy for any stops after the Canyon visit. I felt strangely unsettled each time I glanced at it, where it remained slung across the back of the chair, almost *too* still. Like the paintings in haunted mansions with eyes that tracked the cartoon hero. I scooped my accessories up quickly without even looking at them, grabbing the camera and Kit together. We climbed into Callie and, after barely maneuvering her past the overstuffed parking lot and the granola kids using it as their playground, we sailed down the highway for what would be the most consequential typo we'd ever encounter.

Crucial moments in history often pivot on the smallest details. What if Edward the Confessor had died a few minutes early, before he could promise his throne to Harold, thus precluding William's need to be a Conqueror, the Battle of Hastings, perhaps even the whole Norman invasion, fully changing the course of the English language? What if Gary Gygax had never thought to pair Dungeons with Dragons?

I met my own moment of truth in a parking lot, after we arrived at the first viewing area on the South Rim of the Grand Canyon.

I turned Callie into the lot and pulled into a back corner space. A sidewalk designated the border between the workings of man (pavement) and the beginning of the natural world (some grass and rocks). A little trash can stood on the sidewalk for our convenience. We planned to return to the car for peanut butter sandwiches, so this seemed perfect. Benjamin and I emerged from the car, turned toward the Canyon, and together stood and stared, awestruck—and not by nature's grandeur.

The parking lot had filled like any humdrum lot in front of a mall or grocery store. Everyone had crowded to the front. Now, I don't doubt there were a few older folks in the throng who hoped to see all they could with a minimum of cardiac exertion. Those folks aside, it struck us as strange that at a park where the main purpose was to wander around and take in the sights, a place where, besides gawking, the only thing that you could really *do* was walk, everyone had parked as close as possible. The reasons for parking so close eluded me. No one would have an armful of groceries to bring back from the canyon. Was it an automatic behavior, so deeply ingrained that finding the closest spot had replaced just finding a space in many minds? Benjamin commented on it before I did. "Herd instinct to corral together? My dad told me a story about getting somewhere early—I mean first-in-the-parking-lot early—and parking off to the side to read. Not up at the front spaces near the doors. Next car comes in parks in the very next space beside him, for no reason at all."

I turned back to Callie and reached in for my camera. I touched the carabiner clip that linked the Kit and camera. The moment slowed, as if the wilds had cast their atemporal magic over me, and I had eons to contemplate my identity. The fact that I'd parked so far away from everyone else, that I hadn't thought anything of walking the extra few yards to get to the Canyon, made me feel distinct and alone. Not in a bad, us-versus-them way, but not in a good, I'm-proud-of-my-uniqueness way either. I had merely come to a point of recognizing my *Jeffness*. In that moment of recognition, detaching the Typo Correction Kit seemed a blasphemous act, a retreat from myself. I could not escape my calling. Jeff Deck had become an editor, and editing had entwined itself in Jeff Deck's nature. I touched the brim of my hat unconsciously and lowered the strap gently down around me, and once the camera and Kit had settled to their rightful place at my side, worn like a rapier to be easily drawn in a moment of need, time returned to normal, and Benjamin bounded forward.

Through the parking lot, down to where the sidewalk truly ends, we came at last to the Grand Canyon, a testament to the persistence of erosion. The Colorado River has rolled on for six million years without a vacation day or off-season. Its tireless dedication to carving away rock could give even Iron Man Ripken pause (and should make Sisyphus wonder why he hadn't thought of that). The thing about the Grand Canyon that it took me a moment to understand was that I couldn't see it all. I mean, your first impression is *Wow, that's pretty big.* Then you look off in another direction, and the inexpressible beauty of shadow and light, sharp angles and smooth slopes, and contrasting colors covering a startling range of the spectrum make you fall into the scene (but not physically into the Canyon, if you're lucky). Then funny things happen to your vision as you try to make your eyes zoom in on particular features and patches of color that yank your attention around, jerking your head from here to there, and your depth perception and perspective go all out of whack. So Benjamin, meanwhile, is gazing out to the distance, trying to get a handle on the proportions. That's when the fact—that this is merely one viewing point among many along the rim, not to mention the rim opposite—sinks in, and intellectually collected factoids succumb to the natural reality. The Grand Canyon is so enormous that it's impossible to *see* it. To view the whole phenomenon in its entirety, you'd have to be so high above it that all definition and detail would be lost to you. I knew about bacteria and nanobots and other infinitesimally small things, but I'd never once thought something could be so big as to be equally invisible to the naked eye. I thought back to Galveston, where I'd

observed people focusing too narrowly and missing the larger picture. Now I felt more sympathy for them.

For a bit of extra height, which somebody for some reason had
thought would be helpful, the South Rim featured a faux Native
American watchtower. The Park Service had commissioned its
construction in the 1930s, crafting sandstone and rubble and steel
into a giant imitation of Anasazi towers, as if local peoples had
used it to gaze soulfully out over the Canyon for centuries. It was,
in fact, on the registry of National Historic Landmarks, though we
didn't realize that at the time. Benjamin and I went inside, where
I was jarred by an abrupt switch from unsullied vista to capitalist
hunger for the contents of my wallet, as the bottom floor was a gift
shop. I could have sworn we'd passed a gift shop near the parking
lot, too. The idea of so many trinket purveyors populating what
I'd naïvely assumed would be a meditation on Earth's raw delights
made me dizzy, dizzier even than when I later peered down from
a ledge. Somehow we wended our way around the gnashing teeth
with our pants pockets intact. Before ascending the stairway to
higher levels of the watchtower, I turned momentarily from our
spectating goal. Though there wasn't much text in here, I couldn't
help but examine it now. Since my hopes for a text-free zone had
been dashed, since I knew now that not even the Grand Canyon
could stand as a *last bastion* of the world without our interference,
I figured I might as well interfere. Nothing amiss that I could see,
though, so we left the postcards and T-shirts and other gewgaws
behind.

Up the first flight of stairs we went, the needy roar of the gift shop
still echoing in our ears, when I saw it for the first time.

A little chalkboard sign greeted us, leaning at an angle to catch the
eye of everyone coming up the stairs, ready to explain the significance of the Desert View Watchtower, built in the 1930s. Benjamin
admired the artwork adorning the walls and noted the slightly narrower staircase that ran along the wall to get us to the next level.

Meanwhile, I'd noticed a typo. No, I'd noticed two on this thing. I

WHAT TO SEE IN THE
HOPI ROOM ON THE
A large circular painting depicting the
ll paintings including those of MUYING
mbol of the womens' secret society
ene, the little war god POOKONGAHO
d of echo. The center of the room
sandpainting, religious crooks and w
chinas, snake whips and a tray of

pointed out "emense" for *immense* and "womens' " (a Filene's Basement classic) for *women's*.

One hundred typos. We'd done it. I'd found one hundred typos so far on this trip, and even when I'd meant to take a day off, here I'd continued the streak of no typoless days since I'd started on the quest. I pointed the problems out to Benjamin, who finally turned his attention from the upper levels (this level had no roof per se) to read the sign. The question, however, was, were we going to correct it now that we'd found it? "Can we put that off for a moment?" Benjamin requested. "I have a confession."

Benjamin is afraid of heights. As a small child this had kept him from going up on those taller outlooks at amusement parks and forced him to refuse the chance to go up into the Empire State Building. Eventually he'd struck back against the fear. He started climbing trees when camping and then made himself go up, shaking legs and all, to those greatest heights at amusement parks, even letting a trusted friend drag him onto the roller coasters (which he instantly loved). He'd never gotten over his fear, but he would actively charge forward against it. He had to do it that way, charging forward. He couldn't stand here waiting to go up. I didn't think we'd be getting all that high up, but the height wasn't the main factor. The layout of the tower was. You'd go up a narrow staircase along the curved edge, windows conveniently placed to let you know that you weren't just high up inside the building, but *exceedingly* high above the Colorado's millennia of carvings. The lack of floors/ceilings in the upper rooms, where you climbed in an outer ring from one staircase to another, gave you nowhere to look to pretend you were back on level ground. Once you began going up, you committed yourself to the vertical reality of the situation. So we went in haste, Benjamin promising we'd decide about correcting the sign after we'd played tourists for a spell. The windows proved to be the worst part, but Benjamin made it up level by level to the top floor, a small cage of thick plastic windows. Heavy binocular machines blocked an otherwise appealing view through those full-length windows, offering (for a mere quarter) whole seconds of in-depth scouting. I didn't want to see small bits of it clearer. I wanted to see the whole breadth better. These infernal devices stirred me into a defenestrating mood, but alas the windows were too thick and the machines too heavy even if they hadn't been bolted down. Also, I didn't want to pollute the Grand Canyon with large hunks of metal. We headed back down rapidly and decided we'd best experience the Canyon back outdoors—where it actually existed and where we belonged.

As we transitioned back from the gimcrack/knickknack mind-set to appreciating the magnificence of the Canyon, I started snapping pictures, including the obligatory fake-angled shot of Benjamin clinging for life to a shrub at cliff's edge. We followed a well-worn path leading past the railing that delimited the standard tourist area, into narrowing territory. The Canyon asserted its presence now on either side of us, but Benjamin gritted his teeth and forged on. We descended an outcropping of rock and rose again onto a ledge jutting out into the abyss. Here we again paused for pictures, and my fellow Leaguer snapped a portrait destined for fame, or at least for court documentation, depicting me with nothing but red chasm around me, wearing the camera strap around my chest like a sash, the Typo Correction Kit dangling benevolently at my side.

We discovered that our cell phones didn't get any reception, and

I thought it for the best. The last thing the place needed was a bunch of people shouting, "Can you hear me now?" and attempting—and failing—to describe what they saw before them.

After some navel-of-the-world-gazing, we adventured back to the watchtower. Benjamin had succumbed to the lure of the merchandising machine. He wanted to see if they had any postcards featuring gorgeous shots of the Canyon, which of course they did. Seeing as we were back inside the tower, we decided to return to the second level and its error-tainted sign. The floor was more crowded this time with other gawkers coming and going. I withdrew the yellow chalk that would put this sign to rights. Benjamin inconspicuously leaned forward and touched a finger to the apostrophe in "womens' ". The foul mark didn't wipe off. We looked at each other. "It's not a chalkboard," he said, shocked.

Here we made a fatal mistake in our reevaluation. The apostrophe's permanence was the biggest hint that this was no mere prop announcing a restaurant's specials du jour. Though it had that appearance, we should have guessed then that this sign was an inextricable feature of the place, more permanent than its resemblance to a held-back elementary school kid's social studies project would imply. But we didn't reexamine the big picture, as we were focused so much on the typo. Call it the Forest-for-the-Trees Fallacy, the very typo-hunting trap that I had warned myself against! Perhaps it was inevitable in a place like the Grand Canyon, which itself denies full vision of the whole. Our recalculations, then, centered only on the error: black background, paint on fiberboard, hmm, a marker could cover that apostrophe over. I passed Benjamin my marker. Now that we'd be using more than a finger to wipe it out, he'd have to wait with me for the decrease in traffic. We stepped back, and I noted that another tour was passing through. A ranger in glossy green led people down one stairwell and toward another, waiting for a few tourists coming up the stairs to clear the way. We hoped things would quiet in a moment.

Though *emense* loomed as a ridiculous spelling, I wasn't sure, what with the yellow chalk—no, paint?—if the elixir of correction would look presentable on that. So instead of going for the big correction, we decided to start with the small. To pass our moment of waiting, Benjamin read more of the sign and noted a spot needing a comma, where items in a list slammed together. *The center of the room is occupied by a snake altar, a sandpainting, religious crooks and wands carved wood figures of kachinas* . . . I remember skimming the sentence twice, first without and then with the proposed comma, and thinking in a Trussian way about how easily, in the absence of proper punctuation, sentences can come to grief.

Benjamin nodded at me when a quick look around told him that there were fewer people around. We had little time, so we moved in, striking together. I added two white elixir marks: an apostrophe for *women's* and the somewhat cosmetic comma to help prevent readers' stumbling mid-sentence. At the same time, Benjamin, with a quick stroke of marker, wiped the author's erroneously placed apostrophe from the sign so that no one need ever know. We stepped back, grimaced.

To the discerning eye, the two white marks stood out too boldly. While many passersby might not have noticed the coloration difference, especially in this dimly lit room, anyone looking for something amiss would certainly see it. I didn't bother with *emense*. Since I had discovered that my yellow chalk wouldn't work, I had no correction tool that could make it look good enough. We decided to be glad for what we'd gotten—we'd corrected a majority of the errors in the sign, two out of three, so we'd still get credit in the all-important tally—and head out. Then we went into that other gift shop a hundred yards down the sidewalk and corrected another typo. Now that we'd ruined the whole day-off idea, I didn't want it to be a single-typo day, especially not after such a fine string of high-count days. That accomplished, we returned to Callie for peanut butter sandwiches before driving on to the next site, clockwise around the Canyon.

The next viewing spot was better: fewer people, no tourist shops at all, and a mere wire guardrail to keep cars from going over. We were free to wander right to the edge of a sheer cliff, lie flat upon the rock, and crawl forward so that our heads poked out over the absolute drop.

TYPO TRIP TALLY

Total found: 101
Total corrected: 63

11 | **Pressed**

April 2-10. 2008 (Los Angeles, CA, to San Francisco, CA)

Lights, cameras, and . . . typo hunt! While a new Recruit joins
the ranks, and a faithful companion heads for the hills (or
rather, mountains), our Crusader comes face to lens with the
World of Television.

I paced beneath an umbrella resembling a peppermint at an In-N-
Out Burger stand, somewhere in the cosmic sprawl of Los Angeles. In one hand I held my cell phone. In the other, a cheeseburger
leaked between my fingers. An NBC producer barked at me through
the tiny speaker. I was doing my best imitation of a born Angeleno:
alternately bringing the phone to my ear and the burger to my teeth,
hoping that I would not confuse the routine. Josh Roberts had his
shades off, letting the sun soak into his freckled visage. The abundant luminosity of the West was still a new thing for him.

"Could you hold on a sec?" I said to the partially eaten burger, and
I turned to Josh. "He's playing hardass. Wants to film us *before* ABC,
not after. Says that he called me first."

"Tell him too bad," Josh said. "You just scheduled ABC."

"What if they can't do it after?"

"They'll make the time." He'd finished his own burger a few minutes ago and now plucked survivors from a cardboard dinghy of
fries. Josh had ordered his Animal Style (mustard-fried patty, extra
everything) off the secret menu, jumping into the adventure of
In-N-Out headfirst with both feet (if that's anatomically feasible) as

he had with the trip itself. My new TEAL colleague demanded a fully realized adventure. He'd stepped off the plane in San Diego with a binder full of places to visit, shenanigans to undertake, and cuisine to consume along the West Coast; mustard-fried patties were but the barest beginning.

I returned to the producer and told him our slot with ABC was fixed, but we'd gladly do a shooting with NBC afterward. He said gruffly that he wasn't sure about that, he'd have to call me back. I frowned, looked to Josh again. "I don't know if he's going to be able to do that. Maybe I should have tried to move ABC."

"He'll call back," he said. "Listen, Jeff—I've worked with enough producers to know their act. They'll wheedle you, they'll guilt-trip you, they'll bully you, whatever it takes to get the booking. But you're the boss here. It should be on your terms, not theirs."

I nodded at Josh's hard-won wisdom. He'd been immersed in the Biz for a long time through his commercial production gigs back in Manhattan. He was a pro, a clear-eyed operator who could bash through bluffs and feints with the blunt assertions of a native New Yorker. I, on the other hand, had never dealt with the good folks of the television industry, and my negotiation skills historically consisted of saying "Well, OK," and then running away. The seeming absurdity of the situation didn't help, either. They wanted *me,* an itinerant editor, on millions of TV screens?

The producer called back. He'd relented; the League would have consecutive filmings by the two major networks.

The tale of TEAL had, by this time, proved irresistible to various journalistic outlets. Our coverage snowballed in the typical pattern that media stories follow these days, starting as a tiny sphere picking up jacks and thimbles, gaining greater mass as it went, until the ball of our exposure was gigantic enough to accrete cities and islands and the Earth itself. It began with an NPR morning show in New York. Since at that point I was less than twenty-four hours into the trip, and a thorough neophyte at media appearances, I succeeded in giving as awkward and ineloquent an interview as humanly possible. Elderly listeners developed arrhythmia and high blood pressure, and younger listeners swore off radio for life. The public-speaking industry held an emergency conference to address this new threat to oratory. Yet somehow the piece interested enough people for the *Boston Globe* to pick up the thread. From there, more radio, print, and online outfits put in their nickel on the League, until we arrived at the present surreal juncture.

We headed for my cousin Steph's old apartment in Hollywood; she had moved out the prior week, but the place was available for a few more days. Benjamin was staying with a friend, so we wouldn't see him until tomorrow for the ABC filming. As soon as Josh and I got to Hollywood, we understood why my cousin's move had been a sage idea. We spent many fruitless hours circling the streets for a parking spot, like buzzards in a carrion drought. We ended up stashing Callie overnight in a sketchy garage for a jacked-up, illicit after-hours rate. The neighborhood, however, did have one advantage: with its many stores and cafés and tourist attractions, it would be rich territory for typo hunting.

The next day we met the *ABC World News* filming crew on Hollywood Boulevard, a block or two from my cousin's old place. Benjamin had rejoined Josh and me—in fact, it was the first time that the three of us joined forces for typo hunting. But other factors complicated this auspicious occasion: the giant video camera floating in my wake, and the affable, gray-haired correspondent sauntering at my side. Ordinarily the success of our craft rested on careful wording and subtle approaches—but today the League was a spectacle.

I presented as natural a face as I could to the TV folks, but secretly I chafed with worry. Unsupervised, unobserved, TEAL could work at a languid pace if it so desired, and it was free to fail due to wrong turns or simple bad luck. Now, though, the pressure was on. I *had* to find typos, and quickly, or we'd look like fools. And we had to get at least some of them corrected, or we'd look ineffectual, pointless. The correspondent and the camera guy nodded to each other, and the film began to roll. I smiled nervously and jumped into the nearest souvenir shop.

My eyes scanned the displays, while Benjamin and Josh split off to do the same. Despite my nervousness, it took me all of thirty seconds to snare the first prey of the day for the League. Amid the commemorative sweatshirts and toy clapper boards, a small sign advertised Fine Art Monogram Souvenirs, whatever those were. In the text below the title lurked a classic mistake, one that we had seen before in a California ghost town three days prior: "Stationary", when they'd meant *Stationery*. The sign was talking about notepaper, not standing in place. In normal circumstances I would have had the choice of either correcting the error on the sly or alerting the store manager, but the presence of my entourage made that choice for me. As everyone converged on me, seeing that I had found something, the manager materialized at my elbow.

"Uh . . . hi," I said to her. "We've got 'stationary' here, and it should actually be spelled *e-r-y* instead of *a-r-y*. Could I go ahead and fix that?"

Everyone focused on the manager, including the all-seeing lens. She gave our company an uncertain look and decided that being accommodating on camera could only help business. "Sure."

"Should be a pretty simple fix here," I said reassuringly, markering out the offending letter and painting in an *e* with elixir.

"That's a sign made by some stationery *company*," the

ABC correspondent said to me in disbelief (or at least an approxi-
mation of disbelief for the camera).

I nodded. "You'd think they'd be more careful, but . . . they're not."

As we continued our rounds, I thought about what physicists
and psychologists term the "observer effect": the changes that an
observer inevitably makes on whatever she is observing, by the very
act of observation. With the camera crew in tow, the reaction of
each shopkeeper or clerk was automatically altered before I so much
as opened my mouth. Sometimes the producer would hustle into
a store to negotiate the right for me to enter the place, and often
people would agree to corrections to appease the implied judgment
of the video camera. Whenever the producer asked for permission to
film us correcting typos, he was effectively asking permission for us
to correct the typos as well. It was typo hunting through a skewed,
La-La-Land lens, and it created its own reality.

The correspondent, the producer, and the cameraman converged
with a request. That first catch was good, but could I think a little
bigger?

Bigger? said I.

More *visual,* they clarified. They wanted a big ol' booboo that
would heighten our little drama. They wanted another one of those
Benjamin's-head-sized apostrophes, something that I'd need to
splash with a pail of correction fluid.

"Er—sure," I said.

Aiming to please, Benjamin and Josh and I turned our hawklike eyes to the garish landscape around us. We unearthed errors
in T-shirt stands, marquees, cafés, and of course more souvenir
places. Then we came to The Coffee Bean & Tea Leaf, where our
ABC friends offered to buy us beverages. I walked up to the counter and SWEEDISH BERRIES jumped out at me right away. A chalkboard typo, easy enough to fix, or so I thought. The producer
talked to the baristas and came to us shaking his head: no cameras
inside. At this, the cameraman shrugged, noting that he would have
no problem shooting from the outside in through the large glass

exterior of the coffee shop, so he went out to position himself. I brought the Sweedish up to the barista and requested a correction, and she paused. I knew that look well by now—the look that said *Sorry, ace, I don't know who you are or what you're saying, and I don't care. Brush-off in 3 . . . 2 . . . 1 . . .* But before her dismissal could launch, her eyes darted behind me, and caught sight of the guy outside pointing a giant lens at her through the pane. Lo, how the camera did then perform its thaumaturgy upon her! Suddenly she smiled and said that she would fix the error straightaway, and she turned and transformed two *e*s into one. Josh came over, not to offer his congratulations, but to boast that he'd found two punctuation-deprived signs on the same bathroom door.

Afterward, I conferred with the correspondent, the producer, and the cameraman. How was that for *visual*? Did the spectacle through the window meet with their approval? For that was what I now craved.

Well, they said. It was OK, it was visual, but perhaps still lacked zest, verve, a fresh and clean feeling. Could I be a shade more *daring*?

Benjamin, Josh, and I nodded. We would push back the brushy frontiers of typo hunting. There were certain zones that we had previously feared to tread. We corrected mistakes in a tattoo and piercing parlor, where the proprietor was happy to concede to the producer's requests, albeit with a sardonic smile. I reached up to make the minimum required fix to a sign reading WE DONT CARE!! HOW MUCH YOUR HOMIE CAN DO IT 4!!! We stalked the aisles of an army surplus store, where a sign for a HELLICOPTER HELMET didn't mean to imply that none but infernal pilots could wear it. Both places I probably wouldn't have been brave enough to police without my attendant platoon. Here, again, the camera crew had given me a strange kind of access or influence. Though there were always trade-offs. For every typo I gained thanks to them, there'd be another I'd lose somewhere else, at a business run by camera-shy folks. It was like reciting a poem through a bullhorn.

The ABC crew wrapped its footage of our corrections with their money shot: me adding the apostrophe to TODAYS SPECIAL, which was painted on the front window of a café. The cameraman ran back and forth through the doorway to film the action from both sides of the glass. After they had us take a couple of spins around the block in Callie so they could get driving shots, the first day of ordeals came to an end. I felt exhausted by the combination of typo hunting and pretending to be an interesting, photogenic person. As I calculated the day's reckoning for the blog that night, I was astonished to find that we had netted an incredible total of seventeen typos found, nine of which we were able to correct. In other words, the single most productive day of the entire trip. Still, I couldn't help but feel ambivalent about the whole thing. I was glad that the League's mission would have high-profile coverage, but I also recoiled from the mechanism of the filming. It wasn't so much that I minded playing the clown prince of correction—more that it had felt less personal and more antagonistic than ordinary TEAL practice. When a camera trails you like an unblinking henchman, your interactions with others automatically become more about *you* than anything else, stunts rather than meaningful conversations. We'd never intended to follow the model of Sacha Baron Cohen.

There *had* been a moment, fortunately, that clarified our motives and would appear in the actual piece, during a walk-and-talk that I did with the correspondent.

"You're very nice about it," he pointed out.

"It's not about making anybody feel bad, or, uh, or, uh, making somebody look stupid or something, it's just really about going after the errors themselves," said I with typical eloquence. This stance genuinely seemed to surprise him, as it contrasted with the unsympathetic, commas-and-brimstone temperament of most high-profile grammarians and sticklers. If viewers could take away that message—that blame should have no place in spelling and grammar—then our appearance would have been well worth the trouble.

Not that the trouble was over. We had to do it all over again the next day.

The three of us rendezvoused with NBC's *Today* crew at the Larchmont Village shopping district. The tree-lined street was a lot quieter than Hollywood Boulevard, feeling almost like a neighborhood in a normal city. The correspondent was younger than the ABC guy had been, playing more the hip contemporary than the amused observer. He wanted to find something that he could correct himself, because it would make a great visual. Could we go ahead and locate a sexily obvious typo? he asked us. *That* part sounded familiar.

First, though, the driving shots. Like ABC, they wanted to capture us cruising around in my car, but NBC harvested far more shots in this pursuit. At first I didn't get the fixation on Callie—she was a loyal old gal, but what did she have to do with the meat of our mission? I'd explained to them that we didn't spot all that many typos from the car. Then I realized that they had placed much importance on describing the visual language of the road trip. I am driving from city to city, so the viewer must see me physically behind the wheel, peering out the car windows, not to mention actually turning the key and starting the engine. We must create a simulacrum of traveling. The viewer might not understand otherwise. They lent Josh a video camera and instructed him to lean out the window to film Callie's wheels in motion.

The shortest part of the day was the typo hunting. Benjamin, Josh, and I had our voyeur-friendly routine down by now. We walked down the street and into promising establishments with deliberate steps, turning our bright faces to each other and attempting to make sound-bite-worthy comments. Upon entering Sam's Bagels, I spotted the misspelled varietals JALEPENO and PUMPERNICKLE, and the proprietor was happy to take the signs down and correct them himself. There wasn't much else to unearth on the street, however. We found a few more typos in boutiques here and there, but the haul paled in comparison to yesterday's. Nothing was big and beautiful enough for the correspondent himself to correct, and he seemed disappointed. Before we could try ranging farther for richer material, the crew declared that they had enough footage of our craft. They'd come up with a better idea for the correspondent's stand-up.

A "stand-up" is the correspondent directly addressing the camera, usually at the end of a piece, and it doesn't always involve standing up. For our piece, the correspondent sat at a table outside a café. Josh, Benjamin, and I were supposed to walk up behind him, sit down, and point out his name spelled wrong in the chyron below. Ho-ho, a virtual typo. We walked down that street about fifteen times, squeezed tightly against each other so that we all fit in the camera's eye, while they tried to time his speech to a perfect shot of us sitting down behind his table. It was fun, like we were C-listers making our big-screen debut in *Three Men Walk Purposefully Down the Sidewalk*. Once they gave us the thumbs-up, we TEALers hurrahed. A job well done, now time for lemonade!

But then the producer called me over, gesturing toward the car, and we topped off the day's filming with even more driving shots. Once again, the TV guys had decided that the imagery of the car—us driving around in the car, us getting into the car—was a necessary piece of the visual story. What could visually declare that this was a *Road Trip* better than *guys in car*? Where NBC put extra emphasis on the shots of Callie, ABC had put some extra emphasis on my Typo Correction Kit, an invention wholly my own, built and refined during the westward journey. They'd had me lay its contents on a table for a slow pan, and they made sure to include the Kit in shots of me. Both news teams had to assemble what was basically a two-minute movie, which had to include a proper setup and a catchy ending. I sympathized with the demands of storytelling. I only wondered what stories they were planning to tell.

The NBC folks departed, and then I had to say good-bye to my friend. If Benjamin were not about to hike the Appalachian Trail, I'd be worried about his ability to move on from the visceral thrills of tracking down typos. I was more concerned about his departure's effect on the League. Okay, its effect on *me*. How could I carry on without his zeal?

"Thanks for everything, buddy," I said. "I would never have made it this far without your help."

"Oh," he demurred, grasping my hand in a firm shake, "I'm sure you would have, *geographically*. But maybe not with a correction rate over fifty percent."

A numbers man to the end, I thought. "Well, have a safe flight back," I said. "And when you take your walk in the woods, stick to the path!"

"You get your ass up to Seattle—and Jane—in one piece," said Benjamin, and he headed for the nearest subway station on the Boulevard.

I opened the car door, but then I heard, "Oh, and Deck . . ." So I turned.

Benjamin stood some distance away on the sidewalk, pointing a pen at me. "The League is in your hands now!" he called. "Make me proud."

I saluted him with the Typo Correction Kit. Then he was gone, a champion off to new campaigns.

A few days later, first the *Today* piece and then the *World News* story aired. Josh and I didn't have a TV at our hostel in San Luis Obispo, so I had to catch the ABC clip online the next morning. I sat on the quilted bedspread, eating a Pop-Tart and Googling my own name. Before clicking on the video of the piece, I read the text associated with it—and froze. The toaster pastry fell from my hand.

"Typo Eradication *Assistance* League?"

"Uh-oh," Josh muttered.

The initial wave of stories about TEAL consisted largely of positive, sympathetic coverage, with equally positive reader response. We rejoiced in these pieces, seeing them as a confirmation that people besides us actually cared about the nits and grits of spelling and grammar. A few of the pieces strove for a deeper understanding of the mission, such as a story by the *Chicago Tribune,* which brought up the same dilemma of independent-store identity that I had fretted over in Santa Fe. However, something was missing from most of the stories about the League.

Our journey was, on the surface, simple. Man Drives Across U.S. Fixing Typos. There it is in six words. The *what* of the story is straightforward, which is probably what made it an attractive subject in the first place. The *why* of our story, however, is rather more complicated. Even we didn't have a full grasp of that part, at least not yet. Thus, whenever media outlets tried, in truncated fashion, to address the reasons for our mission, the results were less than enlightening. The *Today* piece on TEAL opened with the anchor saying, "In today's world of text messaging, odd abbreviations take the place of actually spelling out a word, so some would argue it's actually helped many of us forget the rules of the English language."

The blame-it-on-texts meme also popped up in the *Seattle Times,* the *Virginian-Pilot,* the *Albany Times-Union* (quoting a local English teacher), the *Nashua Telegraph,* the *Longmont Times-Call,* and London's *Guardian* ("the barbarous neologisms of text-speak"), though I said not a word about texting in my interviews. It was a general, unexamined answer for why modern spelling often falters—easy, pithy, and therefore useful.* Note the *Today* anchor's use of that slippery word *some.* "*Some* would argue" that texting is destroying English. Nobody specific is actually mentioned here, so the viewer would have to assume that it's common knowledge, and even that we Leaguers had undertaken our trip for that reason. Jack Shafer, *Slate* magazine's curmudgeonly media critic, classifies *some,* along with *many, few, often, seems, likely,* and *more,* as "weasel-words," a favorite tool of journalists "who haven't found the data to support their argument."

Blaming spelling errors on cell-phone argot is silly enough. We veer painfully close to the aching borderlands of irony, though, when

---

* Hopefully, informed debunkings such as David Crystal's recent *Txtng: The Gr8 Deb8* will finally lay this myth to rest.

there are errors in stories about guys fixing errors. Coverage of our mission included a bushel of outright mistakes, all of which could have easily been avoided by taking a second glance at the TEAL website. These weren't obscure bits of arcana, just the answers to basic questions:

What does "TEAL" stand for? Not only did we apparently call ourselves the "Typo Eradication Assistance League," but we were also known as the Typo *Elimination* Advancement League, according to the article in *The Dartmouth*. I admit that I chose a long name for our team for humorous effect, but come on.

What are our names? In the print edition of the *Boston Globe* story about us, a photo caption identified me as Benjamin and Benjamin as me. The identity of my bewhiskered companion came constantly into question. The *Baltimore Sun* ran a photo caption identifying Benjamin as the twenty-third president of the United States—Benjamin Harrison. He appeared in the *World Almanac*, of all places, wearing my middle name as his first, as Michael Herson. The magazine *Utne Reader* inexplicably referred to him as Jeremy, perhaps to help him fit in with the rest of the League, Jeff, Josh, and Jane.

Where did the trip start? The *Guardian* had us beginning our trip in San Francisco and heading due east, perhaps confused by the BBC interview I did in San Francisco. Portland's *Oregonian* got the starting city right, but then blew its spelling: "Summerville," Massachusetts? Sounds magical!

What did I say? Britain's *The Sun* apparently took as gospel an article on TEAL in the satirical magazine *Private Eye*, quoting me as lobbing rather harsh words: "Some people just have no feeling for language." The BBC Magazine Monitor, in turn, dutifully quoted *The Sun* as quoting me saying that. Call me Jeremy if you want, but don't put words in my mouth, mates.

We were only some dudes driving around with markers. It's not like they screwed up reportage on an Iraq offensive, so who cares about whether they got *our* little story right? But every word in a news story presumably rests on research; every dollop of delicious factual nougat has supposedly been vetted by somebody. The widespread occurrence of errors about our trip gets a body wondering . . . what *other* stories have been misreported? One of the most egregious recent examples involved all the major media outlets parroting a story about a California paraplegic being healed by the bite of a brown recluse spider. Turns out nobody stopped to catch their breath and check the facts. The paraplegic was probably never paraplegic in the first place, which doctors only discovered once the spider bite got the guy to the hospital. Plus, there are no brown recluses in California, at least not outside of the arachnid zoo. Even if it had been one, the brown recluse's venom is cytotoxic—it breaks down cells instead of repairing them.

Sounds ridiculous, until you consider that if a paper or website or cable channel doesn't jump on a breaking story right away, they'll look slow, out of touch. We, the consumers of all massively distributed information, made them that way. We demand information faster with each passing year and each emergent technology, heedless of that information's accuracy, seeking only to keep the data IV pumping into our ravenous vessels. What is actually said matters less than its *immediacy*. It doesn't have to be this way, though.

O fellow slaves to the datastream, I exhort you! Rise up and shuck your shackles!

Ahem. All right, I'm not an expert, I just played one on TV. Already far too much media criticism bobs around the Oceanus of the Internet, unsolicited and often hooting and jeering. The media are overextended and fighting to stay afloat, with shrinking revenues, massive staff layoffs, and unsustainable business models. So I won't join the harpoon-slinging pack. I'm a guy who likes to read every piece of text he passes by; I tend to amble and ruminate. My ideal mediaverse would feature fewer, longer pieces in print and online; trading the cable-news trend of obsessively gnawing a few lean story bones for more measured, thoughtful coverage; and journos who have time to get the story right because readers and viewers chill while the fact-checkers earn their paychecks.* I suspect we could all live with considerably less fluff in our news diet, as well. Nonprofit investigative news outfits like ProPublica and public radio programs by NPR and American Public Media provide an excellent antidote to shallow stories, but they rely on donations to survive. I'm not suggesting that everyone run out and get an *All Things Considered* tote bag, or that television networks altruistically cut the entertainment angle from news programs, returning them to their original loss-leader status. I merely offer an observation for your consideration: Every time we change the channel or click a link, we determine the path trod by the media beast.

Days later, I steeled my nerves and stepped out in front of the slow surge of cars. I was on a steep hill in San Francisco; I'd had to wait for a trolley to clatter by. Across the street, an attractive blond producer named Zoë beckoned to me. A blight upon sexy British accents, I thought as I clomped along at a deliberate pace, trying to ignore the blare of horns and the menace of nearby bumpers. After about five lonely weeks on the road, I would have walked into traffic for just about any winsome smile. Jane was nearly a hemisphere away, and I missed her terribly.

The BBC's coverage of the League had hardly turned out more sophisticated than that of its American counterparts. They opted for a Wild West theme, thanks to the Santa Fe hat that I still wore as a spur to the mission. At this moment I found myself participating in a staging of the lone cowboy forging ahead through a herd of steel cattle, or at least that's what they seemed to be reaching for. I'd recently completed a slew of takes of me walking up the hill, and then back down to come back up again. The theatre of the piece had required many other shots—even more, it seemed, than either of the TV crews had wanted in Los Angeles. These folks needed me walking and tapping the "holstered" Typo Correction Kit at my side

---

* Six-fifty an hour, as I recall from my intern days.

and walking some more. They needed the hat, and the shadow of the hat. The correspondent had performed little magic tricks between takes, to stave off monotony.

At a Beat Museum dedicated to Jack Kerouac and his cohorts, the BBC correspondent had seen something Kerouackian—Kero-*wacky*, if you will—in my mission and thus deemed the locale appropriate for a walk-and-talk that would end the piece. This piece of stagecraft would involve us waltzing by a bin of books, picking one of them up, and then me explaining to the correspondent why TEAL stood for all those who did not have the faculty to express themselves as well as Kerouac, or some bollocks like that. They wanted a smooth sound bite from me that would encapsulate the mission's purpose. What they got was several takes, with us continually walking back over to the bin while I mumbled something different each time. Sometimes when I picked up a book, I'd drop it on the floor. At take five or six, the correspondent looked like he'd rather be doing a magic trick, or anything else.

Probably the most awkward stop had been at a sex shop in the North Beach neighborhood. As with the tattoo parlor and the army-surplus place back on Hollywood Boulevard in L.A., I became filled with the compulsion and courage to go into a more unconventional venue to correct typos, in large part due to the camera crew at my back. I found a pair of typos right away in an ad for a lube that apparently possessed the following traits: MIMICS THE BODIES OWN LUBRICATING FLUIDS, and COMPATIBLE WITH CONDOMS & DIAPHRAMS. The subsequent awkwardness was caused not by the owner of the shop—who turned out to be a nice guy who was happy to let me correct the mistakes—but by the mere, leering presence of me and a British news outfit in such a place. We had barged into the establishment essentially for an expected comedic payoff. I felt more like a feckless mountebank than ever. Sheepishly I made my correction with the camera rolling.

Now, if I made it to the curb without dying, my ordeal would be over. I pressed on, steadily avoiding a peek at the annoyed San

Franciscans in their hybrid Priuses and Jettas. When I reached the sidewalk, Zoë exchanged signals with the far cameraman and then clapped me on the back. "Right, then, brilliant," she said. "How about a beer?"

We headed back to their car, where we saw that the correspondent had fallen asleep, his face pressed against the window. The cameraman took some optional footage of this, and we all headed to their hotel's bar. I enjoyed three rum-and-Cokes on the BBC and inwardly toasted Benjamin with his favorite drink.

In the morning I did an interview with a Minnesota Public Radio show called *Grammar Grater,* which assembles thoughtful weekly episodes on spelling and grammar. My confidence on air had power-leveled since the NPR stutterfest on the second day of the trip. Of course, I could also credit my alertness in the interview to the coarse wakeup of the morning's previous interview, with a pair of Iowan shock jocks (though, how shocking could they be, interviewing a grammarian?). As the style of my interviewers swung from fart jokes to engaged questions, I could see the contradictory forces yanking at the public over the airwaves, some daring to offer us insight, some quailing to go near such a thing. I couldn't have guessed that an altogether different tug-of-war lay in store for my mission, with ropes taut and combatants ready to pull.

Typo Trip Tally

Total found: 183
Total corrected: 104

12 | You Got a Friend

April 12–17, 2008 (San Francisco, CA, to Vancouver, BC)

As they round the treacherous curves of the PCH, our Hero and his new firebrand companion do great Deeds in the name of their mother Tongue. Yet all is not well. There is a traitor among them, and a frightening revelation, in the manner of an evil Chicken, is coming home to roost in the head of our Hero.

Josh cracked San Francisco open like a mussel, seeking the sweet creature within. He did the same with every city on our itinerary, but this, the jubilant locus of northern California, came the closest to satisfying his voracity for new experiences and sights and craft beers. His wide-ranging enthusiasm helped to revive me somewhat from the travel-weariness I felt at this point. Without Josh, I would not have ventured into the recondite shops of Haight-Ashbury, would not have encountered the drugged-out denizens of Golden Gate Park, would not have sampled the city's finest Vietnamese and Mexican, nor its nonfigurative and quite tasty mussels themselves. Nor would I have wound up at the Cartoon Art Museum, concealed in the financial district's thicket of towers.

At the time of our visit, the museum featured an exhibit on "Sex and Sensibility," profiling ten female cartoonists and their work. What a splendid way, I thought, to honor some of the lesser-known players in the comics game, artists and writers and humorists who deserved more recognition for their talent. Then I started reading the biographical plaques—and the fires of righteous fury licked at the periphery of my vision.

It was a whole *gallery* of errors. They ranged from relatively minor mistyping ("... raised in one of he lesser parts of the greater Chicago area", "Her father often said in is jovial way ...") to words that were garbled ("I admit I became kind of a bif fishas flounder of Kirshenbaum ...") to places in the text where it appeared that whole words or even phrases were missing ("Interestingly, while she did not have a favorite Beatle, she did have a minute-and-a-half and then went on to work at numerous jobs ...", "I always loved to draw and really loved in a cartoony way"). There were mistakes littering every one of the ten biographies.

Josh shook his head upon seeing the errors. "To think we paid six bucks a head to see this," he said, disgusted. With stunning ease, he shed his tourist mantle, and his New Yorker aggression kicked in. "Let's go tell them right now. Let's make sure they fix every single typo!"

"In the name of the League!" I agreed, but Josh was already moving.

He marched over to the woman at the front desk; I hurried to follow. Thinking that his problem-solving approach might involve a quick jab to her face, I subtly shouldered him to the side and took over, asking to speak with the curator of the "Sex and Sensibility" exhibit. I explained that typos riddled all their biographies. Her eyes narrowed and she opened with a self-defensive maneuver. She said that they'd had a high-school intern type up most of the signs, as if it were acceptable to lay the blame on that poor kid.

"Why don't you come and take a look at the errors?" Josh said. He had decided to go with verbal pugilism rather than physical, so he added, "FYI, you'll need a good ten minutes to see them all."

She walked over to the exhibit with us. I pointed out the "I became kind of a bif fishas flounder" one as an example. Before I could catalog the other mistakes for her, the museum associate changed tactics. She might have seen that these textual sins were too heavy to lay exclusively on the thin shoulders of the high-school intern. She now said that all the biography signs had been copied from a book that had inspired the exhibit. She claimed she'd done a couple of the signs herself and had noticed errors in the book biographies.

Hmm. "So you faithfully copied the errors over into the exhibit signs?" I said.

She didn't respond to this, perhaps realizing that whatever answer she'd give would make her look even worse. Instead, she directed my attention to the book (itself titled *Sex and Sensibility*), which was in the museum gift shop. Josh and I leafed through until we found the biographies.

"Aha!" Josh said. "Look, it's right here—this woman was 'kind of a *big fish as founder* of Kirshenbaum'. Not a freaking *flounder*!"

A flounder *is* kind of a big fish, but I was sure the correlation was coincidental. We read on, realizing that the museum had to be the culprit for the mistakes. The book version of the biographies, the source material, was error-free. Only by reading them could we understand what the exhibit versions had been trying to say.

We went back to the associate and I explained what we had found. For the integrity of the exhibit, and respect for the cartoonists themselves, could the museum fix the signs?

The woman sighed. "You're the first person who's ever said anything about the mistakes. Here's the name of the curator." Then she added, "I really doubt that they'd get fixed even if you tell him about them." With that, she delicately removed the gauntlet from her slender hand and threw it to the floor. I bent down and picked up the damascened steel glove, accepting the challenge, and Josh and I walked out. Given the hostile response from the museum associate, I didn't hold out much hope that the curator would listen to little old me.

So I set my readers on him. My *minions*, cropping up in ever-greater numbers each day on the TEAL blog. I'm not sure how many people harassed this poor caretaker through beseeching e-mails and phone calls, but from the reports that readers sent me,

I'm guessing that the guy had a full in-box. The curator popped up on the blog a couple of days later saying that he'd had the signs corrected and begging that I call off the TEAL devotees, who apparently were still inundating him with "vitriolic and speculative" messages. I did, satisfied that justice had been wrought. When certain factions online questioned my judgment in loosing the pack in the first place, Josh stepped in—acting as my second in comment-section duels, on my blog and elsewhere—and vigorously defended me.

We left San Francisco, raring to tackle the rest of the West Coast. But man, was there a lot of it left. North of San Francisco, the coast's population drops sharply, and doesn't pick up again until halfway into Oregon, somewhere around Eugene. We weathered six hours' worth of driving—including a single typo correction at a remote deli—up to Klamath, California, where the very last hostel of the TEAL journey awaited us, a lone wooden house tucked in among endless woods by a stony shore. Somewhere along the way, the temperature had taken a sharp dive, marking our welcome to the Pacific Northwest. There were no typos to find near the hostel, nor indeed even a speck of civilization. Originally the plan had been to take in the nearby forest of redwoods, but by the time we arrived, night had fallen. We stepped out into the drizzle and smuggled booze into the hostel along with our food, knowing that we'd not leave the place until the light of morning.

The next day we powered on all the way to Portland. Jane was in my thoughts constantly now. Her arrival at the Seattle airport was not far away, so every mile brought me closer to her. Again we found ourselves on the road for about six hours, and didn't get into town until evening. Josh had proven a doughty companion for the road, taking intermittent shifts at the wheel, which were crucial at times like this for meeting the demanding pace of the itinerary. I'm not sure whether this trek or that of the previous day took the technical cake for longest travel day of the TEAL trip. All I know is that the consecution of two epic slogs made for tired Leaguers. Nonetheless, soon after we checked into our hotel, my brother in error-sleuthing said, "Let's hit the town!"

I remained in a state of collapse on my bed. "Can we do that from here?"

"Man up!" said Josh. "We only have two nights in Portland, and *I* intend to enjoy them." He began to search online for the most succulent dinner and distinctive spirits in the neighborhood.

Yes, get out there, but forget grub, rebuked a voice in my head that sounded a lot like Benjamin. *You haven't done your hunt today.*

I'm hungry, and beat, I argued back. Tomorrow would be fine. Before Josh, I had spent more than three weeks on the road with the real Benjamin, who possessed a whole-minded focus on the mission and relative disinterest in sightseeing and cuisine. Why *shouldn't* I now follow Josh's lead and allocate a little more time for enjoyment?

You're on a daily mission, yo, said the haranguer, still in Benjamin masquerade. *You should be . . . HUNTING!*

Hunting for typos in the dark?

My internal interlocutor hesitated. *You could have found some already today. That's two days in a row of slacking.*

Where? Where in the textless hills and vacant roads should I have gone looking? Was I supposed to conjure typos to fix from the insensate air, during all those lonely miles between San Francisco and here?

The voice did not respond, so I considered the argument won. Josh and I headed out for burgers at an independent brewery. We ate well there and everywhere else during our brief stay in Portland, including a great breakfast place that through the power of their pancakes could be forgiven for refusing to let me fix their chalkboard. It was feeling like a real live vacation. Still, I could not help but remember the chiding voice in my head, accusing me of dereliction.

Perhaps that was how I came to folly the next day. We met up with David Wolman, an enthusiast of the League whose book on the history of English spelling, *Righting the Mother Tongue*, would come out later that year (not to be confused with Bill Bryson's *The Mother Tongue,* also a book about English language history). Wolman obviously had the same orthographic topics near to his own heart, but he expressed surprise upon meeting me that I wasn't more of a hardliner. As a chronically poor speller, he'd suffered through countless indignities at the hands of unsympathetic schoolmarms and grammar cops. I wondered how he'd gotten the impression that I was like them; did I come off that way in the blog? As we chatted about wayward apostrophes and such at a bistro on Alberta Street, I mentioned a sign that I'd noticed on our way over, in the window of a restaurant closed for the day: "He was a bold man that first eat an oyster", attributed to Jonathan Swift.

"I keep mulling it over," I said. "Obviously grammatical syntax was not quite the same in Swift's day, and yet it seems . . . *wrong* to me."

Wolman agreed but could not be sure.

"Why don't we look it up online?" Josh said, offering up another brindled calf to the voracious elder gods of technology. I agreed to this, as Josh's Google spellcheck trick had served us well back in San Francisco, when we'd confirmed the spelling of *bustier* in a second-hand clothing shop.

Wolman pulled out a device with browsing capability and punched the quote into Google, both the way that the restaurant had it and the way that I thought it ought to be, "the man that first *ate* an oyster." He announced that my way had returned more results than the restaurant's way. The virtual jury had spoken.

After our rendezvous with Wolman, Josh and I went back to the closed restaurant and taped a small sign over the window with our correction. Below it, we left a business card. We congratulated ourselves for bettering the restaurant's image in the eyes of the dining public, and went off to grab some seafood.

Only problem was, the virtual jury had been wrong. Later in the evening I did some Internet research of my own and discovered that "first eat an oyster" was, in fact, the correct wording of the Swift quote: "He was a bold Man, that first eat an Oyster" says the Colonel in Swift's *Polite Conversation* (at least according to an 1892 printing). I felt the flush of terrible shame redden me from toe to crown. I knew then that I should not have rushed to fix something that I wasn't absolutely sure was incorrect. Tie goes to the proprietor. Though we made no permanent alteration to the sign, the Swift blunder is still one of the two moments that I truly regret during the TEAL trip.*

On we journeyed to Washington State the next day, and the sun broke the gloom, lending considerable beauty to Puget Sound as we arrived in Tacoma. My friend from kindergarten days, Carson, lived in an attractive neighborhood right by the water. He grilled some salmon and the three of us stayed up for a while that evening, getting drunk on wine and watching stupid television. This traditional display of camaraderie helped things feel normal for a while, until I realized I was still wearing my cowboy hat.

"I've got to put in time at the base tomorrow," said Carson. "Hey, if you want, I could—"

"*Show us around?!*" Josh interrupted, slamming down his empty glass. "Oh *yeah*!" He clapped me on the shoulder, and I tore my gaze away from the bright parade of ephemera onscreen. Maybe it was an afterimage from the TV, or the wine, but I thought I could see jets swooping and barreling in Josh's fervid eyes. "Don't we, Jeff? We do, don't we."

"Of course we do," I said. McChord Air Force Base would be a poor venue for typo hunting, what with all the men with guns and all, but I wasn't about to deny Josh the latest bounty on his quest to see the coolest stuff ever.

"I considered being a fighter pilot," Carson said to us the next day as we walked beside him on the tarmac of an airstrip. He was dressed

---

* The restaurant closed its doors the following year—though probably our note didn't have anything to do with it. Portland experienced what alt-weekly *Willamette Week* called a "Restaurant Apocalypse" starting in late 2008 and lost many great independent spots, thanks to the economy tanking.

in full lieutenant's regalia, complete with jaunty hat. "But then I realized that I would rather just go someplace and have lunch."

Hence his decision to fly transport jets. Which still impressed the stuffing out of me and Josh. Carson had shown us the interior of a C-17 Globemaster III. It was a giant machine that would climb into the air and convey teenagers with guns to foreign lands. We met a few of these kids in the plane. I couldn't help but feel silly. Here were guys several years younger than me with the means of war in their hands, and what was *I* doing? Semantically skirmishing with markers and elixir of correction? How could my frivolous quest even compare to the *vitality* of the lives these young men led?

I came away from that C-17 troubled by doubts. The airmen I'd met could be certain that they were making a difference, protecting their country from fanatics and evil hearts. By contrast, the Jonathan Swift incident the other day had demonstrated the fine line I myself walked between helping and harming. What kind of good could I be doing, if it could so quickly turn to wrong? As we walked off the airstrip, Carson swiveled toward me and barked, "Jeff! Don't step over that."

I had come close to crossing an innocuous red line painted on the tarmac, near the fence. "Why?"

"Because if you do," said Carson, "an alarm will be triggered, and the base police will come and shoot you."

"Oh. All right."

I stepped well clear of the mortal line, which upon closer inspection was accompanied by a legend saying something about "authorized deadly force." Yes, it would have been helpful to see that earlier. Never had text been so vital to my well-being. Though I had broken many rules so far on the trip, I preferred to do so when the consequences were a little less severe—say, involving an angry shopkeeper instead of a squad with M16s.

Way back in January, Josh had suggested a daring revision to our West Coast schedule: that we forge a path past Seattle and land in Vancouver for an evening, before doubling back to meet Jane's arrival at Sea-Tac. So now we pushed on past Seattle and across the Canadian border, keen to spice up the Typo Hunt Across America with a dash of foreign savor.

At the crossing, a gruff customs officer interrogated us about our purposes for visiting, trying to get us to admit that we were potheads who intended to harass the honest Canadian populace with our grubby mid-continental ways. We elected not to mention the true purpose of our visit, since it did, technically, include at least a minimum of harassment. Annoyance and discomfort had revealed themselves, I thought, as the golden core of TEAL.

Using the interwebbing skills for which he is renowned, Josh landed us semi-swanky accommodations in downtown Vancouver for a decent price. My initial impression was that the city did not diverge in any noticeable fashion from many of the American cities that I'd already seen. But for the chill in the air, and the vaguely British twist to the spelling on signs, Vancouver could have been San Diego or Atlanta. The following day, we'd take a stroll in the giant park capping the north side, and that generous amount of wildness would lend some character to the city, but this evening's perambulation along lively Robson Street gave a familiar impression. Our search yielded pretty much the same types of errors we'd been finding stateside (mostly missing letters and punctuation). Our correction rate remained low to nonexistent. We wished to be on our best behavior in a foreign land, and unfortunately most of the typos could not be fixed without risking an international incident.

Then we stopped.

LONLEY? asked the chalkboard. YOU GOT A FRIEND IN BOOZE.

Josh was the one who'd pointed out the sign. We peered at the specimen, and I felt a thin rivulet of confidence feed into my heart's murky pool. I had done plenty of chalkboards on this trip. We could fell this typo for sure. There was an apostrophe mistake on the other side, too. Josh gave me a determined nod. I smiled. After all we'd been through, I could count on him as a hardened veteran of the League. He said, "Nobody's looking right now. Let's just do it—give me half of that chalk, and I'll do one side and you do the other."

"Sure," I said. "You get the apostrophe one, and I'll do *lonley.*"

"What?"

"Lonley," I repeated, confused now. "The typo you so astutely pointed out on this side of the board."

Josh peered at the chalkboard. "Oh yeah, that's a good one!"

"Uh . . . what were you looking at, if not that?"

He indicated the next line down. "See, there. *You got a friend.* Should be *You've got a friend.*"

"That's not a typo. They're trying to be slangy."

"It's not *right,* though."

"It's a style thing. You have to allow room for self-expression."

Josh shrugged. "All right, let's do our corrections."

He went around and added the apostrophe needed on the other side. As carefully as I could, I converted the *e* to an *l* and vice versa in LONLEY on my side. When Josh came back, he decided to add his own correction below that, regardless of what I thought. Thus, to my dismay, a 'VE appeared, like a dark djinn summoned to fulfill the wishes of the black-hearted.

"Dammit, Josh!" I said. "That wasn't a typo. For real. Take that out." He refused. And then it was clear to me: an insurgent had somehow entered the ranks of TEAL, right under my marker-flecked nose.

How did we get here? First I had to take a hard look at the siege engine I had set grinding toward the citadel of English. What was the League about, *really*? Not the idealized form in my head, but its literally stated goals, and our practices in carrying them out. The original mission statement read, in part:

> [S]lowly the once-unassailable foundations of spelling are crumbling, and the time has come for the crisis to be addressed. We believe that only through working together with vigilance and a love of correctness can we achieve the beauty of a typo-free society.

There was no room for subtlety or individual expression in those words. It was a call to war. I had created a dread automaton that chugged along according to inexpertly programmed instructions. I could see now how in line Josh was with our mission according to its very definition. As in every other aspect of his journey, he had jumped into typo hunting with surpassing vigor. He had overfixed the chalkboard because that meant extra points, giving a 110 percent effort to the mission. Josh wasn't the traitor to the cause. *I* was.

No wonder I had gotten so many puzzlingly fanatical comments on the blog from people who decried the decline of America through bad spelling, who wanted me to correct the way that people *talked* as well as the way that they wrote. No wonder Wolman had assumed that I'd be a hardliner until he'd met me. The League was carrying out the dream of hardliners everywhere. That wasn't what I'd intended at all. I had sought to overstate things a bit in the mission statement, to recognize through self-parodying pomposity that my journey bordered on the absurd; e.g., referring to typos as "vile stains on the delicate fabric of our language." I hadn't expected anyone to nod gravely at my words, missing the hyperbole.

Josh's approach to YOU GOT A FRIEND IN BOOZE was perfectly consistent with his previous actions. He had displayed a straightforward approach to typo hunting from the start. Back in L.A., when I'd pointed out a fuel pump label that said HARMFUL OR FATAL IS SWALLOWED, he was unimpressed until I went around and corrected each instance of the error on all seven pumps. It was a concrete task for him, a checklist in which each box must be filled in completely with a No. 2 pencil. Fix every occurrence, change every wrong into right, and then you can have your beer. Upon noticing how often we ran into "owners expense" signs, Josh proclaimed them the "bread and butter of TEAL," seeing each instance as basically another job to be done. Now I realized the implications of this functional approach to language: Josh was a prescriptivist.

The popular perception of English-y folks, or language nerds, is that we are a fairly monolithic group of preposition-obsessed finger-waggers. But bitter ideological divides are a characteristic of every field of interest, and spelling and grammar are no exception. O how the fires of battle rage between the two camps of dogma! To all those who ordinarily give change junctions no more than a passing thought—beware!

The Prescriptivist is typified by Lynne Truss and the Old Guard of English conventions, columnists in the tradition of William Safire, and many language-based humorists. Call this one the Grammar Hawk. The Hawk swings and punches in the cause of linguistic tradition, i.e., the way that we've habitually been spelling and punctuating words for a long time. The philosophy here is that there is one proper way to go about orthography, and one way only: what the dictionary and grammar textbooks instruct us to do. These are the standards that have arisen from consensus and that provide the greatest clarity in writing. The Hawk tells people how they *should* spell.

The Descriptivist represents most academics (linguists, English professors, cognitive scientists) and dictionary staff. We can call him the Grammar Hippie, for he advocates a passive, observational approach to spelling and grammar. The Hippie merely notes how people *do* spell, here and now. They refer to "Standard" English rather than "correct" English because many equally valid variations exist; Standard English possesses no absolute, data-proven superiority over other dialects. All of orthography's supposed conventions and rules are ultimately subjective, sometimes even with oppressive agendas behind them. Language is in a continual state of growth and flux.

I hadn't thought about this conflict much when starting out on the mission—I'd been focused on my own personal interpretation of what typos were, of when to consider something an error. Now that I was forced to examine it, typo hunting looked completely antithetical to Grammar Hippie beliefs, but I didn't feel comfortable with the pure Grammar Hawk approach, either. Black and white could not by themselves paint the complex portrait of American English. (Or rather, *North* American English, here in the dark streets of Vancouver.) Ideally, people would see the nuances, would recognize that something like LONLEY would never be right, but that they were free to bend their speech to a certain degree in the service of dialect and individual character, that indeed such practices were healthy and necessary to the ongoing evolution of a language. However, everyone ended up choosing one side or the other, donning either the feathers of the Hawk or the tie-dye of the Hippie.

Even the triumph of the Cartoon Art Museum corrections seemed sour now, considering the mass bullying it had taken to get anything done. I'd needed to resort to an unsubtle, Hawklike maneuver; I couldn't imagine marshaling the troops on a regular basis. For a moment I feared that TEAL's entire mission was misguided on some fundamental level—or even futile, like flinging thimblefuls of water onto a beached whale. One typo correction at a time hardly seemed an adequate pace for bringing about a better world.

Coming back to the present, where Josh still fixed me with challenging eyes, I capitulated. I let the hated 've stand on the sign, and we moved on. We grabbed some mediocre Japanese food and headed back to the hotel, and I spent a restless night thinking about what I'd become.

Before departing the next day, Josh wanted to buy some Canadian beer to bring back with us across the border. The shop we chose turned out to be overpriced, but that was not its sole failing: one sign proclaimed a particular vintage A DELIGHTFUL WINE JUST TO SIP ON IT'S OWN.

That morning, I'd seen a restaurant marquee promising GREEK

FOOD AT IT'S BEST. I was beginning to think that Canadians had as much trouble with the *its/it's* thing as Americans. But who could blame them? *Its/it's* confusion is one of the most common and pervasive types of errors in modern English. We're taught that apostrophes go with possessives like fish with chips, and so when making *it* possessive, the natural choice is to add that obligatory apostrophe. Oh, but our instincts betray us! *Its* is different thanks to its status as a pronoun, much like *his* or *her* (e.g., *Josh Roberts at his best*). *It's* can only mean *it is*. The apostrophe's dual role as both possessive-maker and contraction-maker causes a conflict of interest here, which nineteenth-century printers did not adequately take into account when cementing apostrophe rules in the first place. The distinction is stupid and arbitrary, yes, and until someone comes up with a better idea, we can at least take comfort from knowing that it's the fault of long-dead printers and not us.

All three members of the liquor store staff were watching me with cold and suspicious eyes. One of them approached and asked if she could help me. I told her that she could, actually, and pointed out the *it's*.

Her reaction was frosty. "Does it really matter?"

"It does," I said. I held back from explaining the mission, from elaborating beyond those simple two words. Suddenly I didn't feel like identifying myself by the greater scale of my efforts. I didn't want to be a Grammar Hawk in her eyes. "Do you mind if I fix it? I can just make the *s* bigger to absorb the apostrophe."

"No, no, don't worry about it. *See you later.*"

I didn't need the boot physically in my butt to get the picture. I left the place and reported my failure to Josh outside, as we walked on from the shop. He said, "Well, you didn't tell them about your journey. That's why they didn't listen."

"I want them to care," I said. "Without the gimmick."

"They don't care without the gimmick."

Of course they don't, I thought darkly. I would revisit this exchange with my friend Frank the next day, during a stymied attempt at the Space Needle. *Shouldn't they care that there's a mistake, even without the funny story?* I'd ask. And Frank's reply: *They need the story as a reason to care. Otherwise, you're just a guy pointing out a mistake.*

But that was supposed to be the important part. The ridiculous acronym, the animated map with its bouncing cartoon heads, the florid words of the blog, even the crossing of thousands of miles in the name of punctuation—those were all trappings, frosting, not the point itself. In each moment, I *was* just a guy pointing out a mistake. The point of the mission was to inspire other ordinary people to speak out when they see mistakes. The prospect of that actually happening had never looked so dim.

TYPO TRIP TALLY

Total found: 213
Total corrected: 123

13 | **Run-Time Errors**

April 22-25, 2008 (Cataldo, ID, to Rapid City, SD)

At long last, the romantic reunion of our Champion and his demure, computer-literate Sweetheart. They turn Eastward and begin the long course home. If only she didn't believe his mission was utterly Pointless.

The afternoon should have been perfect. Underneath my feet, green grass struggled into spring. Snow-crowned, evergreen-carpeted mountains speared a blue sky studded with clouds, and Jane was at my side, tresses fluttering in the breeze. A thawed pond lay beyond bare trees preparing to bloom. It still wasn't warm enough to shed our winter coats, but we could at least leave them open. The undulating landscape had been nothing short of stunning on the drive here. I could enjoy all this with the girl I'd waited so long to see, so what was the problem?

"Issac I. Stevens", that was what.

"Hey, Jeffbear," said Jane. "You're squeezing my hand."

Josh and Jane and I had spent the weekend in Seattle, temporarily joining forces for typo hunting. Yesterday Josh had caught a plane home to New York, and Jane and I had struck east, stopping last night at the dubious way station known as Spokane. She brought a much different vibe to TEAL than had her predecessors, and not only because she was my girlfriend. At corrective crossroads where Josh would have been unyielding, and Benjamin kinetically aggressive, Jane chose to be accommodating. She grew up as the middle child in her family, consequently becoming well versed in mediation and compromise. Her chief objective in any given situation was for everyone to get along and not feel unhappy. Obviously, typo hunting ran rather against these conditions, so Jane preferred not to do the aggravating of others herself, instead standing back and offering conciliatory suggestions when my observations ignited somebody's ire. Often she ended up performing a valuable function missing from the heretofore testosterone-dominated League: a voice of reason.

r Travelers

Some of the prominent travelers who visited the Mission and possibly stayed in this building were:

Issac I. Stevens, Governor of the Washington Territory; Captain John Mullan, builder of the famous Mullan Road; and General William Tecumseh Sherman, of the Civil War Fame.

The sign featuring the seemingly odious name "Issac I. Stevens" stood along one of the paths through the grounds at the Cataldo historic site, a mission house used long ago for the Christianizing of native peoples in the area. I'd gotten a vague hint from a guy at a gas station back in Coeur d'Alene that this would be a fine place for Jane and me to stop and eat our sandwiches, before pressing on to the day's destination across the Montana border, Missoula. The site had turned out to be a fine diversion, but I'd already spotted a couple of obvious typos in and around the mission house, and now there was this one. The sign listed a few of the notable historical figures who may have crashed for the night in the guest house—fun facts, but didn't misspelling the first name of the governor of the old Washington Territory muddy the educational aspect a bit?

"This is a classic screwup," I muttered. "So many people mix up the *s* and the *a*. Could be that the double *a* feels unnatural to modern English speakers. I remember back in junior high, one of my classmates—who would go on to become valedictorian, no less—proudly showed me the glossy cover that he'd designed for his report for science class, and there it was. 'Issac Newton.' Even back then, it jumped out at me as wrong."

Something more interesting had caught Jane's attention during this musing, a pretty bird or the sun glinting off the surface of the water, but now she nodded and took a look at the sign again. "Well," she said, "keep this in mind: if Washington State was still a territory when this guy was around, it had to be a while ago."

"True."

"Could he have spelled his name that way? It could have been a variation on the name back then."

At first this rationale struck me as suspiciously similar to the one that a park ranger had trotted out for me back at a reconstruction of an old mining town in the southern California desert. One store had promised STATIONARY on its marquee, clearly intended to be an advertisement for its goods and not an indicator of its mobility or lack thereof. When I brought the sign up to the ranger, he had said dismissively, "That must be how they spelled 'stationery' back in the Old West." That had been mere days after "St. Frances of Assissi", the so-called Spanish spelling. Apathy masqueraded as an awareness of language change and divergence. Granted, names could change their spellings over time. My own first name is an update of the Old English name Geoffrey (e.g., that lewd rascal Chaucer). In this case, though, sorry—they *didn't* spell it like that back then. Here, I already knew that Sir Isaac Newton, whose birth had preceded Governor Stevens's by a couple of centuries, was an Isaac, thus I knew that "Issac" was not historically the norm. Or, of course, I could look further back, to the biblical origin of the name, and at least by the King James translation, he was a double-a-not-double-s kind of kid.

But hold on—Jane had suggested that it might have once been a *variation*, not the standard, and that was entirely possible. In the next state over, Montana, visitors to Glacier National Park could stay at the Izaak Walton Inn, named in honor of a seventeenth-century fisherman. Today you can find all sorts of mad alternate spellings of names not long ago regarded as canon, such as Michael (Micheal, Michale—or Makayla for girls). Probably at least a few Issacs roamed the nation at this very moment. What I had to figure out was whether *this* Issac, Governor Stevens of the Territory of Washington, had actually been an Issac. I suspected he wasn't, but Josh wasn't around to confirm this via his handy-dandy traveling Internet, which I also wasn't willing to put full faith in since the Jonathan Swift botch in Portland. I said to Jane that she could be right, and we soon got back on the road to press on to Montana.

I thought about the Issac-Isaac question all day, though, and even verifying later on the Internet that, yes, the late Governor Stevens did go by *Isaac* did nothing to quell my growing unease. I became irritable. That night, after the kids at the Missoula Pita Pit botched our order, I savaged them in the blog, both for their poor customer service and the fact that they worked in a place with HER's written on the bathroom door. Jane got irritable at my irritability, and we skipped our customary evening session of the popular card game Phase 10 and went to bed.

Jane and I endured some long, desolate drives on our journey through the northern Great Plains, and the road from Missoula to Billings was no exception. Indigo mountains were nice, rolling plateaus and fields were cool, but even pleasing scenery can grow monotonous and lonely after a few hours. Such a drive offered plenty of time to reflect and ponder, especially when my fetching companion took a turn behind the wheel. Somewhere in the lower tract of Montana, I began to realize why the Issac business bothered me so much—what makes *Isaac* more "correct" than *Issac*? It was a slipperier question than it appeared. We regard *Isaac* as the standard spelling for the name, treasured as the Truth of this particular patch of the given-name landscape. It was in the Bible, no? Except that *Isaac* is an Anglicized version of a Hebrew name. The original is *Yishāq,* so what is *Isaac*? It's a variation, a noodling of *Yishāq* into English. The translation could have turned out as *Issac* instead. The study of people's names, anthroponomastics, can yield histories as long and twisted as, well, the word *anthroponomastics.*

Then something else occurred to me. I'd gotten used to hashing these kinds of things out with my old buddy Benjamin, echoing the dialectic rhythms of our days as roommates, but somehow I'd failed to solicit help from the one closest to me. Here Jane had come all this way to join me in my crazy mission, even now giving me a rest from the wheel, yet she hadn't been included. She'd done her Jane thing of being there for everyone else without voicing her opinion. I suspected that I hadn't asked her to voice one because I thought I knew what she'd say, and it wouldn't be what I wanted to hear. "Jane?"

"Uh-huh?"

"What do you think makes double-a *Isaac* more 'correct' than double-s *Issac*?" I asked.

Jane had gone into a kind of trance herself; now she lowered her speed from ninety-five miles per hour to a more reasonable ninety. "Mmmm, I don't think it *is,* necessarily. I mean, whatever the guy's name is, that's his name, so if someone else writes it down wrong, then bzzzt—wrong answer. But I don't think one's better than another."

"So . . . what about words that aren't someone's name? Where there's no one person to decide the right version."

Jane shrugged. I waited her out, and she smiled one of those self-conscious smiles that comes from knowing someone's staring at you. I certainly wasn't going anywhere. "Um, okay. Well, to be honest, that's why I don't really see the point of your mission, Jeffs. Who's to say what spelling is *right,* if the version that you're insisting on is historically as arbitrary as the 'typo' version?"

That had been harder than I'd expected—on me. I didn't want to argue against her, but rather, explain my position, since she'd so carefully mentioned that she didn't see the point. "It's . . . it's still important to make the distinction," I said. "Because we all have to agree on *one* of the versions. For clarity."

She gave me a doubtful look. "Clarity. Uh-huh. Would anyone not get that *Issac* was supposed to be *Isaac*? Would it affect their comprehension of that sign? I know that stuff like that will always bug you, because you know how the dictionary would spell it. But as long as everybody basically understands each other, then dang, what's the problem?" She patted my leg to take the edge off *dang*, which was strong language for her. "When you're writing the code for a computer program, you can potentially make a few different kinds of errors. Run-time errors will cause bad glitches or freezes, and compilation errors prevent the program from even running in the first place. Logic errors, on the other hand, aren't as bad—they can at least get through the compiler. You'll get some funky results, but . . . I feel like these typos are little logic errors. Not enough to crash the program. If people started walking into walls when they saw a typo, going bonk, bonk, bonk—" Here her pantomime would have been more amusing and perhaps adorable if we had not been traveling at our current speed with her behind the wheel. "If people were having real problems with typos, I guess I'd understand better why I only get to see my bear for one week out of three whole months."

Like a deftly coded function, Jane had returned the precise value of what troubled me. I was losing my grip on what the problem was, besides the fact that I had one. The media's repetition of that *why* question had jostled any hope of certainty right out of my head. First I reassured Jane that my mission (an idea I'd come up with before even meeting her) could not ever measure up to time devoted exclusively to her. That accomplished, I stared out the window at sere grass and thought about prescriptivists, aka the Grammar Hawks, who loved to perpetuate the notion that English had a "pure" form. This monolithic set of rules about spelling and grammar, cemented in an ancient age, had supposedly remained unchallenged and unassailed until recent times, when ignorant barbarians besieged its gates with their poor spelling and lazy constructions. History shows this not to be the case.

First, it's important to note that this complaint about the corruption of the English language is not new—it is very, very old. Perhaps the first professional Hawk was Giraldus Cambrensis (or, more familiarly, Gerald of Wales), a chronicler in the late twelfth century. In his *Descriptio Cambriae (Description of Wales),* he proclaimed the English spoken in the county of Devon as the purest form of the language, and lamented how the dastardly Danes and Norwegians were corrupting English dialects everywhere else. (Giraldus also had the distinction of being one of the first anti-Irish bigots on record.) A couple hundred years later, in the late fourteenth century, John of Trevisa made the same complaint—but this time the corrupting culprits were the Norman French. As the son of an Anglo-Norman baron, Giraldus would have disputed this. And the English language of, say, the early-to-mid-twentieth century—the version seen by current Hawks as the pure form to defend from today's orthographic miscreants—would give both John and Giraldus the most terrible night sweats.

Who's corrupting whom? Who is/was the guardian of the *pure* version, the *right* version of English? The situation gets very mucky when you consider the whole patchwork journey of the language. Old English, spoken for about seven hundred years by shepherds and reformed pillagers, was phonetic in its written form. You spelled the way you talked, and any kind of consistency—even on the same page—could go jump in the moat. Dictionaries weren't even a glint in a scrivener's eye. So much for stylistic uniformity, and the language's ethnic purity had hardly maintained its chastity, either. Even at this early stage, outside influences poured in, not just from the Germanic tribes that had mashed the language together in the first place, but also Latin (from the remnants of the Roman Empire), and Viking marauders (the ones that Giraldus Cambrensis had complained so bitterly about). Then came the Norman invasion in 1066, and French began its long hold on English, shaping it into Middle English over the centuries. Only in the early 1400s do we see the beginnings of standardization, as legal and governmental clerks agreed upon a common written form (known as Chancery Standard) that kings and Parliament could use to address the whole nation. Even then, that was just the unified language of The Man; the lower classes of society preserved English, and the literate among them had neither cause nor desire to fix up their own spelling and grammar, which was still heavily regionalized.

It wasn't until the seventeenth century that people cobbled together the first dictionaries, and those were aimed first at listing words as a reference, and then at *defining* all these new words flooding into English, plus of course the heaps of words that already existed. They hadn't agreed upon the exact spelling of those words quite yet. That would take a whole other debate among the nation's literate and influential that often turned rancorous. For the first time, the Grammar Hawks surfaced in real numbers, arguing that the language should be peeled back to its purest state—in this case arguing for the old Germanic form as the purest. Obviously they didn't win out, but a later, similar wave backing Latin as the pure form would have better luck.

Only with the publication of Samuel Johnson's dictionary in 1755, less than three hundred years ago, did the dictionary move from mere reference to being regarded as the central authority. As Seth Lerer points out in his book *Inventing English,* Johnson's baby "created the public idea of the dictionary as the arbiter of language use." Dr. Johnson had high hopes of being able to *fix* the language into a single solid and stable form. But the eight-year task of being the sole arbiter, navigating among regional variations and the abundance of spellings for difficult words, without a pole star (or more than the barest twinkling of phonetic principles) to guide his many decisions, eventually mellowed him from being a strict, self-made Hawk to taking on decidedly Grammar Hippie tendencies. Quotations from well-known sources littered the dictionary, backing up the choices he'd made, as if to direct attention away from his role as the decision-maker.* He ended up admitting in the preface that his purpose had become "not to form, but register the language; not to teach men how they should think, but relate how they have hitherto expressed their thoughts" (quoted in Lerer's book). That's the Hawk-versus-Hippie dilemma crystallized.

The scenery rolled on. Jane yelped in delight and jabbed her finger at my window. "Look over there! Buffalo!"

I saw them, brown shaggy blots on a hill. "Yeah. Buffalo." I slouched further in my seat, staring at the dashboard. Taped to it was a yellowed sign that Josh had bought for me in San Francisco, at a pirate supply store: IF DECK IS SALTY, THERE WILL BE LASHINGS. She saw me looking at it.

"You're a salty bear right now, huh? Does that mean you're lashing me to the roof for the rest of the trip? It's okay. You know how I like fresh air." When I didn't laugh heartily enough, she knew I was still lashed to the mast of some stubborn mental frigate. "Aww, come on, I didn't mean to say that your mission's pointless. You've made a lot of people happy by fixing their signs. You have even more people cheering you on every day in the blog."

"Yeah, I know."

"Good!" She brightened. "Hey, I should be making more corrections, right? I've only done a couple so far. When we're in Billings, you tell me when you find one, and I'll grab the Wite-Out. You point, I correct!"

"Deal," I replied, though I wondered if I'd even bother pointing them out for correction. Battered by my own adventures in language investigation over the course of the last month and a half, I felt like weary Samuel Johnson, though with considerably less to show for my efforts. If English is ever-changing and ever-mutating, if no pure form exists and never existed in the first place, then *what was I doing?*

---

* The *Oxford English Dictionary* would expand upon the use of quotations in quantity as well as depth, as the makers of this comprehensive and literally *exhaustive* dictionary didn't just add sample sentences to show the words in use, but also worked to track down the earliest written appearances of the words.

I found that I'd never discovered a satisfactory answer and could no longer sail full speed ahead without one. I had set out to protect the language from errors born of both carelessness and ineducation, but now I didn't quite understand the creature I had taken as my ward. It wriggled to get away from me, it twisted and eeled.

Perhaps, I thought, what I regarded as typos were not "mistakes" at all—they were part of the natural evolution of English. How could I know how the speakers of my native tongue would spell a hundred years from now? They'd alight from their potato-fueled urban gliders and laugh at my present efforts. "Check this out—back in 2008, there was a guy who wasted his time on *apostrophes*! Im sure glad we aint usin *those* anymore." Was I standing in the way of an inevitable, continual, necessary transformation? I felt like I was trying to guard the tides from the moon. Grammar Hawks had erred in regarding English as a fixed, carefully sculpted entity—in other words, treating it like Latin.* An on-the-ground, vernacular language simply behaves in different ways from a rarefied and static tongue. Now I had to face the possibility that the mission of the Typo Eradication Advancement League was as outmoded as . . . well, Latin.

We finally trundled into Billings that evening. I got out of the car and stretched. Here I was on an epic road trip with my beautiful girlfriend. I had been behaving like a misguided Hawk for too long, swooping and darting at mice while the great grinding world moved on. Maybe it was time to do some strolling, enjoy a nice dinner with Jane, and see if I could *spot* a few typos here and there. Maybe it was time to roll like a Hippie.

When the Holiday Inn concierge handed me a map of the hotel, featuring a blaring typo in their near-nonsensical slogan (A FRONTIER OF IT'S OWN!), I barely even blinked. "How about that," I said blandly to Jane, indicating the interloping apostrophe. "I'll point it out to them later." It was too late for much hunting, so we headed into a lively bar/meat market downtown and enjoyed great food

---

* More on Latin specifically next chapter.

and two-dollar local drafts, then retired to the hotel to play a rousing game of Phase 10. I drifted to sleep afterward with a sense of relief—I had learned to stop worrying and love the typos.

In the morning we returned to the downtown area, ready to track down errors now that businesses would be open. I saw by the light of day that Billings actually couldn't boast all that much of a downtown, but there were a few shops and cafés available for our perusal. So we wandered, and soon enough I came across a typo, in a commemorative plate on display. It occurred in the middle of a paean to bears: "Be gentle enough to follow natures inspirations and be strong enough to make the world a better place." To the left of the doggerel was a stoic and somewhat self-conscious ursine face.

"Look at that plate," I said.

"What a bear, bear!" said Jane, clapping her hands. Even after she spotted the typo, her enthusiasm for a plate dedicated to her favorite animal could not be diminished. I thought, oh whatever, the manufacturer (American Expedition) won't ever bother correcting this. I ought not to be a killjoy when the plate can still move bear enthusiasts like my TEAL companion.

Next we came upon a shop that carried, among other things, products by local artists. The proprietor came up to me with a warm smile and we exchanged pleasantries. As she chattered on, my eyes wandered to a display of framed poetry by Billings-area wordsmiths. There it was, buried in a poem about rural routes or something: "Our dusty road winds its' way through sage . . ." Like Vancouver, Billings sure seemed to be having a problem with its *its*es. I opened my mouth to point out the typo to the nice lady in front of me . . . and I closed it again. I would say nothing. What tattered standard did I think to wave in the faces of the state's honest citizens? I had only the grammatical snapshot of this mere moment in history to flaunt. The whole thing was pointless, as Jane had intimated. Thus spake, or *didn't* spake, the newly minted Grammar Hippie. I snapped a quick picture of the poem and hurried out onto the street, Jane following me with a puzzled look.

"What happened?" she said outside.

I told her about the typo and my hesitation.

"I'm glad you didn't say anything!" Jane asserted. "It's a *poem*."

"And?"

She squinted at me in the sunshine. "In poetry, language belongs to the poet. Would you go through e.e. cummings's poems and add capitalization? Like Emily Dickinson's old editor, removing all the dashes from her poems?"

Ouch. She had pierced right to the heart of the matter: I was presuming too much. The gentleman who'd come up with these verses was more poetaster than poet, but he still enjoyed citizenship in a country beyond the League's jurisdiction. This had been obvious to Jane from the start. She was, now that I thought about it, the quintessential Grammar Hippie—not just due to her fondness for nonconfrontation, but because she recognized the mutable nature of truth. In my pre-League existence, if I complained to her about somebody knocking me over in a subway car, she would play devil's advocate and suggest that the offender could have been having a bad day, or maybe he had bad eyesight. Jane understood that we are trapped within the cage of our own perceptions and biases. From my perspective, the subway brute existed *only* as a jerk: that moment of transgression defined him. But from his viewpoint, it was a passing instant in what might otherwise be a life of unblemished charity, hardly the action for which posterity should remember him. Unlikely, perhaps, but *possible*.

In language, as in life, we cling to what we were taught and what we have always done, making it difficult not just to understand the quirks and seeming peccadilloes of others, but to relinquish beliefs that have become outmoded. If I saw a sign that said *ice tea* instead of *iced tea*, I'd judge it as a mistake. But *ice cream* started off as *iced cream*. So many people left off the hard-to-enunciate *d* when spelling the word that it eventually disappeared. Whether I like it or not, *ice tea* might be vindicated someday by a shift in spelling norms. Why, then, should I sweat small distinctions that may eventually prove irrelevant? I had plenty of reasons to rejoice in our language. We speak, and write, in one of the most diverse, gloriously ecumenical tongues on the planet. In English, there is a word or phrase for pretty much anything we want to say, and if there isn't, *we make it up,* and it is welcomed into the family. We can express ourselves as complexly or as simply as we like. We can be magniloquent didacts, or we can talk plain.

A pretty realization, so why did I feel empty?

Billings would be, in retrospect, a time of tranquillity. Soon after we left, Jane and I faced no end of traveler's woes. Snow drifted down from the grayness, thickening gradually. By the time we crossed into Wyoming, we found ourselves cutting through a full-fledged storm. This was right around when Callie began to demand service for her engine, for the first time since the Southeast. We lost two and a half hours to car repairs in Sheridan, and all the while snow fell in sheets. We didn't roll into Rapid City until almost nine o'clock at night. Here it was Authority's turn to rebel, steering us amiss and leading us to a darkened mall instead of our hotel. Half-maddened by the worst drive of the trip and blinded by fogged windows, I swung Callie back around in a reckless turn. A police car materialized from the shadows, as if it had been waiting for someone like us to come along. The adolescent officer admonished me to "stop driving so crazy." That I did not get a ticket was the sole mercy of the day. We finally reached the hotel, to discover that (a) it had a real live indoor *waterslide* and (b) the waterslide was now closed for the evening.

Still, we were able to simmer in a hot tub for a spell, and that helped. We went back to the room and drank a couple of nips, and I wrote the day's blog entry while Jane embarked on a steamship for dreamland. I closed my laptop and glanced at the bed. She was sleeping with her mouth open, her arm curled around a little plush buffalo I'd bought for her. She'd come all the way out here, to drive across trackless plains and support a mission she didn't believe in, only so that she could be with me. I already missed her. In a couple of days we would arrive in Minneapolis, and Jane would fly home, and I would be alone. The stretch of territory that remained after that, the final leg all the way back to Massachusetts, seemed vast and futile. If I had truly become a Grammar Hippie, an observer instead of a fixer, I no longer had much use for the aims of the League.

I could just speed home. I had a lot more stops on my itinerary in the Midwest and the East than were strictly necessary. I could lay aside my Kit and my hat and dedicate myself to the enticing prospect of getting back to familiar environs as soon as possible. Then all these ambiguities and conundra would be over, and I could return to a normal life.

My cell phone rang.

"Check it," said Benjamin. "There are two main categories of spelling junctions: plus-junctions and change-junctions. *To* plus *morrow* equals *tomorrow*, that's a plus junction. *Copy* times *ed* equals *copied*, that's a change junction. Your very first spelling catch—after the shower curtain, I mean—was 'referal'. *Refer* times *al* equals *referral*, a consonant-doubling change-junction. They couldn't handle the junction, man!"

I regarded the wall for a moment. A standard-issue hotel print hung there, flowers in a field that could have been anywhere. Finally I said, "Isn't it about two in the morning on the East Coast?"

"Screw that, man. I can't put this stuff down. I found some great books on grammar, and I'm beginning to understand how some of these typos keep happening."

Jane muttered something about radio buttons and turned over in her sleep to dream further web-designer dreams. "That's cool," I said, "but—wait a minute, aren't you supposed to be huddled in a tent in Georgia right now?"

"I've been thinking a lot about what we found during my leg of the trip, and I've been following the blog since then, and . . . I don't think my part in this is over yet. Reading your entries from the last few days makes me all the more sure of that."

"What do you mean?" I said.

Benjamin whooped into the phone. "You're slipping off the track!

It takes you five days to make ten corrections. From the numbers you just posted, you've dipped under fifty-one percent—you're in danger of dropping below fifty percent corrected!"

"I'm in the middle of nowhere. They don't cotton much to words out here."

"Excuses!"

I couldn't hold back anymore. I spilled all of my doubts and frustrations. I told him about the internal war that the Hawk and the Hippie seemed to be waging in the guts of our mission.

He didn't sound surprised in the least. "I could already tell that something was different. I'm not sure I have the answers you're looking for—but we'll figure them out as we go."

"We?"

"You heard me, dude," Benjamin said. "TEAL needs me back on the team. I know that shotgun seat is opening up once your Jane heads back home. So, Deck, I'm putting the Appalachian Trail off for a year. It'll still be there in 2009."

I didn't know what to say. Light began to diffuse into the dark future of the League.

"I'll see you in Chi-town," said Benjamin.

TYPO TRIP TALLY

Total found: 276
Total corrected: 140

14 | The Epic Chapter Wherein Heroes Battle and the Scenery Flashes Past

April 27 – May 1. 2008 (Minneapolis, MN; Madison, WI; Chicago, IL; Bloomington, IN; Cincinnati, OH; Newport, KY)

Reunited with his faithful friend and foil, our Hero charges into the last battle for the soul of the League. Taking opposing sides, these Allies spar through the snowy streets of Madison, tread carefully around mental land mines in the Windy City, are nearly mad driven on Indiana roads, and finish Once and For All over the Ohio River.

I shall skip describing the scene at the Minneapolis airport, where Jane and I bade each other farewell, lest the upwelling of your tears streak the ink of these pages and damage this highly collectible book. I returned to Callie, alone for the first time in seven weeks. Perhaps if I could have crawled into some eremite cave, the sudden aloneness wouldn't have been so *loud,* but as it was, I had a mission. In the Twin Cities, my destination was clear: the Mall of America, a monument to capitalism and testament to Americanism—complete with roller coaster—that could not be passed over. Unfortunately, the typos therein were all too easy to pass over. I failed to correct a single one of the eight I found, dropping me under the fifty-percent correction mark.

Back in the infinite warrens of the mall's parking garage, I called Benjamin to find out when he'd arrive in Chicago.

"Hey man," he said, "if your typo hunting's done this early, you could always move on to your next stop. That's Katie and Lisa, right? You sound way down. Madison's your best bet."

I set off on the four-and-a-half-hour drive without hesitation, stopping briefly to unfurl my limbs and void my bladder. Western Wisconsin was still lonely territory, and I considered how, when I'd first envisioned the trip, it had been as a solo run. The sun set behind me and darkness fell like a coconut on an animated noggin, eliciting a swirl of stars in the open sky. I pulled up to the home of my college friends, and Katie bounded out into the cold night to bear-hug me. A cat tried to dash through the screen door when I greeted Lisa. I looked around, noted the futon already unfolded into a bed, and the paused image from *Collateral*. From a chair pointed at the television, a face popped up, belonging to a guest I had not foreseen. Benjamin smiled his wily smile.

"Surprise!" he roared. After more than three weeks away from the mission, my old friend looked refreshed and geared up to tackle orthographic chicanery once more. "I couldn't come all the way out to the Midwest without seeing these two crazy kids—I haven't seen them since the wedding!" The girls, of course, were laughing. I joined in, and my curdled heart squeaked with joy.

The next morning, Lisa suggested a promising neighborhood for typo hunting, and a faithful reader had posted the address of Brennan's, a combined produce market and local food store. In spite of the temperature hovering at the freezing point, I felt ready to dive in, but I cautioned Benjamin that I might be more of a spotter than a corrector. "I may be seeing it Jane's way. Maybe I'm more of a descriptivist."

"No, you're not, Deck. A Grammar Hippie couldn't have dreamt up this mission. You may not be a true Hawk, either, but what we need first is momentum. We'll talk on the way. You tell me what you think, and I'll—"

"Play devil's advocate?"

Benjamin shrugged. "No, tell you why you're wrong."

I responded with equal sarcasm, channeling Bill Murray: "I love this plan. I'm excited to be a part of it. Let's do it."

At Brennan's, I mentioned the possibility that I'd been lying to myself about the value of these corrections. Plenty of the typos we'd found had gone long unnoticed, and few clouded comprehension. Over at the apple stand, I found a perfect example. No one needed the first *n* in Washington to recognize the name. I wondered how many people had even heard of Washington Piñata apples, and if they started calling them "Washigton Piñata," so what?

"A slippery slope, that's what. You gonna fix this? I want strawberries."

"I'll go ask." I went up to a woman at the center of the store and told her that I'd found a sign missing a letter, offering to fix it since I was going around the country fixing typos. I practically spat it out in one breath as I saw her eyes starting to glaze over.

"Oh no, we'll take care of it," she said, though I hadn't told her what or where the typo was. Then, in a voice reserved for the pre-adolescent set: "We have a *special marker* for those signs." We moved on to the other part of the store, but not before she said—as if to a co-worker, but loud enough so we could hear it—"Oh, whoops, looks like I spelled 'strawberry' wrong." I started to turn back, and she added, *"Oh wait.* No, I didn't." And she glared at me. In that moment, the cashier eerily resembled a few of my exes, making me grateful for Jane's sweet presence in my life all over again.

"Mm," Benjamin commented. "Now I'd *really* like to fix that typo. Anyway." He proceeded to argue that words used to have multiple spellings, and they'd been understandable, sure, but reading was much easier now. As an example, he offered his father. Due to his dyslexia, the goal of correctly processing what he was reading had trumped learning how to spell, which he'd never quite come back to pick up. "It takes more *effort* to decipher his e-mails, man. His choices of phonetic representations don't always make sense to me. If everyone decided spelling conventions don't matter, we'd get a growing variety of spellings for each word, and when you factor in accents . . . good luck." Agreed-upon spellings made the act of read-ing much quicker for society as a whole. If we relaxed our standards, we would still understand most text, but it would be more difficult, and it would take more time. Issues of wrongness aside, ignoring those spelling norms was really just *rude*. Benjamin said, "So you mind that slippery slope, man. The next step's a *doozy*."

We paid for the food and went back into the part of the store with the apples. Benjamin grabbed my green marker and walked up to a guy stocking the shelves from a box across from our "Washigton" apples. "Hey, check this out. There's an *n* missing in 'Washington'. Mind if I write it in real quick?"

The guy shrugged and said, "Sure."

I caught my jaw on its way down. Benjamin inserted a tiny letter, almost like an apostrophe, thanked the guy, and headed for the exit. "So yeah," I said, by which I meant, It's great to have you back.

"I know," Benjamin said. "The wonders of apathy." Sometimes it works against you, sometimes with you. That's the thing about apa-thy; it doesn't care. "The ol' 'If Mom says no, ask Dad' trick. Works like a charm. Actually, it never worked on my parents." Even so, that had been golden delicious.

A cold wind pushed against us as we headed to the car, and the first squadron of snowflakes descended from a dull gray sky. As we headed to State Street, Benjamin and I began a conversation that blurred our surroundings into a similar gray. The stores and scenes and text we passed faded, save for the insistent luminescence of the typos that continued snagging my attention as we swept by. The conversation became the single tangible element of our world, a clamor of argument and counterpoint, with neighborhoods and cit-ies swishing by unnoticed as swords swung and shields clashed.

Benjamin *was* right that spelling standards had helped. Once that printing press began to crank out words, perhaps a *fixing* (in terms of freezing in place) of the language was inevitable. Wider access to the written word meant a greater need for standardization. Increasingly better dictionaries offered not only a growing volume of words, with meanings, but also spellings that came to be viewed as authoritative. That's when some rode the swinging pendulum too far: they tried to *fix* (in terms of correcting) the language. A true breed of Hawks hatched, and things got messier. An upper-class campaign chose Latin as the gold standard of languages and worked to alter English accordingly. They played havoc with the spellings of words, altering some to be more like their Latin roots, and even Latinizing words from other languages. That's how we got silent letters in words like *doubt* and *island*. The Hawks also added grammatical rules to make English function more like Latin (or seem to); one rule finally dying out is the prohibition against splitting infinitives. Back at the publishing house in D.C., my boss had pulled me aside to note that I'd let a split infinitive "get past" me. I drew him up a quick little poster in which his own cartoon head informed him that "to blithely split" infinitives is perfectly acceptable, allowing us "to fully utilize" our language's range of expression. We've been friends ever since.

"Hold on," Benjamin interrupted. "You haven't changed any split infinitives. You wouldn't. You invented the rules for TEAL in the first place—so you can decide how much of a stickler you want to be. We can discard all of those nonsense dicta that limit expression and don't truly enhance clarity. What we're after are obvious errors, helping correct slip-ups, not forcing people to bend to our grammatical will." Benjamin seemed to think I could walk some mediating line between Hawks and Hippies, but I had trouble seeing it through the thickening snow. "We're too binary, stuck on ones and zeros, ones and zeros. Forget who you fit with or don't. Stick to what we're actually doing."

Fine. We greeted a woman with her hands in a customer's hair. "Uh, the sign in your window has a couple letters flipped," I said, indicating the "ect" in place of *etc.* "Do you mind if I fix it?"

"Go ahead."

Well jab me with an apostrophe and call me a contraction. I had not expected that chipper reaction. We removed and reversed the sticky letters. "We've gotten comments on the blog from the Hippies that language changes," I said, wiping out a plural apostrophe as we passed it on the sidewalk. "Grammatical rules, words' meanings and spellings, it's all in flux, and that can't be stopped. Is my mission at odds with a natural process? Language can't be *preserved*. Anything that fixed is dead. Like our late friend Latin." I grabbed a Counting Crows album from the rock-pop rack as a prop. "Isn't that why you love these guys? They put their songs through new arrangements, rather than playing the studio versions at concerts." Benjamin nodded. He didn't go to shows to hear the album again—that could be done at home. "If there could be one final form of English that remained truly pure, we'd soon need a new language for actual *use*."

"Point to you," my companion conceded. "But *ad* instead of *and,* like we saw in the Atlanta parking garage, isn't language change. I doubt Las Vegas's extra *s* in *greatest* is going to catch on because I have never heard anyone say 'greastest'. These are errors, unquestionably. Language change is so gradual that it's mostly invisible." In *Watching English Change,* Laurie Bauer notes that most specific changes can only be pointed to after the fact, and more amusingly, that the one real sign of shifting meanings or spellings at the time is the complaints of Hawks trying (and failing) to stop them. "How about that 'seafoood' back in New Mexico? Come on, man.

"And what about people's names?" he added as I made corrections to CAPTAIN BEEFHART and JIMMY BUFFET. "That's not how Jimmy Buffett spells his own name, so end of story."

My thoughts returned to e.e. cummings. Didn't the true sovereigns of the language often buck literary conventions that didn't serve them? Shakespeare invented words at his convenience. Kerouac had his own style of punctuation that made sense for his writings. Twain, who pushed for some spelling reforms of his own, used true phonetic representations of words to re-create the accents of his characters. Cummings used all of those tricks and more to force people to read his work exactly as he wanted them to. Even if you can't fake a passable Russian accent, reading the poem "kumrads die because they're told)" aloud will force you into one.

"Kids in school need to get the basics straight so that they can experiment wisely," Benjamin replied. "There's a huge difference between using sentence fragments like Hemingway, for effect, and using them erratically and inelegantly because you don't know how to construct a basic sentence. This is the part that the Hawks would get right if they stuck to concerns about clarity—without limiting expression."

Rules that aided the clarity of a sentence had an internal logic, like the rule about where to place antecedents (nouns being referred to by some other word) to avoid pronoun confusion. "When he took a deep sniff of the black marker, Benjamin deduced that Jeff needed a break from typo hunting." This is not a great sentence because the pronoun *he* could refer to two possible antecedents—either Benjamin or Jeff. So who sniffed the marker? Did Benjamin take the sniff and thus gain deductive powers? Here's a clearer sentence: "When Jeff took a deep sniff of the black marker, Benjamin deduced that his friend needed a break from typo hunting." Note that I cut the pronoun out of the picture altogether—if I'd said "Benjamin deduced that *he* needed a break," it would still be unclear which guy the *he* referred to.

Guidelines masquerading as rules, on the other hand, operated from caprice rather than logic, like the one about not starting sentences with *but, and,* or *because.* That might help elementary schoolers avoid mistaking dependent clauses for sentences, but later on, no one remembered to tell the kids to remove those training wheels. "Because of that prohibition, I couldn't fully utilize *because*," I pointed out. The outer fringes of the vast dorsal mantle of Chicago oozed onto the horizon. "Besides, people speak in sentence fragments all the time."

"Let's keep the written separate from the spoken for now," Benjamin said.

"Some of these arguments are going to cross over," I said.

"Yeah, but TEAL's mission is focused on the written word, and we should zoom in on that stuff. You even said it on NPR." When my story had been featured on *Wait Wait . . . Don't Tell Me!*, they'd pulled a sound bite from me on how written mistakes can linger forever while a verbal remark disappears into the ether. "Lots of the mistakes we're finding are specifically written mistakes that aren't about *language* at all. They're about the mechanics of our written system, the sound-symbol correspondence, the way we add the suffix to the root on paper. Those are the ones I got kinda intense about when I hit the library. Am I making any sense?"

Two separate levels of symbolism were at work here. Language, the oral process, is a single level all by itself. Somehow, in our separate tribes, we've agreed upon sounds to represent most every conceivable thing, action, descriptive detail, et cetera (or "ect" if you prefer). The sounds *dog* and *blue* are not onomatopoeic, like *vroooom* or *whoooosh*—they don't have any connection to what they represent beyond the significance we've given them. This first level is innate to our species. Babies naturally acquire and then begin to utilize spoken language, both the lexicon and grammatical patterns of a given language.

The use of written symbols to represent the sounds we make, and the combination of those symbols to create the word-units, is a second and very different level. The written word follows behind the oral, but written language is not a natural creation. It has to be taught to us. This is why failing our kids on the educational front leads to illiterate but not mute children. When children can't—or won't—speak, we assume something's physiologically or psychologically wrong with them.

I looked up and caught a massive sign for MILWUAKEE FURNI-TURE. The letters were definitely bigger than the Arizona billboard apostrophe, making this the physically largest error yet. The *Chicago Tribune* reporter who'd been shadowing us for the last few blocks nodded appreciatively; there was an error worthy of the paper. Benjamin shot me a glance: *See, there's another one.* This wasn't about language change. It was specifically an editorial problem, an issue with the written word, an error born of inattention.

Stick to what we're actually doing, Benjamin had suggested. TEAL concerned itself only with the written word. No wonder both Hawk and Hippie perspectives felt wrong. I'd brought checkers onto the chessboard. After spending time with Josh the Hawk and Jane the Hippie, I'd gotten too spun around by the extremes when so much of that debate didn't apply to TEAL.

"I personally," Benjamin confessed, "have descriptivist leanings. Your mission certainly feels prescriptivist. Like I said, it's not something a laissez-faire descriptivist could have come up with." On the Kinsey scale of linguistic orientation, he suggested the following: Josh = 0, Jeff = 2 (though I'd perhaps started as a 1), Benjamin = 4, and Jane = 6. What I'd first thought of as zeros and ones was in reality zeros and sixes. I'd missed the whole range in the middle.

"So let's figure out what TEAL is really about," I said, "and that will naturally be the middle path."

"I thought you'd never ask," Benjamin replied. "I have trouble admitting it, but this typo hunt is a blast."

"Thanks."

"Though it's not the typos themselves I care about," Benjamin said. "For me, it's mostly about—" A barking ball of stir-crazed energy drowned out the rest. We found ourselves in the furniture-chewed apartment of our Bloomington host.

"Uh, I didn't quite catch that," I said.

Benjamin shook his head. "Forget it. Wasn't important."

Even so, I hated when that happened. Which got me thinking. "Everyone deserves to be understood," I declared.

"What's that?"

"What TEAL's really about."

He looked like he'd just downed one of the apocryphal eight spiders annually consumed by the average person. "First, didn't we agree that typos rarely have an impact on clarity?" Before I could respond, he added, "More important, I disagree with the basic proposition. We have freedom of speech in this country, but that doesn't extend to a freedom *to be understood*. Adults are responsible for putting in whatever effort is necessary to communicate. Not everyone does that; therefore, not everyone deserves to be understood. Maybe I'm right not to trust the meat from a store that can't get the spelling of *grocery* right, so they get less business due to a lack of professionalism. Sometimes you get what you deserve."

That sounded shockingly Hawkish for Benjamin. It came back to judgment. We'd been worried about the Atlanta typo on the Obama shirt, fearing that not merely the wearer, but our candidate himself, would be judged by that missing apostrophe.

My eyes strained at their nerve tethers, nearly jumping out of the sockets in pursuit of something I'd glimpsed while driving past. Benjamin hadn't seen it. I doubled back and pulled Callie to a stop in front of the billboard. RESTUARANT!

"I've got it!" I declared as we ambled into the field. The billboard wasn't up on a scaffold, but the error was still sufficiently elevated to make this a difficult correction. "I was close before." We craned our necks up at the transposition. "People judge you by your mistakes, so we can help people avoid the scorn and judgment of others. If they don't want the typos fixed . . . I guess they're comfortable being judged." Ugh, now *I* sounded overly Hawkish.

There was no way to fix this artfully. The best we'd be able to do was add little editorial arrows above and below to show where the letters should go. After a test leap proved inadequate, my lighter colleague placed himself immediately underneath the troubled letters. "Give me a leg up?" Clutching the marker in his teeth and walking his way up the sign with his hands, Benjamin let me hoist him up as high as we could send him, but even then he could only reach high enough for the bottom arrow. He got back down and I flexed my weary fingers.

"Afraid not," Benjamin said as we marched back to Callie. "Keep working. I have a problem with your hypothetical judgmental people. *You*, Jeff, are the one who cares! Referring to some other person who might come by and make judgments sounds too much like . . . like what you hear on TV. '*Some people* think that Obama's relationship with Reverend Wright is very telling.' No, they don't; the TV pundit wants to justify covering an attention-getting, ratings-boosting nonstory. These hypothetical—these fictional—people give that pundit latitude to push his issues on us, or blatantly replace news with entertainment. You can't slip into the comfort of doing the same, man. *We* correct typos because *someone else* might be bothered by them? It's too circular, and you're better than that."

"Right. I'm getting closer, though. Give me a moment to rejigger my thoughts and try again." We arrived at the home of my mentor from the *Rocks & Minerals* days, Marie. An editor herself, she dove right into the typo hunting while expertly tour-guiding us around Cincinnati.

Waiting for us to resume verbal fisticuffs, Benjamin wandered past something in the gift shop of the Krohn Conservatory. After pulling a double take, he read a note out loud: "The wood chopsticks stamped with an eternity design and are nestled in a double fish brocade pouch." After a quick discussion over the best way to correct this, Benjamin added an arrow to indicate where the "are" should be moved to. "There, now future readers won't get dizzy puzzling that one out." He smiled.

Then I smiled. "It's rude not to proofread."

"You're onto something, Mr. Deck, but be careful there." As the eminent linguist David Crystal has pointed out, grammar and etiquette have long been tied together. The post-dictionary craze about *proper* grammar went hand in hand with an increasing obsession over proper rules for everyday interaction in polite society. Start with the fork the farthest out and work your way in; a *gentleman* walks on the right side of his lady. While some of these rules are merely anachronistic with a faint trace of logic in their origins, many simply popped into existence as the demand for such rules increased. The self-perpetuating emphasis on the "proper" way to handle all manner of minutiae demanded more rules, so more rules there would be. I could understand why people might throw up their hands at all the little grammar rules that feel much like table-setting details—which one of these is the salad fork, and why does the number indicating the footnote go after the comma?

While I might bend toward the Hawks here, I don't want to twirl a baton in their parade. Lynne Truss manned a float in this parade when, succeeding her angry-panda grammar rant, she wrote *Talk to the Hand,* an intolerant little etiquette manual that bemoans the state of society today. What *is* the world coming to? Even as I felt repelled by the idea of becoming a maven of grammatical etiquette, the point remained that a certain inattention was rude, or worse. The Cartoon Art Museum had evidenced a disdain for its paying customers, tossing up signs that became utter nonsense in places; they couldn't be bothered to check them over.

As Marie led us onto the Purple People Bridge, which crossed the Ohio River into Kentucky, Benjamin mentioned to her how much he'd enjoyed tormenting me over the past few days. "He tries to figure it all out, and I kick back and act profound by saying, 'Um, not quite.' "

"All right, sensei," I said. "What's wrong with 'It's rude not to proofread'?"

"Nothing and everything. It's all a matter of emphasis, grasshopper."

In the mall on the Kentucky shore, a plural PHOTO's sat on a light blue background painted with traces of white representing clouds. I tried to use the elixir of correction to cloud over the apostrophe, but it was too blatant that way, with the two shades of white not quite matching. Instead, I made a white elixir bird to fly up there in the sky with the clouds. I hope they liked it. Our Kentucky typo corrected, we left the shopping center and turned right back around.

"It's *rude* not to proofread," I said. "No. It's rude not to *proofread*. Why don't people proofread?" The author who doesn't proofread may leave trouble behind for his readers. They're now forced into exerting the extra effort to decipher what the author had meant. Then again, many readers won't bother. Benjamin was right that the author didn't automatically deserve to be understood. What readers deserve, though, is that the author present his message with the greatest possible clarity.

The shifting weather mirrored my inner exultation, as the wind picked up and the waves below the bridge chopped and frothed. We paused, occupying neither Ohio nor Kentucky, but some strange liminal zone.

"You're an editor, Jeff."

"I'm an editor."

"As am I," Marie chimed in.

"Yes! We're *editors*! By the plow of Cincinnatus, we're editors!" I shouted on the bridge, my words dispersed but not dispelled by the rising winds.

Our mission wasn't about the mere typos, those little errors. Our message surpassed typos on its way to the greater realm of clarity. At some point an English teacher got through to me that I shouldn't just write a paper and turn it in, that I should take the time to edit it. Maybe even edit it again. The first draft of writing was only about getting it down from your head and onto the page. The editing stage was where you made it work: refined what you were trying to say, figured out *how* to say it better, and polished it to maximum effect. In fixating on the niggling little rules, the Hawks were reading only sentences and not paragraphs, pages, or books.

Back at college, Benjamin had reorganized the whole first chapter of his thesis, cutting it up into pieces and shuffling them around on his floor, until he'd gotten all his information into a logical flow that helped his argument. My thesis adviser had sent me back through every chapter I wrote to cut the excess fat, redundant sentences and words that didn't add anything new.

I didn't want to stop at raising awareness of typos. They were the obvious mistakes. I wanted to help everyone attain new levels of clarity, to recognize the editing process as a part of writing. "TEAL's mission should be about raising *editing* awareness."

"And hopefully without being jive-ass arrogant punks about it," Benjamin added.

"Without rancor," I agreed. Yes, we could offer a new voice of grammatical reason, a voice that wasn't screaming or jeering.

I stopped short. "What about the typos then? Do we leave that all behind?"

"No," Benjamin said. "Dude, the typos have led us into so many other things we'd never thought of . . . that's what I got stuck on, why I had to come back. If I get a vote, it's that we keep riding on this course. See what we find. I'm curious about what happens next."

I tugged at my cowboy hat. "Yeah, me too," I said. We'd come to a kind of koan: the path you're on is the path you need to find. "Let's go blog our finds. If my count's correct, we've got eight for nine today, and I think that might push us back over fifty percent." Benjamin and I stepped onto Ohio soil once more, ready for whatever revelations awaited us. We wouldn't drop below fifty percent again.

TYPO TRIP TALLY

Total found: 328
Total corrected: 165

15 | **Why Hudson Can't Read**

May 2-6, 2008 (Athens, OH, to Cleveland, OH)

Here, an Ironic tragedy brings our Heroes to a juddering halt,
as wounded and wailing as foundering school Standards. The
torch of Education burns low in a toy store with auspices of
a loftier, educational purpose.

During a car-bound lunch of peanut butter sandwiches and
graham crackers, Benjamin discovered a surprise on his voice mail.
We'd parked on a residential street near Ohio University, killing time
before meeting up with my sister. As he listened, a strange expression stole over his face. He hit the replay button so that I could hear
the message his friend from the bookstore had left. "Hey man, this is
Semajh. Uh . . . I don't know if you've been peein' on bushes or *what*,
yo, but the Park Service is *really* wanting to talk to you. They called
here looking for you. I told 'em you don't work here anymore, but I
don't know, man. It was weird."

We debated the merits of trying to call the Service, but we
decided that the odds of finding the person who'd been looking
for us, when we didn't know his or her name or what it had been
concerning, would be pretty slim. We probably should have tried
anyway. Benjamin tried to call his old co-worker back, but he wasn't
around, so Benjamin left a quick message. After speculating about
what interest the National Park Service could possibly have in talking to Benjamin, we honestly forgot about it for a while and headed
off to typo-hunt.

The following morning, we journeyed up to the pleasant sub-urban town of Hudson, where my father and stepmother live. I'd planned to spend several days with them, since I passed through northeastern Ohio infrequently and I had some filial duties to catch up on. Though Benjamin and I enjoyed the respite, the town would yield one of the strangest and most appalling interactions of the entire trip. I had rarely spent much time in any one place, and a week in Hudson could have been pushing it. Realizing our proximity to Cleveland, Benjamin played nothing but Bone thugs-n-harmony during our outings, and that also made our stay seem longer. Even with plans to spend our last couple days visiting Cleveland proper and my other sister's college, Kent State, we were scraping the bar-rel for fertile typo ground by our last leisurely Hudson hunting day, despite Dad's best efforts at searching out new venues in the area. Fortunately, we'd saved a patch of the town square, and here we went into every single store, finding little in typo quantity, but much in sinister quality.

My first impression of the Miracle on Main Street shop was appreciative: a weird amalgam of office/school supplies and toys that weren't mindless junk to clutter kids' rooms. This place had a laudably educational orientation, with products ranging from the *learning is fun!* extreme back to the more natural *give kids some-thing more interesting to* do *than watch TV.* Craft kits adorned the walls, and a spinner rack featured an abundance of energetic play aids, including jump ropes and hula hoops. Alas, before I could picture a pastoral landscape filled with sickeningly bubbly children leading delight-heavy existences under a friendly sun, that destroyer of dreams inter-fered once again. I gawked at the sign upon finding it. YEAR AROUND FUN! PLAY IN DOORS & OUT!

- **Increase Agility**
- **Year Around Fun**
- **Improve Balance**
- **Play In Doors & Out**
- **Expand Motor Skills**

Hm. Playtime in America might have been a wee bit . . . outsourced. While the policy of the League involved not picking on speakers of English as a second language, this was different. The sign had likely originated somewhere else, but it had landed in northeast Ohio, and here in an education-oriented store of all places, it was perfectly fair to address the idiom trouble that the makers of this sign had run into. I went for a clerk. Benjamin and I were the only ones in here at the moment, so I didn't have to be shy about stealing time away from an actual customer.

When I pointed out the sign's strange claim of "year around fun," the clerk replied, "It just means that you can enjoy this in spring, summer, winter, or fall." She didn't *sound* like she was making fun of us, but I didn't know what to say next.

At my silence, Benjamin stepped in, presuming that she hadn't known what I was talking about and so, not knowing how to respond, had offered a ridiculously obvious clarification. He saw her bet: "See, the uh, problem is that it says year *around* fun instead of *year-round,* which is the usual expression."

"Oh," she said, looking over. "Well, I believe they're making a pun."

Okay. Jump ropes, hula hoops. Year *around* fun. Right, ha ha. I might have accepted this defense of her sign if it hadn't had another quirk: PLAY IN DOORS & OUT. I let her pun theory pass with a quick dubious glance and switched to the other offender. "Okay, but check this out. 'Play in . . . doors'? It should be 'play indoors.'" I spoke too confidently, certain she'd have no objection here. The absurd images conjured by the typo would do my work for me, I mistakenly assumed. Talking about it later, we realized that even the two of us had interpreted it differently. Benjamin had pictured someone attempting to work a hula hoop or skip rope within the confines of a door frame. I pictured something even more literal: playing in the doors like you'd play in the playground, which is to say *within* it, like termites. *Mom! My hula-hoop matter-phasing shut off, and I'm stuck inside the door again!* To my dismay, the hula-hooping child wasn't the only thing out of phase.

"No, I think that's right," the woman replied, yielding to the sign all judgment and authority. Someone had *printed it* and released it to the four winds, so by God, it must be right. Who were we, mere individuals, to question the will of the toy manufacturers?

"That's definitely wrong," I replied. Should I go into why? Should we talk about clarity of meaning? *Now* who would be explaining the—I'd believed—obvious?

Then she made a move that could very well have spun my opinion of her right around. She reached for a true authority to consult, a handy dictionary. I sighed in relief, ready to christen her as redeemed while she flipped to the letter *i*. That was the value of a store emphasizing education. In the end, education isn't about how many facts you can cram into your head, it's about knowing *how* to get the information you need. Even Conan Doyle's polymathic detective kept encyclopedias and atlases close at hand for quick reference.*

Consider my shock when, in a vindicated tone, she declared herself right and put the dictionary nearly in my face with a smug "Look!"

We looked.

In and doors were separated by a dot. Many of the other words on that page, and the rest of the pages in the dictionary, had words broken up with dots. Though he looked somewhat peaked, Benjamin graciously accepted the weighty and irksome charge that now fell to us. "Um," he said. "That's a dot that separates the syllables of a word. That doesn't mean it's two words."

---

* Said Holmes in his first recorded mystery, *A Study in Scarlet*: "I consider that a man's brain originally is like a little empty attic, and you have to stock it with such furniture as you choose. A fool takes in all the lumber of every sort that he comes across, so that the knowledge which might be useful to him gets crowded out, or at best is jumbled up with a lot of other things, so that he has a difficulty in laying his hands upon it. Now the skillful workman is very careful indeed as to what he takes into his brain-attic. He will have nothing but the tools which may help him in doing his work, but of these he has a large assortment, and all in the most perfect order."

Silence. All the hidden host of the grammatical divine awaited her verdict. She gave Benjamin a look like he was trying to trick her, so I added, "Look at the other words. They have dots between their syllables, too." Oh, I'd been right about my opinion of her spinning around when she reached for that dictionary. Unfortunately, it had spun a full three-sixty. I would like to applaud her decision to bring the dictionary in as the decider, but at least a passing familiarity with how a dictionary works would be helpful. The worst part, and we couldn't have known this at the time, was that she wouldn't be the last person we'd encounter who'd been smart enough to reach for a dictionary but then failed to be informed by it.* The bitter irony of being in this educational store with an employee who'd never been properly introduced to the dictionary was not lost on me.

"Oh, all right," she said finally, "but that still doesn't mean this is wrong." She gestured toward the sign.

Time to roll out the rusty old gimmick. "We're going around the country correcting typos," I began, and asked if perchance we could . . .

"No." Emphatic, like scolding a toddler with an uncapped permanent marker who was heading for pristine walls.

I couldn't let this one go. I just couldn't, and I used the reason I couldn't let it go as my next argument. "We were thinking that since this store has an educational bent, you'd appreciate knowing about these typos, and that we could help out by fixing them."

"No, you cannot. My boss wouldn't like it. The corrections wouldn't look good."

At this point, another employee decided to join us. The first woman showed the newcomer the sign and explained that these two boys *claimed* that "year around" wasn't right. "It *isn't* right," she replied. "It should be 'year-round.'"

"And *I* was saying that it might be a pun."

". . . maybe."

---

* See chapter 16.

"They were also saying that 'in doors' was a typo."

"It is. It should be 'indoors,' one word."

At long last! She'd finally gone to a source of recognized authority who had issued a definitive confirmation of our claims.

I tried to address the second woman, in the hopes that she could take over. "Can we fix these for you?"

"Well, I don't know. What did Hortense* say?" Uh-oh, she'd deferred back to the first woman. What was it with the reluctance to take authority here?

"I told them no," she said, as if that were the end of it. As if she hadn't been telling us no because she'd thought the sign was right. Then it occurred to me that perhaps she *hadn't* been telling us no because the sign was right. That she'd been claiming the sign was right to make it easier to tell us no. I pushed that thought away—I couldn't face what it implied. Perhaps knowing that I was about to ask her to reconsider, given her co-worker's opinion, Hortense intoned, "I would rather have a sign spelled incorrectly than a tacky-looking sign."

Benjamin, who'd moved to the side at some point, pulled out his poetry notepad. He wrote down that resonating, cynical statement word for word so that we'd have it later for the blog. It had a compelling meter to it, I had to admit. And as good poetry can, it transcended the moment and spoke for more than the PLAY IN DOORS sign. In that moment, Hortense spoke for many like-minded people, all those who emphasized style over substance, appearance over accuracy. I nodded. In the end, she'd managed to impress me after all—impress a fist right into my gut.

"That's a good line," I said, and we left.

"So much for an educational store," Benjamin said as soon as we'd hit the sidewalk. " 'I would rather have a sign spelled incorrectly than a tacky-looking sign.' Wow. That's deep."

"It does tend to sum things up, doesn't it?" Indeed, that concern

---

* Name has been changed to protect the irrational.

had prevented us from winning permission a number of times. God forbid anyone should see evidence of an error corrected. You'd hardly appear infallible by not correcting the error. Ahh, but the correction, if not done to blend in perfectly (as I always strove to do), would draw attention to what most people might not otherwise notice. You could *get away with it*. Sigh . . .

I mused on the cultural trend toward style over substance, and the more I thought about it, the more pervasive it seemed. Movies don't need a plot so long as we get lots of explosions and/or enough topless women. The whole idea of a fashion industry, offering clothing for their visual appeal, has somehow supplanted the actual utility of clothing. So much glitz and glam, so much money spent on marketing, and I wonder if that number correlates to what's spent on actually improving the products or services. I remembered in Las Vegas, we were visually stunned by the whole effect. "Looks like fun," we'd agreed, not realizing we'd captured the true spirit of the city. Yeah, it *looks* like fun so it can distract you as the greenbacks fly out of your wallet. What would a Las Vegas of substance over style look and feel like? *Charlie Rose* Land?

I forced myself to lay these thoughts aside for a while and grabbed the volume of the complete works of Shakespeare I'd somehow left here the last time I'd been at my dad's. I'd have to remember to bring this along when we left Hudson.

The next day we headed into Cleveland and began our hunt at the Great Lakes Science Center, located between the Browns Stadium and the Rock and Roll Hall of Fame. Yesterday's troubles had inspired us to check out other educationally oriented sites such as this. I confess that we got a little lost in the fun of hands-on activities aimed at scientific minds somewhat younger than our own. We shouted echoes through tubes, balanced beach balls on air, set rubber rings spinning in place on a rotating metal disk, and sent puffy clouds of sublimating dry ice up to the ceiling. A couple times I had to turn myself around, saying, "Wait, I forgot to check for typos."

Having then checked, the place reassured me. For all the text we scanned, we uncovered only three mistakes, all of which could have been true typos in the typographical error sense, missing a key or hitting the wrong one. The emphasis on being a *science* center hadn't kept them from performing better than average on the English front. I think I expected a certain rivalry among the core subjects. *I don't care about multiplication tables—this is civics!* The Center gets an A in English for finding room for copyediting while journeying through the many steps of the scientific method.

We found, encased in glass, a plaque announcing a winning "eight-grader" 's science project. That one we couldn't touch, but the other two we amended. A simple mark indicated "no where" should be brought together, elsewhere. Finally, "Galileo Galilel" was an extremely easy fix, as we merely converted the top of that final *l* into a dot, making it an *i*. For spelling one of their main dudes wrong, Benjamin votes that they get an A-minus instead. Of course, my A rating could be too generous for a different reason. We made the corrections ourselves since no one seemed to be anywhere around to ask. I shudder to think we might have gotten the same reaction we'd gotten at Miracle on Main Street; the discovery that another education-oriented environment disdained our similarly intentioned efforts would have cut too deeply. The context was different here, though. The Science Center had a strict focus on content. No one here could have produced anything similar to Hortense's final remark without being laughed out of the halls of science. I could hear her now: "I'd rather misspell Galileo and confuse hundreds of children a day than have an ugly-looking exhibit explanation." "I'd rather have a broken flight simulator than a homely-looking flight simulator." No, I expected that the minds behind these accessible, effective exhibits wouldn't have much trouble using a dictionary.

We strolled around Cleveland and found a few more typos before heading back to my dad's, Bone Thugs blasting all the way. That night we shot some pool in my dad's basement. Benjamin, still riled up from the Science Center, explained the physics behind each carom. Eventually I went to bed, but not to sleep. I'd put off going to bed because I knew that I couldn't drift off, not yet. I suppose I ought to be grateful to Miracle on Main Street for bringing my attention to something that should have been obvious to me from the start: that "year around fun" means fun through spring, summer, winter, and fall. No, wait: that my mission had at its very foundation an eye toward education. How had I been able to count on this many mistakes, knowing that I could find at least one daily? More than probability was at work, and more than a casual malaise. Was spelling and grammar education missing a few pieces? As much as TEAL had decided to act as editors rather than "defenders" of the English language, our treatment of perceived mistakes was only half the story. Before people could make mistakes, or not, they still had to learn the basic mechanics of spelling and grammar. As we collected more typos, we thought we saw evidence that these essentials weren't being fully acquired by the populace.

The contrast between what I'd found and what I'd expected to find gave me my first clue. I'd thought I would find a greater variety of typos. Sure, misspellings had caught my eye originally, and I'd known from the start that apostrophes would be problematic. Still, I'd imagined myself dealing with some of the more nuanced rules, earning thanks for explaining, "*Couple* is a tricky word. Like *number, all*, and *none*, these subjects can be singular or plural depending on context. While *a couple* (say, a couple of the toddlers in the room) could *hold still* for a picture you're taking, in this case, *the couple holds still*. This couple functions as a single unit that happens to consist of two people in love, while the couple of toddlers are separate entities. *The* versus *a* is usually a good hint." Even Benjamin, who hadn't known if I was serious about the mission, had identified subject-verb disagreement as his archnemesis, and homophones as his weakness. We'd seen fewer than a dozen homophones, and the barest suggestions of subject-verb disagreement.

By the time we reached Ohio, TEAL had already caught more than three hundred typos. What we'd found first was lack of apostrophic confidence and then misspellings galore. It was the misspellings, Benjamin had explained, that brought him back. He'd seen a pattern, as if he were Alan Turing. Many of the problems were oral-to-written conversion problems. Even the apostrophe fits in here since there's often no difference between the *sound* of the plural *(watermelons taste great but peaches are better)* and the possessive *(a watermelon's seeds get everywhere, but the peach's pit is easy to deal with)*. With misspellings, intelligent people obviously knew the word they wanted and knew how to use it properly, but they just didn't know how to spell it. So we knew where the problem was, and Benjamin hoped the specific examples we'd found would point to why.

As previously noted, English appears to be quite a mess. One could make vulgar analogies about the way it allows words from other languages to, um, enter into its own lexicon. But English's ability to continually assimilate and grow is also a strong argument for its genius and beauty—and could even be a factor in its increasing dominance in world affairs. Certainly it improved our word selection to have similar words come in from different languages. Take a word like *kill.* Deriving ultimately from the Germanic *küllen,* it's a short, punchy word that serves the basic idea of ending something's life. It has a brutal and blunt sound. But if we're talking about legally sanctioned killing, we don't want to sound brutal, so we turn to the more technical *execute,* derived from Latin by way of Old French, which was long the language of law in Norman-conquered England (as mentioned in chapter 13). For other specialized contexts, we can employ words such as *assassinate,* which hails (in corrupted form) from Arabic. In spite of foreign influxes, written English remains about 84 percent phonetically logical. The thing is, the words we found during our trip didn't seem as though they came from the 16-percent exception side of the aisle.

We were finding things that fit the rules, like "scalion" for *scallion,* "puding" for *pudding,* and "occassions" for *occasions.* Double-letter problems ran amok, but even they couldn't compete with the vowel confusion, including "braclets" for *bracelets,* "absolutely" for *abso-*

lutely, and "lemonaide" for *lemonade*. It's easy to see the pattern now, even sticking to the ones we found in March, the pool of data from which Benjamin drew his conclusions. Vowel trouble and double letters. "Absolutly" and "braclets" together indicate a second category, along with my first real find, "referal" for *referral*. Both types of difficulties would often take place at the junction between a root word and a suffix. The larger pattern into which these pieces fit, however, was an impression that the speller operated by guess-work. If these words were botched in defiance of their own phonetic logic, then what was the principle that guided the speller? There wasn't one. Many were guessing, as if they'd never been taught to pay attention to the letters while learning to read. When Benjamin stumbled upon a list of often-misspelled words in the 1955 classic *Why Johnny Can't Read*, he was shocked to behold that, fifty years later, the book still held predictive validity for our findings on the road. Vowel trouble and double letters ruled the list, and the author, Rudolf Flesch, addressed them directly.

Were students taught to memorize the word lists and not taught *how* to spell? That's how I remembered spelling class. We'd use a single set of words each week, then move on to a new set the next week. If you could spell them right on the first day of the week, you'd opt out of having to do that week's spelling homework; otherwise you'd work with those words over and over. The hope was that the word lists would add up to a vocabulary. Later we'd get vocabulary words plucked from whatever books we read in English class, and thinking about the vocabulary words made me consider those spelling words from another angle. The idea of vocabulary words had been to teach you words you didn't know, definitions and all. *Felicitous*, *incessant*, and everyone's favorite word from *Siddhartha*: *courtesan*. But I knew what most of the words in my spelling book meant by the time I saw them. It was rare for the spelling book to add any words to your spoken vocabulary. The purpose was what it claimed: to teach you how to spell those words. Except that there'd been one simple oversight in methodology. There was no instruction toward teaching anyone *how* to spell the words. You just memorized them.

Oral language is a natural process, and the written correspondence has to be taught. When it comes to *knowing* words, children have budding oral lexicons that get a head start on the written. If we want to get kids spelling, reading, and writing, we have to teach them with a system of acquisition. We need to help them translate between the oral system they already possess and the written system. Looking back at the mistakes we'd found pointed to rules of spelling mechanics that hadn't been firmly planted in the spellers' minds. A doubled consonant makes the preceding vowel short, which might have been a helpful hint with "scalion" and "puding". More than helpful, it should have ruled out a double *s* in "occassions", which has a long *a*. Then there's the silent *e*, which sits after a consonant and makes the vowel preceding that consonant a long vowel, or, as teachers might explain it, the silent *e* "makes the vowel say its name." Hence the long *a* sound in *brace* or *bracelets*. I suppose I'd known these things on some level, with words like *hope* and *hop*, which became *hoped* and *hopped*, respectively. I couldn't remember explicitly learning about it. Then Benjamin had returned, carrying notes he'd taken from crawling through a segment of the library. While he might be a Hippie in dismissing complaints about "the degradation of the language," he did believe some helpful, basic facts had been missed by the methods that schools had their teachers using.

"They can't handle the junction," he'd said, back when I was in South Dakota. "Braclets" and "absolutly" were particularly painful for him to see as they were supposed to be the easy kind. Plus junctions: *absolute* + *-ly* = *absolutely*. Being able to recognize when to simply tack on the suffix and when something had to give, that was the first step. Then with that other kind of junction, the change junction, came the mutually exclusive consonant-doubling and *e*-dropping rules. *Hop* × *-ed* = *hopped*, and *hope* × *-ed* = *hoped*. Note that with these rules you preserve the phonetic integrity of the original words.

Hortense from Miracle on Main Street came to mind once more. Wasn't the problem she'd had with the dictionary the same problem that everyone seemed to be having with spelling? She had the dictionary *right there*, but she hadn't been taught how to use it. Teach kids to use a dictionary and give them the basic construction of phonics, and they ought to be able to spell most of the words they can say.* Once they actually get reading, the engine turns over, and they begin acquiring words both from conversation and from what they see on paper. We could give them the proverbial fishing pole rather than carping on lists of words. Otherwise, it'll all depend on what you can cram. In that case, I guess I'd have to thank my parents for a great verbal memory.

I thought back to the dozens of spelling mistakes I'd seen along the way. We're all using way more words than *anyone* can simply memorize. I suppose if you hold yourself to a limited vocabulary, you ought to be able to remember how to spell all the words you use, right? Or, if there's no dictionary handy, you should avoid writing a note to someone that uses words you can't recall, effectively making your written representation slightly less well versed than your spoken self. Those were my half-hallucinatory thoughts as I finally drifted off to sleep. I dreamed of classrooms with rows and rows of students, all taking a spelling test on the contents of the entire dictionary. Some students looked harried as they tried to remember the words and keep up with the monotonous teacher-voice listing the words; others had given up. I saw one little girl coloring a picture. She smiled up at me and said that the teacher won't mark her off as long as her paper looks pretty. Another kid was repeating tricks he'd learned for spelling individual words: "Wed-nes-day, *Oh, see* the ocean, desert is barren and only has one *s* but dessert is yummy and has two of them, there's *a rat* in separate, Feb-ru-ary . . ."

"Isn't this the information age?" I shouted. "What's the point of

---

* Dealing with the exception words is typically the last part of phonics instruction.

memorizing the whole dictionary?" My words echoed pointlessly on through the scholastic corridors of my nightmare.

TYPO TRIP TALLY

Total found: 358
Total corrected: 192

16 | How Do You Deal?

May 11-16. 2008 (Albany, NY, to Manchester, NH)

Comedy or Tragedy, 'tis sometimes difficult to see when one lives
the Play. Though in sight of familiar territory, the Journey
nearly at its end, still the unwavering armies of error must
be beaten back. From an Albany Fair, through the very Knowledge
Halls wherein the idea of TEAL has its faintest beginnings, and
at last into our Hero's stomping grounds of yore, astonishingly
varied responses muddle the Duo. Sic vita est.

Reader, I would like nothing more than to spring immediately
into the story of my triumphal return to New England: first our
brief alighting in Hanover, where my friendship with Benjamin was
forged, and then further backward in time to my hometown and a
stay with my mother. The multifarious wonders that Benjamin and
I encountered shall be related in due time, but I fear that before
every dawn come the primordial frights of deepest night. The deeds
done in Manchester, and the wisdom won there, cannot be complete
without an account of important events preceding them. Had I my
druthers, I would not speak of Albany at all, but the truth of the Tulip
Festival must out. I plead with you to conceal the following episode
from your children, until they've passed the age of nightmares and
can understand the virulent course that world events too often take.
Further, I bid you steel yourself against the horrors I am compelled to
describe, for you shall bear witness—in as brief and muted fashion
as I can manage!—to the hoary, pustuled flank of iniquity. For in

Albany I faced the worst day of typo correcting I would ever experience, and I pray that none of us ever sees its like again.

As we pulled up to the curb at my uncle and aunt's place, we discovered that Uncle Bill had been waiting for us, seated out on the lawn playing with his dog Harley. He sported a bright yellow TEAL shirt, the first I'd seen in action since I set up the store online. Harley, too, was ready; the clever black Labrador bounded up to us, a favorite stick clamped in his mouth. Not to be outdone by husband or dog, Aunt Kristen appeared with a hug and a big tip: down the road in Washington Park, Albany's annual rite of spring, the Tulip Festival, romped and rollicked, much like Benjamin upon meeting Harley.

Finding a parking spot down near the festivities proved to be a trial that required advanced skill checks in Patience, Navigation, Creativity, and Eyesight. "Everybody remember where we parked," Benjamin remarked as we set off down the long road to the festival, which teemed with people celebrating the heritage of the oldest Dutch settlement in the country. Booths of assorted arts and crafts lined the dirt paths, and at the paths' intersection stood a cluster of food wagons. We merged into the masses and began to visit the little tents, which ranged from mundane trinkets to some inspired pieces of art or its close facsimile. Oh, and gifts and treats galore. Candles and chocolate and perfumes and potions. And typos. Yes, we'd come to a swollen canal of errors, and now needed only to unplug the dike.

It began at the candy stand, with a tough one. They were selling chocolates called "non-pariels", which I pointed out to the attendant should actually be *nonpareils* (from the French word meaning "unequaled" or "peerless", testifying to the candy's excellence). He nodded quickly, somewhat busy with sweet-toothed Albanians. I didn't believe he'd do anything about it, but I also didn't want to make him drop a sale, so we moved onward. Already I worried that if everyone was working in high gear, trying to fit as many sales as possible into the fleeting window of the festival, we'd seem more intrusive than usual. The first incident had been candy, though, always a sure sales bet, and the next tent where we spotted an error didn't have the same feel. Here a few people browsed the paintings for sale, but no one was ready to actually purchase anything. One lady actively introduced herself to people while a large tattooed guy—the one in charge?—reclined in a seat at the back corner of the tent.

A laminated sign advertised that pet-centered art had been created by an "internationally renown artist" who shall go unnamed, lest the source of her renown become reknown. When the woman didn't seem occupied with anyone else, I casually caught her attention, but upon mentioning the word *renown*, the tattooed man broke in, anticipating my objection. "That's spelled right."

The woman wandered away without having spoken a word. Clearly she didn't want to be in the conversation if he'd claimed it. I turned, awkwardly addressing him across the tent while standing in front of the sign. I didn't want to come *at* him, and he made no move to rise. I attempted to clarify, though I already felt put on the defensive by the ferocity of his claim. Well, yes, I told him, renown had been spelled correctly. "It's just that it should be renown*ed*."

"No, listen," he almost shouted, pointing an accusing finger in such a practiced motion that, for a second, I thought he might be Bill O'Reilly in inked-up disguise. "I wrote that sign, and it's right. First I thought the word had a *k* in it, so I checked the *dictionary*. It said renown is a word—so it's *right*."

"Oh yeah, of course *renown* is a word," I agreed. "It's just that *renown* is the noun and *renowned* is the adjective. If you'd said she was a person of international renown, that'd be one thing, but internationally *renowned* needs the -*ed*."

"What school do you teach at?" he replied. I couldn't be certain if he was checking my credentials to see if they outranked his use of the dictionary, or merely mocking me.

I settled for my standard response: "We're going around the country correcting typos." For proof, I reached for a TEAL business card, which he immediately told me he didn't need—because he *wasn't changing it*. I wondered what would have happened if I'd said, "Actually, my dear fellow, I teach Platonic rhetoric and postmodern orthographic theory at *the* University, but I've deigned to give a guest lecture at your risible local college." Would he have stuttered into an appreciative tone and asked me to proofread his entire tent—if I could spare the time? Somehow I doubted it.

I winced from his rebuke and trudged onward up the dusty track, Benjamin at my side. I hacked some grit out of my lungs and commented that we couldn't do worse than that ugly scene. When will I learn not to say things like that?

We got a much more polite rejection of our offer to fix the next problem we saw. In yet another tent, a man in a smart beret allowed us to handle a small apostrophe problem after recognizing us from one of the news stories last month. Had our fortunes changed? Alas, he would prove to be the radical exception for TEAL's day at the fair—and I'm not just talking in terms of fashion sense.

A triply erroneous sign taunted us from its lofty position upon a tent. *Vidalia* is not a word with an obvious spelling, especially if you don't know how to pronounce it (hence, "Vadelia"—or even "Vidaria", as I noticed in a produce market in Hoboken), and *vinaigrette* is moderately challenging, so I could see how "vinegarette" had happened. But "tomatos"? *A ladder! a ladder! my sidekick for a ladder!* As we continued to breathe in kicked-up dirt and tried not to rub too much against our many neighbors, I spied the promise of Island Noodles, complete with the authentic taste of "Hawiian Island Sauce". Benjamin immediately rated this typo correction as a high degree of difficulty. The sign had been placed within the tent, up past the grill where they cooked their Noodles until the food achieved maximum tastiness, or, in island parlance, *broke da mouth*. We headed around the tent to where an underling wandered around without a clear purpose. Woe betide the traveler attempting to merge onto the road paved with good intentions, which too often forces you back down the exit ramp. Though we'd tried not to perturb the chef himself, the underling merely turned and began to relay our request. The busy Noodler raised his beefy head from that steaming grill and aimed a broad smile directly at us. Then, inter-rupting the question being passed to him, he provided a single word in a flat baritone: "No." His eyes sparked with glee in the instant the word popped out, as if this was the most fun he'd have all day, though, granted, it probably was. His head fell back into the steam, our existence forgotten; the underling returned to his hesitant cir-cles at the back of the tent.

"I once fell in love with a girl from New York," Benjamin said.

"Oh yeah, and how'd that work out?"

"I got rejected. Pretty much like that. Though her 'no' was in a higher register."

We spied some fresh produce and made a stealth correction to a sign offering "tomatoe" (*there* was the missing *e* that had migrated from "tomatos"!) before deciding we'd had enough. Benjamin looked exhausted, which isn't something you see every day, and I confess this place had an ill effect on me—I was turning grouchy. Escape, however, wouldn't be so simple.

As we headed down the lane lead-ing out of the park, I caught sight of an oddity ingrained in wood, amid hand-carved goods in one last tent. "Excuse me," I forced myself to say to the woman seated behind the table, "I noticed on one of your signs—"

"We don't sell any *signs* here," she corrected. "We sell *artwork*."

After the beatings I'd taken, this response made me much less interested in sparing her feelings. I blurted, "Okay. There is a *typo* in your *artwork*. Unless it's a pun? 'Bon Appetite'?"

"It's not a pun; it's a phrase."

I could tell she enjoyed the rhythm she had going. Oh wait, sorry. *It's not a rhythm, it's a sentence structure.*

Rather than take her artwork and slam it against my skull, I replied, "It shouldn't have an *e* on the end."

"Well, people are still buying it!" she replied. Then she loosed a long, evil cackle. *Fool, the free market has triumphed over your silly normative spelling conventions! WUAH-HA-HA-haaahhhh* . . . With her laughter ringing in our ears, we hurried from the Tulip Festival, gladdened at least to have escaped with our souls intact. Back in Callie's steel-reinforced safety, I checked to make sure my own name was still spelled correctly.

After having been shouted down by the renown guy, shut down by the Hawiian noodle chef, and cackled at by the *artwork* woman, I expected to feel saddened, confused, and angry, seasoned with a generous helping of weariness. Brutal as the festival had been, though, some magic note of dissonance produced in me an ironic reaction against the attitudes I'd experienced. Yes, an incongruous lighthearted feeling descended upon me, and I opened myself up to the world with a curious receptivity. As Benjamin had noted in returning to the adventure, the value of the experience might lie in rolling with whatever came our way, and seeing where it led.

The next day we went hunting through Albany again, with a newspaper team joining us for the tour of basically a couple blocks. We introduced them to the inevitable towing signs warning of "owners expense", and some assorted merriments typical of our quest, including a sign above a small flowerbed that read, THIS IS NOT A TRASH CAN PLEASE DONT LITER IN IT! Alas, with hate speech like that, the metric system will never find a home Stateside. The tour didn't last long—we discovered that many businesses were closed on Monday in Albany, at least in the neighborhood we visited. With the hunt done, we had dinner with one of my pals from the old Washington publishing days, and met the young man to whom this book is dedicated. When last I'd seen them, Henry was a mere mound rising from the midsection of his mother.

Here our eastward return offered a strange reflection of the westward venture. As New Orleans had followed Mobile, so too would

Albany be counterbalanced by a more hopeful locale. No place could have served that purpose better than our alma mater, where Benjamin and I had first met, as well as being the site of the first stirrings of my mad destiny. Somehow I couldn't quite believe this adventure had nearly come to its end. I felt as though I'd only begun to pull it all together, that I needed more time to synthesize it and start doing things right.

It had been nearly a year since the perfect June weekend that had seen the genesis of the League. Now I found myself on the same postcard streets, on an equally stunning day. Sun warmed the Georgian brick of the campus, and the green crests of nearby mountains seemed to beckon. This time, however, I wore a desert-dweller's hat on my head and a vinyl bag full of curious implements at my side. Benjamin and I had planned in advance to meet up with our respective senior-thesis advisers. Upon our arrival, Benjamin made for the Religion Department, and I took the opportunity to prowl around for fond memories and typos. I thought it appropriate to ply my trade in the very place that had prodded me to leave behind the nine-to-five office life, if only once, and go out and *do* something.

I'm pleased to report that, save for the single exception of a sign using tack-on letters that had no spare apostrophes available, every typo we battled on the Hanover Plain met its end. The town provided ideal typo-hunting ground, greeting me with a receptive heart or, if not that exactly, at least good humor. Main Street held few shops you'd recognize as national chains, and the friendly folks I found in these local businesses were exceptionally receptive. A candy shop featured a much sweeter experience than I'd had with the non-pareil seller in Albany; the girl behind the counter consented to my request to fix the spelling of "cocao", but only after first explaining to her little brother, who was helping her, why the change needed to be made. She printed a new label and let him find the difference. At a local sporting goods store, the owner became defensive when I pointed out the WOMEN'S WINTER HAT'S sign, starting to say that someone else had made the signs—and then he stopped himself, declaring that he needed to take responsibility for the error. He granted permission for the fix and even hastened to point out a MEN'S WINTER HAT'S sign that I had missed, so that I could amend that one, too.

I don't want to give the false impression that Benjamin slacked off while at his favorite Hanover restaurant. In fact, he introduced his professor to his newest hobby during lunch. Once you check the text around you with an eye to grammar and spelling, he explained, they leap out at you. By pointing to the chalkboard opposite their table, he immediately validated his claim. Therein lay a rendering of *Guinness* that seemed to lack its usual thickness ("Guiness"). Professor Susan Ackerman responded by noting that the *Zinfandel* had turned "Zinfendel", smoothly bringing herself into our ranks. Benjamin brought me back to Molly's as soon as we reconnoitered, advising me to have my chalk at the ready. The bartender, well used to obnoxious Dartmouth kids pulling stunts and tricks in his domain, still readily consented to some quick fixes. Fortunately, whoever had originally chalked the sign used approximately the same colors that I had, so nothing stuck out too badly. We had a *Cheers* moment as wait staff and patrons alike—including one who'd seen us on the news—joined in on the fun, asking us about our journey and giving us heartily up-flung thumbs.

We headed out to drinks with my own thesis adviser, Professor Ernie Hebert, who'd also taught Benjamin once. The specials sign outside the pub, Murphy's, listed a curious element in one of its hors d'oeuvres. Mmm . . . "coconunut". I wondered if it came with any Hawiian Island Sauce, though perhaps the extra syllable was enough to ensure extra flavor. Benjamin and I shared the tale of our journey with Ernie. As an English teacher, he could appreciate the TEAL mission, but he was amazed that we had survived a near-entire circuit around the country without getting our noses punched inside out. A professor to the last, even as we relaxed and knocked back beers, he pressed us for answers about what we'd learned from our travails, backing up Benjamin's Chicago assertion that we were in it for us now, for the experience more than for the typo correcting. I appreciated his ability to dive right into a deeper discussion of the mission, even as I faltered in my attempt to draw satisfying conclusions about what we'd seen and done. After the drinks, Benjamin and I stood around for an extra moment outside, long enough to make a quick swipe (Benjamin taking out most of the second *n* and the *ut* after it) and slice (my own strike of the chalk against the board, converting the left side of the decimated *n* into a *t*).

We drove south that night to Manchester and my mother, Benjamin blasting his new Filter album to keep us awake. Reflecting on the "coconunut" correction after a day of such great responses, I made a decision, one that may well resound throughout the future of the League. "Tomorrow in Manchester, let's not do any stealth corrections."

"Yeah?"

"I've been around the country, and now I'm going to be back in the town where I grew up," I shouted above the music. "I shouldn't have to sneak around—I'm a native son!"

"I don't know that everyone's going to see it quite that way," Benjamin hollered back.

"That's okay. I . . . want to try it this way."

He nodded. "That's fair."

The pot I'd stirred in Albany would soon begin to foam over. By dealing directly with the people closest to the typo, I invited the citizens of Manchester to reveal themselves to me. I'd realize eventually that I could have done this with anything—say, carrying around jars of pickles, asking people to taste-test. In calling for a day without stealth, I'd effectively called for interactions of all manner and degree, and Manchester delivered more than I ever could have anticipated.

It all came down to Elm Street, the heart of Manchester's once-and-future downtown. For the largest city in New Hampshire, with more than a hundred thousand people, old Manch Vegas (as certain wags referred to it) possessed a conspicuous lack of character.

Elm was the only place where you could find a few independent businesses huddling together for shelter from the chains. The city had been making more of an effort in recent years to spruce up the downtown area, and Elm Street did boast a few newer restaurants and bars, but nobody *shopped* there. Why deal with the sparse parking and sparser selection of wares when you could head over to the mall or the Walmart on South Willow? A couple of blocks west, the red behemoths of former industry sulked over the Merrimack River on both banks. Some parts of the old cotton and locomotive mill buildings had found a second life as restaurant or condo space, but nobody had figured out how to use the considerable real estate to its fullest advantage.

We parked on Elm outside a used bookstore, which drew Benjamin in like an iron bee to a neodymium honeypot. I picked up the book *Red Mars*, deciding not to wait for the copy that Benjamin had offered to lend me. He called me over to the back run, where he'd caught not only a classic apostrophe for a plural (ALL AUDIO'S 25% OFF), but a new category of fiction: COMTEMPORARY. I could tell by the look on his face that he wanted to ask, "Are you *sure* about this no-stealth-correction thing?" These errors were at the opposite corner of the store from the register, where the only clerk in the store was ringing someone up. We were well concealed by overstuffed bookcases. How easy these could be to right. I shook my head no.

"Hear me out. I know we're a solid twenty-five corrections over fifty percent, but *that*"—and here he pointed to COMTEMPORARY, which he must have spotted second—"is just wrong."

"Then I hope this bookstore cares as much as we do about words." I considered other bookstores we'd examined across the country, realizing how few of them had yielded typos. I'd made them a stop in nearly every major city. I could remember only Galveston's bookstore typos now, and that place had been one of our best responses. I approached the counter, and the woman asked if I was ready to check out. I looked at *Red Mars* in my hand—I was, wasn't I? After we did that, I asked about the signs.

"Oh, we had a volunteer who made those signs." Ahh, right. Volunteers are apparently held to a different standard. It was the Cartoon Art Museum all over again. If you're getting paid, you ought to be professional, but what can they do to you when you're a volunteer? If they'd written "maid by valunteeerz" on the signs, I could have saved myself the trouble of asking. I don't know if the employee could read these thoughts from my face, but she must have read something (though clearly not the signs in her store). She added another reason not to bother: "They've been up for a long time and nobody seems to have noticed the mistake."

Seems, Madam! nay, it is; I know not "seems."

Okay, so now she'd passed the buck and projected her apathy onto everyone else, as if signs only became the store's responsibility after multiple complaints had stacked up on her desk into a thickness sufficient to be bound and sold here: *Please Fix Your Signs Already,* by Your Customers (2008). I hoped it was merely the idea of having to do the work herself that had made her react so negatively, and so I offered to take care of the mistakes myself, presenting a phial of elixir to vouch for my sincerity.

"No, we'll take care of it," she lied. Upon hearing how unconvincing she sounded, she switched lies. "The volunteer's going to be making new versions of those signs anyway."

I'd heard all of these lines before, but never in such rapid succession, out of the same mouth. We'd gotten a bravura performance in the unlikeliest place; perhaps the bookstore clerk had missed her true calling on the stage. Benjamin laughed as soon as we hit the sidewalk. "Wow! You'd think she'd been following the blog to have come up with all those!"

"What was the problem?" I nearly shouted. "I mean, *why*? I don't understand why she wouldn't at least let me white out that apostrophe?"

"She could be an agent of FLAME," Benjamin offered.

The rain—or perhaps reign—of errant apostrophes continued to sluice onto our sunny day. We caught a whole row of plural apostrophes trapped in one sign behind glass. The juice bar hadn't even opened for business yet, and already it drowned under the weight of excess punctuation. I wished it good luck and better proofreading as we continued on along the street.

No quarrel with apostrophes would be complete, however, without at least one confusion of *it's* and *its*. We stared at the dry-erase board, set on an easel outside the storefront of the Benton Shoe Company, which was NOW IN IT'S 16ᵀᴴ YEAR. Okay, this could be an easy fix. They'd let us wipe out that apostrophe, right? Before I even thought about it, my finger had stretched out toward the board, touching it, trying to wipe the little mark away. It failed to disappear. At that moment an employee popped through the front doorway, having noticed us staring at the sign. As much as

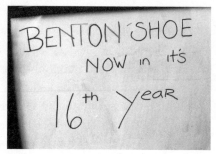

I'd insisted on no stealth corrections, I'd been caught failing at one. "It's the *it's*," I said lamely. "It should be *its*."

"Without an apostrophe," Benjamin clarified.

She must have been the person who'd written the sign—months ago, for the dry-erase marker had dried and become permanent. Her initial reply, without the defensive tone that the words implied, was, "I never promised that I was brilliant." She said it with a casual shrug, but she didn't slam the door in our faces. I wondered if we still had a chance at this one, as bad as we'd already made the situation, and as miserable and—dare I say—nightmarish as Elm Street had become. "An apostrophe," I said, "that we can't rub off—it won't come out."

"Here," she said, perhaps taking pity on us, " I know." She reached for my Typo Correction Kit, and I offered her the closest color, which didn't match the sign. She shrugged this detail off as well. "That's all right." Then, with my marker, she turned the apostrophe into a little star. Next she added another star to the board, and another, and another. She'd made a parallelogram constellation, or quadruple fireworks for the store's obsidian anniversary. The apos-

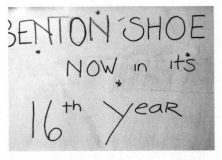

trophe had been hidden amid the decorations. She handed back my dry-erase marker and with a quick, quirky smile, she zipped back into the store, humming a quiet tune to herself. No, she'd never promised to be brilliant—she'd just proven it.

"Dude," Benjamin said, "that was freaking amazing."

I wished, when I'd started the trip, that I'd had the foresight to create some kind of awards. "For Excellence & Creativity in Eradication, I award you this beribboned Typo Correction Kit." Our fortunes had reversed course. As we moved farther down the street, I bounded nearly as high as Benjamin normally does.

Another dry-erase board with a problem greeted us: STEAK CEASAR SALAD. The cashier initially told us not to worry because they'd be erasing it tomorrow, which seemed plausible as the salad was among the daily specials. When I told her of our quest and added that this stop represented the triumphal return to my roots, she bade us onward to correction with a heartfelt "Okay," holding back the "whatever" that still spoke through the rustle of her shrug. Benjamin had caught a "ceasar" salad back in Hudson, and now I'd evened the score. My blue dry-erase marker didn't quite match their light green, but it'd be gone tomorrow anyway. As I wiped it away, I turned to Benjamin and cried, "Me too, you brute! Then fall 'ceasar'!"

After noting that a like-minded individual had added some apostrophes to a sign desperately needing them—quickening the manufacture of good spirit in my heart's grimy mills—I decided we'd successfully covered the main chunk of the street and should head back to the car. We agreed upon one last stop for drinks, mayhap smoothies, at the Bridge Café. Benjamin noted that the café had to be a cool place because it hosted poetry slams.

Of all the typos I'd ever noticed, this would have to be one of the slightest infractions. Even apostrophes or lack thereof come down to a single mark, but this was in effect a sliver of a letter. *Gorgonzola*, up on the chalkboard, had been spelled "Gorganzola". I smiled at how easy it'd be to have someone to reach up and, with the slightest finger-swipe, take the tail off that *a* to make it an *o*. I approached one of the two men behind the counter, and he accepted a TEAL card and heard us out, turning to see if he could spot the error. Before he had a chance to say anything, however, the other guy jumped in, practically shoving the first employee to the side. "So who says it's wrong?"

The first guy stepped back away and let his supervisor (was he that?) take over, which was too bad, since he'd seemed open to making the correction. Now I had the privilege of talking to this other guy, whose style of service had been a tad abrasive even with his last customer. "Well," I said, "the first *a* needs to be an *o*. It's the tiniest of changes . . ."

"Everybody makes mistakes," he replied, which I felt I could nod along with, except for its immediate postscript: "Why should I fix it? Because you say so?"

"No. Because it's wrong." His logic had caught me off guard. Since everyone makes mistakes, there's no reason to fix them? The ball bounced over the shortstop's glove; why should the outfielder bother to run it down?

"We'll be *sure* to take care of that for you," he said in a sarcastic and challenging tone. I couldn't believe this guy felt the need to stare me down over a typo, but that's what he'd decided to do. His jaw was set, and his eyes hard: full macho mode.

"It's just taking the tail off the *a*," I reiterated.

Again using a contrary inflection, he said, "Thank you. Anything else?"

I looked to Benjamin, who'd already picked out what he'd planned to drink. He shook his head no. We'd slake our thirst somewhere else. Sometimes you have to walk away.

As disappointed as I felt for not fixing literally the easiest of all the typos I'd ever detected, Benjamin looked even lower. Apparently he'd expected a very different atmosphere, judging solely on the basis of the café's poster about its slam nights. "Poets gravitate to places with the right *atmosphere*, man. That completely caught me off guard. What was that guy's problem?"

"His misspelling? Everyone makes mistakes, like he said."

"Yeah, everyone makes mistakes, but that doesn't mean we all defend them."

And defensive was exactly what we'd seen, which brought me back to Albany and *renown*. As Benjamin and I began talking over the various responses we'd had over the last few days, we realized they'd covered a surprising range.

Forget the typos. Mission aside, I'd taken a tour of basic human interactions. We'd seen a wide sampling of how people dealt with challenges, problems, or general requests made of them on a fundamental level. We're fast approaching seven billion people on this little blue period in the text of the cosmos, and every day we bump into dozens of each others. Each interaction does not necessarily equate to one person wanting something from the other; sometimes they possess a common goal. (My mission was supposed to be the latter: enlisting people's aid in improving their own surroundings.) When someone initiates an interaction with us, we have to decide how to react. I'd noted earlier how the customer service aspect that dominates many of these situations provided a basic script, but over the past few days I'd caught a lot more reactions of the unscripted variety. As human beings, how do we choose to react in that instant when someone walks toward us, smiles, and begins to speak?

As I sat down to my blog, I couldn't shake the Bridge Café guy's skewed recognition that we all make mistakes. I titled my day's entry: *We All Make Mistakes. Now How Do You Deal?* I played with the idea, but I felt fettered by the single day's events. I couldn't tell the whole story that way. Albany, Hanover, and Manchester felt like a family of experiences, much like the Three Bears (a simile that would win Jane's approval). Papa Albany Bear had been too aggressive. Mama Hanover Bear had been gentle. And Baby, no, Teenage Manchester Bear had been juuuust . . . all over the place. Benjamin and I continued to debate motivations and explanations through the next day's hunt, again in Manchester.

With the renown guy, I'd had no hope right from the start. He'd immediately changed the discussion from focusing on the typo to the question of who's right. Once we'd devolved into "I'm right and you're wrong," his position had become entrenched because his very identity—as the person who is *right*—was at stake. "That's a huge thing that I see in customer service. When customers feel like they're being told they're wrong, they get hostile," Benjamin added.

The renown and gorganzola affairs had shared that confrontational defensiveness. "Why should I fix it? Because you say so?" "What school do you teach at?" They'd responded to my request by asking who I was to be correcting them. As much as I'd tried not to blame people for mistakes, focusing instead on the mistakes themselves, some people refused to let that distinction play. Anything they did became linked to their identity, and anyone who suggested the slightest tail-off-a-letter change to what they'd done became the enemy. I marveled at how, once again, tiny little typos had led me to a much larger communication issue, one that could apply across the broad spectrum of our daily experiences. Too often, we get stuck arguing from that perspective, placing egos like roadblocks into the situations. Perhaps I should have invested first in the appeasement of those egos, before even broaching the topic of the mistakes, with a sincere "How's your day going?" In his book *I'm Right, You're Wrong, Now What?* the clinical psychologist Dr. Xavier Amador sums up his approach to conflict resolution as, "Why would anyone want to listen to you if he felt you had not first listened to him?"

So what about the other reactions we encountered? For some, the ambivalent nature of apathy rears its fuzzy-logic head. We'd already witnessed how apathy could be boon or bane for us, but now I could field effectively alongside that most infamous of all shortstops, I-Don't-Give-A-Darn.* The prerequisite for apathy was creating a boundary line between oneself and the rest of the world. Once that boundary was set, apathy could take root, either from basic frustration at forces outside one's control or from a consciously predetermined refusal to allow the outside any concern. Our Noodler represented the latter, and as soon as he identified us as "not my problem," he could shoot us down with practiced ease. We didn't even have time to state our relevance; we were interlopers, and we stood outside the boundary. On the obverse of the apathy coin, my ceasar-salad correction had been allowed because the woman hadn't cared about the words that would be wiped away. Telling us yes had been the fastest way to resolve her sole concern: eliminating our existence from inside her boundary line.

Still more intriguing to me had been our bookstore lady, who'd gone out of her way to lie for no reason we could nail down. She'd lied so consistently that I couldn't even hazard a guess as to her motivation. I can't be sure if this was the case, but Benjamin did observe, "There *are* people who have a problem with everything, no matter what. They argue for the sake of arguing." Yet even if this explanation fits, how would such people get through an ordinary day? Does that kind of argumentative nature confer a feeling of superiority, or do the topics of argument truly feel that important to the arguer? It might come down to control, a narrow focus on insignificant details as the only controllable things (e.g., no customer's going to tell *me* what to change in *my* store). Or by sticking to the molehills and minutiae, one gains an excuse for not facing the difficult mountains that do loom outside the kitchen window. (Uncharitable persons might claim this about the TEAL mission itself.) Beyond our speculations, I fear I haven't the insight to definitively draw back the veil.

---

* Or, depending on how Abbott and Costello judged the sensibilities of their audience during their routine, he might manifest as I-Don't-Care or I-Don't-Give-a-Damn.

Hudson's Miracle on Main Street fiasco returned to my mind then, but that hadn't been arguing for the sake of arguing so much as it had been a desperate groping for authority (the makers of the sign must know better than any of us; the dictionary will tell us; here's a woman I work with, know, and trust).

Not everyone had to react so negatively. I thought back to Hanover, where one guy caught himself passing the buck and took responsibility for it. He may not have created the typo, but he was there in the moment and could make the change happen. He'd even pointed out the brother typo of the one I'd caught, so we'd nabbed that one, too, working together. I considered that to be an excellent model to carry across life's vistas of possibility. Who cares who made the mistake? I only care about how it gets fixed. Immediately following that one, I'd come upon the candy-store clerk, who turned a mistake into a teachable moment, the epitome of lemonade from lemons. At Molly's, they'd rolled with our request so well that I had to revisit my thoughts about judgment, which Benjamin had shot down back in Chicago. While others might judge the mistakes and think less of a restaurant that had them, their response to our request had offered so much more vital information to judge them by. In showing such good humor and letting us correct the typos, everyone nearby feeling comfortable to join in the moment, they'd *proven* themselves. The very atmosphere that Applebee's, T.G.I. Friday's, and their ilk simulate in their advertisements actually existed here; we felt it. Thinking about it gave me a pang for Hanover like I hadn't experienced even during my reunion.

Topping it off, though, was our Benton Shoe lady. That had likely been her own apostrophe, placing her with the many Americans who lack *apostrophic confidence*. In the end, though, what mattered most about her was her creativity and easygoing nature, as she casually made one of the most inspired typo corrections of our entire journey.

As if to screw the point deeper into the paneling of my head, the next two days offered almost perfectly symmetrical experiences.

Once each day, we spotted a sign from the car, parked, and went inside the establishment to speak to someone. Both people we told used an air of professionalism to cut our interactions short. In spite of those surface similarities, the results were radically different. Outside The Derryfield, a restaurant and nightspot that my mom had patronized back in the day, an LED sign flashed a string of red messages, including one that advertised PRIME RIB NITGHT. We had to wait as it cycled through a couple times, timing the moment right to get the picture, which we used as our evidence inside. A hostess grabbed a manager, who said he'd fix it and then walked away. The curt nod punctuating his sentence let us know he'd heard us and that the interaction had therefore concluded. Had we been lied to, or had he done it? We drove on for more typo hunting, and when we passed by later, we saw that the offending *t* no longer existed. Benjamin had offered a smile as he thought back and said, "That guy's a pro. He might have seemed abrupt, but that's the attitude of someone who gets things done." That nod had probably reflected this latest item entering his mental to-do list, and I didn't doubt that everything that went on that man's list got crossed off.

By contrast, in the second instance, our efforts received a "No . . . we don't do that." We stood inside a credit union, where the marquee outside advertised a HOME EQUTIY SPECIAL.

I stared at the woman behind the desk, confused. I'd explained our mission and asked to borrow a ladder, but she seemed to be answering a different question. "Uh. Don't do what?"

"Buy whatever you're selling." Spoken with the professional authority she'd swaddled herself in, using it as a flak jacket to protect her from really hearing us. Even as I tried to clarify that we weren't selling anything at all and only wanted to point out that they'd misspelled *equity* (which I'd thought to be a key term for a banking institution), I could see that she'd given us her official decree. The conversation had already ended, regardless of how long we kept talking.

"What a piece of work is man," Benjamin began to muse. As for me, I'd done enough investigation into the knotted guts of human behavior to last me for quite a while. The time for home had come.

TYPO TRIP TALLY

Total found: 432
Total corrected: 233

17 | The Welcome-Back Committee

May 17-22, 2008 (Somerville, MA)

Home once more, his mission complete, still the unslakeable fires
for communication clarity blaze mightily, and new vision begins
to bubble in the cauldron of our Hero's mind, a reaching out to
all those who—actually, no, the Government has other plans.

We took the last miles of the TEAL journey at a tear. Surely only
Odysseus returning to Ithaca had experienced the depth of eagerness
that I did now. The drive from Manchester to Somerville took about
an hour, but felt longer. So many times had I traversed this bland
stretch of I-93 on visits to my mom, but never had there been such
import to my return. I had traveled nearly twelve thousand miles on
my monumental circuit around the country, and now I returned to
where I'd begun—albeit with a ton more stuff in the car and a short,
bearded fellow in the passenger seat.

No welcoming parade greeted us as we pulled off the highway. No
flotilla of floats impeded our progress as I turned Callie onto Cherry
Street. It was a cool, sunny May morning. The neighborhood looked
as I had left it. My house was as gloomy and dark as it had ever been.
Nevertheless, I sprang out of the car, sensing that *I* was different,
and that I had only begun to comprehend the enigmas underlying
mankind and cacography.

We entered the silent apartment; my roommate was away for the
weekend. I stood in the dim hall for a moment, my keys still in my

hand, as the entire trip rushed back over me in recall. Seventy-three days of travel, more epic an adventure than I had ever undertaken. I had hunted typos through frigid snows and baking heat, in teeming cities and lonely outposts, amid mountains and plains and dreaming shores. I had put myself in various perilous situations, but none of my fears about the journey had come to pass. I had not met violence, nor lost my car to theft or the elements, and I had averted both greasy-spoon-induced *E. coli* and chassis-twisting calamities. Surely some higher patron of grammar had gilded my path. Then I glanced at the sloping range of mail on the foyer table and winced. The nice folks at Emory University Hospital at Atlanta apparently expected recompense for fixing my eye. Other creditors had been awaiting my return with varying degrees of patience. I had a welcome-back committee after all, it seemed.

"Come on, man," said Benjamin. "There's a heap of junk in that car that we've gotta unload."

"Sorry, it's just hard to believe that I'm back here," I said. "And just when we got a handle on why typos happen. Too bad this is the end, huh?"

He chose to take my query at face value. "No, we've still got one last hunt to do with Jane, remember?"

We went back out to the trunk and started hauling our bags and other detritus inside. During these labors, I realized that my return was missing something, a certain crucial action that would close the circle of this journey in satisfying, Campbellian form. I checked my watch. We still had time to kill before Jane came up from Allston.

"Why don't we take a stroll to Davis Square?" I said, strapping on the camera and Typo Correction Kit. "There's a score I have to settle."

We headed down the street, and when we came to a particular sign hanging on a particular fence, I stopped and stared it down. Benjamin whistled. "That's the one, isn't it?"

"That's the one," I affirmed.

NO TRESSPASSING.

"Do it, man," said Benjamin. "Time to drive the ruffians from the Shire."

I knew how best to handle this ancient foe—with the final dregs of the bottle of elixir that had served me so well in skirmishes around the nation. I uncorked it and slowly painted over the second *s*, not with malevolence, but with a sense of justice at last being done.

"Tresses shall henceforth be *freely passed*," I declared in ringing tones.

We circled the Square, if that's possible, and headed back toward my street. Jane called me then, on her walk to my house from the Porter subway station. We spotted her rolling her overnight bag behind her farther down Cherry Street, and she hid behind a telephone pole—then burst out and pelted into my arms. "You're not gonna leave me again, right?" she said into my shoulder.

"I'm here to stay," I murmured back, closing my eyes and enjoying her nearness. And I would have stayed put, had the choice been up to me, but an awful destiny awaited Benjamin and me.

Jane and I reluctantly disengaged, remembering that we had one last hunt to do. We swung by my apartment to drop off her bag and prepare for a longer outing. I'd kicked off my mission in Boston, and searched out and corrected typos in various strange territories. Now I would have to complete what my NO TRESSPASSING correction had begun, and face my own neighborhood, here north of the Charles.

The three of us crossed into Cambridge and took a stroll down Massachusetts Avenue. Our party lent a nice symmetry, I thought, to the circuit of the League. Josh, Benjamin, and I had hunted in L.A.; Jane, Josh, and I had hunted in Seattle; and now Benjamin, Jane, and I plied TEAL's trade here at home. The afternoon remained brisk. We strolled under a bright blue sky.

Independent shops and eateries festooned the road down to

Harvard University. We popped into them along the way, enjoying the day and browsing their wares. How this hunt contrasted to that first one I'd undertaken in Boston. Then, I had not known where to search out typos, and when I had stumbled across a few, I drew back from them, hesitant and afraid. Now we wielded our corrective tools with impunity, buttressed by the solid stone of our experiences.

As we wandered through a craft shop, Jane asked, "Is TEAL all done?"

Benjamin chuckled. I said that I'd like to see us go on and do more, that we ought to carefully expand our mission. I also had an interview coming up with Boston's Fox News. This would be the last typo hunt for the trip, though, so in that sense we'd reached the end.

"Can I help you prepare?" Jane asked, her eyes anime-wide with enthusiasm.

"Sure. Ask me a practice question. I'm ready."

She maneuvered over to where Benjamin was. Though they'd only met today, they were already getting along well. He whispered something to her.

"So," she said, holding out an invisible microphone, "where did you guys end up finding the most typos?"

The classic question. Everyone asked it sooner or later. "Everywhere," I said. Starting out, I'd heard many snarky comments about where I'd be most likely to find typos, born out of stereotypes about certain sectors of America. In practice, though, we had found errors in every geographical corner and on every socioeconomic stratum. Typos were a universal, class- and region-blind phenomenon. "Pretty much everyone could use an editor."

"Case in point over here," Benjamin said. Jane and I saw that his old foe, subject-verb disagreement, had returned: ". . . each draws like a pencil, doesn't rub off on hands, and—amazingly—take about 10 years before it disappears." Even here in a shop full of cleverly manufactured goods, in one of the wealthiest and most educated communities in the state, typos could still happen. I added the *s* to "take" and we moved on. Benjamin brushed his hands together. "Glad I got to see one last disagreement go down."

Farther down the road, an extraneous apostrophe in neon vexed us, for old time's sake. A pox on PASTA AND SALAD's! We stared at the restaurant window, knowing that the owner would not likely replace his expensive fluorescent tubes just because we said so. "I wonder how much they paid for that," Benjamin said.

"Those plural apostrophes." I sighed with mock despair. "It seems we'll never be rid of them."

"Why not?" Jane asked.

"Self-perpetuating," Benjamin said. "Other people who aren't confident about their apostrophe use will see this. Then they'll be adding plural apostrophes to their own words."

"Viral, huh? So maybe you need a viral *solution*." And like that Jane gave me an inspiration for what the League's next move might be. She saw it in my eyes, too. "Uh-oh, bear. Why do I have the feeling I'm going to be helping you design something in Flash soon?"

"Hmm," I said significantly. "I wonder what that solution would look like."

We sat down for lunch in Harvard Square and batted around some crazy ideas for what the TEAL site—and what the League itself—could grow into. I devoured my food, barely registering it. I should have been exhausted from my travels, flinging myself back into my own bed for a marathon snoozefest. And yet, now that I was back, armed with everything I knew, I wanted to charge forth and do more. The possibilities seemed boundless and yet within the bounds of my ability. This wasn't the end at all, more like a phase shift, or maybe our quanta ascending to the next state.

We talked over some ideas as we ate, and agreed that today's hunt wouldn't be the last post. Next I'd start a contest, soliciting typo corrections. I could post entries on what counted as a typo or not, and on strategies for typo hunting—emphasizing the kinder and gentler approach, of course. We had enough ideas for at least five posts, maybe more if people began submitting their fixes.

Having clung to one side of the street on our way down, we headed back up Mass Ave. on the other side and again ducked in everywhere. Anything to prolong and enrich that last hunt. I hooked my arm in Jane's, and Benjamin strolled along behind us, examining our environs more carefully. For someone who'd begun the trip with no interest in the typo aspect, he was pretty intent on the mission now. He stopped us and pointed out something we'd stepped right over, a workman's graffito on the sidewalk: TO CLOSE TO N-STAR. Benjamin took my chalk and knelt by the error, scraping in an extra *o*. Not quite satisfied with that, he augmented his work with marker.

"Ahh!" Jane said as he worked. "The typo tried to get our toes!"

"They attack from every angle. They're everywhere." We'd taken out many, but they remained abundant.

"Well then, I guess you better get to work with those ideas," she said, and I petted her arm. Despite her Hippie tendencies, I had her support. I'd explained to her via e-mail and phone how she'd helped me reshape my orthographic worldview after Benjamin and I had slugged it out in the Midwest. I wondered if I could explain my position to everyone sufficiently for both Hawk and Hippie to align themselves with me, to push for a few crucial changes in the way we approach language. E.g., that people could be their own editors, that all it took was a second look at whatever you'd written.

"You know, Jane's right," Benjamin said. "There's work to be done."

"Are you saying you're in for the next phase, too?"

Benjamin handed me back my chalk and marker. "I haven't bought a ticket back yet. I should wait a week to head back south. We could kick things off right now. What do you say?"

In a gift store, we came to my final typo find and correction. Perhaps unsurprisingly, it manifested as an *its*/*it's* confusion. The typo hid in a legend accompanying a little packaged plastic gnome: THIS MYTHICAL CREATURE IS SAID TO BRING LUCK TO IT'S OWNER! The mythical creature in question would bring only grammatical confusion to its owner if I didn't step in, so I markered out the apostrophe. Jane watched me as she played with some toys nearby.

"What a tiny apostrophe that was," she said. "The gnome itself looked like a giant next to it."

Such a tiny thing, but such a big difference it had made. The episode seemed a fitting end to our quest. Though I might have made a mistake in not buying the little garden dweller, as I could have used the luck.

When we got back to the apartment, Benjamin hauled his bags into the living room and commandeered the couch. After blogging our finds, I concluded that last post suggesting that everyone should "stay tuned" for more to come, and over the next few days I kicked off a typo-hunting contest (offering a free TEAL shirt as a prize) and wrote posts *about* typos and the practice of their elimination, leading up to some bigger discussions . . . that circumstances would soon prevent from flowering. Benjamin and I began to put together big plans for the future of the League.

A couple days before Benjamin left, a visitor arrived at my apartment. Jane and I were out at the time, so my roommate answered the door on that fateful Thursday morning. Benjamin sat in the living room reading Arthur C. Clarke, and overheard the interloper ask for either Jeff Deck or Benjamin Herson. Benjamin popped up and introduced himself to a tall, muscular fellow squeezed into a tan uniform that reminded him of his Boy Scout days. "Is Jeff Deck here as well?"

"Not at the present time, but this is his place," Benjamin answered. "I'm the one just visiting. What's . . . this about?"

The uniformed man handed over some photocopied documents, and his card. "This is about a sign you vandalized at the Grand Canyon."

Appalled by the man's characterization of the act, Benjamin replied, "We corrected it."

"It was a hundred years old," the ranger said.

"Oh." Benjamin signed that he'd officially received the documents, for both of us.

The National Park Service was not grateful for the correction that we'd made to the sign in the South Rim watchtower at the Grand Canyon. Their response was, in fact, the opposite of gratitude. The pages, which were hasty copies of the first couple of pages of some longer, absent document, described how we had first conspired to vandalize and then vandalized a precious national historic treasure. The federal government very much desired that we travel back to Arizona in the near future for a chat with a man in a long robe. Benjamin and I had both been summoned to court, unwilling participants in a case called *United States of America v. Jeff Deck and Benjamin Herson.* Now *there* was a phrase to make you soil your breeches. If the title of the case wasn't enough to communicate the gravity of our plight, the consequences of an unfavorable verdict certainly were. Six months of federal imprisonment was one possible outcome.

Suddenly the saga of the Typo Eradication Advancement League had taken a bleak twist. We frantically tried to figure out what to do next. Our first conclusion was that when faced with court summons, one ought to seek out some sort of representation. This went double when the plaintiff was a disgruntled federal agency. Jane promised to follow up on some meager legal connections for us. Meanwhile, I stripped the Grand Canyon entry out of the archives. Not long after that, after speaking with a couple different attorneys, I realized that I'd have to bring down the rest of the website, to avoid further self-incrimination. The shutters went dark on TEAL. Whatever plans we might have concocted for furthering our cause would have to wait—perhaps for a long time. Perhaps forever. One bad correction had the power to negate hundreds of good ones.

Benjamin returned to Silver Spring, where he obtained a copy of the entire complaint document and forwarded it my way. It described how "law-enforcement personnel were notified of a website . . . which described the vandalism of a historical sign inside the Desert View Watch Tower." The document insisted on calling me "Jeff Michael Deck" throughout, presidential-assassin style. They must have pulled my middle name from my driver's license (though they forgot to import the *rey* for *Jeffrey*). I tried to read through the sober text, so that I could more fully understand the grave charges arrayed against us. However, I couldn't quite concentrate on the actual content. The customary scanning of my editor's eye had uncovered much to abhor. No matter that this was a legal document, with every word presumably holding jurisprudential significance; typos had still crept in at every turn. Early in the document, Benjamin and I were said to have violated certain "criminal statues," rather than *statutes*. I shuddered to visualize what violating statues would entail. Then, in a less kitschy context than explaining gnome magic, *its/it's* confusion popped up: "The website describes the mission of it's group . . ." Also, "this a 28 year old Benjamin Douglas Herson", lacked some small but crucial word, plus he was from "Silver Springs, Maryland," rather than Silver Spring. Surely the personified *United States of America,* as complainant, knew the spelling of the city that was home to such important federal agencies as NOAA and the FDA.

Attachment B

Package containing markers

In the face of catastrophe, some turn to drink, others to God or denial. I, apparently, fell back on proofreading.

The last page of the document was a picture labeled "Attachment B". It was me standing at the edge of the Grand Canyon, cowboy hat on, Typo Correction Kit at my side. Someone had helpfully drawn a thick arrow across the picture, pointing at the Kit and labeling it "Package containing markers". The smoking gun! I laughed at this picture until my sides ached.

When I could finally manage to reread the document for meaning, it only became more perplexing. The Park Service apparently thought we'd been specifically targeting government-owned signs on our trip, and even that we'd attacked the watchtower sign specifically for its historic status. The architect of the tower, Mary Colter, had written the sign herself seventy-odd years ago. Benjamin and I had not known that, though. During the trip, we never intentionally corrected anything of historical and/or artistic value. Back at Kitty Hawk, we'd noted but never considered correcting a mistake in the picture of the newspaper edited by the Wright Brothers. In Santa Fe, I pointed out the problem of "St. Frances of Assissi" to the tour guide instead of acting on my own. In Ohio, my father had produced a clipping from his glory days of high school baseball, in which he'd pitched a no-hitter, the prize coveted by all who stand atop the mound. A mistyping had left a reference to a "hti", but I'd held my father's bit of history as sacrosanct. Though my eyes be keen, they can't compare to those of an art historian, and both Benjamin and I deeply regretted our failure to recognize that the sign had belonged to that domain. The thought had just never occurred to us as we stumbled onto, in our view, an ugly little sign up the stairs from a gift shop, a sign that explained the purpose of the watchtower it occupied, but had no accompanying plaque or other indicator of its own age and value.*

Neither Benjamin nor I had any pals in Flagstaff, Arizona, never mind pals of a legal persuasion, so I scrambled blindly to find a barrister who could represent us in the town's federal court. One lawyer

---

* We *had* misjudged one other thing about the sign: we'd thought "emense" was a misspelling of *immense*, though we didn't correct it. Benjamin would discover that the *Oxford English Dictionary* considers "emense" to be an acceptable alternative rendering. A critic, Ammon Shea, who had consumed the entire *OED* and evidently got indigestion for his trouble, also pointed out that Renaissance printer William Caxton, as well as Lewis and Clark, used that rendering of the word. Perhaps Mary Colter habitually used archaic spelling, for yuks. So at least we'd only corrected the mistakes that were in fact mistakes. I'd never unfixed an item during the TEAL trip.

gave me a promising initial evaluation—and then disappeared without warning on vacation. Our appointed time in court was looming. I went back to my random Internet searches. I would have asked for assistance on the blog, but hey, the blog wasn't there anymore. Finally, with the appointment of our ruin dawning on the horizon, I found a lawyer willing and able to represent us. She scored us a continuance, or postponement, of the court date, and was familiar with the prosecutor. I felt reasonably confident in her ability to represent us well. That is, until I received the contract in the mail that I had to sign for her services.

The contract listed my name as "Jeffrey Deek".

Up to this point, I had refused to entertain the notion that Benjamin and I might not return from Flagstaff. Now my only thoughts were whether the federal pen out there had air-conditioning.

TYPO TRIP TALLY

Total found: 437
Total corrected: 236

TYPO TRIAL TALLY

Total found: 2
Total corrected: 0

18 | Court of Opinion

How far our Heroes have fallen. They are brought before an
unsympathetic judge to answer for their Crimes against America.
The punishment, like a banged gavel, will have a resounding
Impact, and the future of TEAL hangs in the balance. The media
join the assault and twist TEAL into a forced punchline. A year
of misery begins . . .

Benjamin sat at the gate among other Phoenix-bound travelers,
reading a book but looking miserable. Not for the first time, I felt a
touch of guilt at what I'd gotten him into. The plane tickets had not
been cheap. Our lawyer had been expensive, and I had yet to understand why. In total, one typo correction would cost us ten thousand
dollars. As a bonus, though, we'd receive a crash course in the justice
system, a civics class with armed bailiffs.

"And don't call me Shirley," I said, coming up behind him. We'd
each taken a flight here to Dallas–Fort Worth and would be sharing
the connecting flight to Arizona.

He set down Kim Stanley Robinson's *Red Mars*, to my surprise; I
was reading *Red Mars*, too. When I pulled my copy out to prove it,
he shook his head. "Surely you can't be serious," he replied. "I don't
know, man, I'm not feeling good about this."

Benjamin had called for a free consultation from another lawyer,
who'd laughed, "You know the saying 'Don't make a federal case of

it'? Well, the Park Service did." The lawyer suggested that the outcome was set. The court had the blog's admission of our deeds, so they had nothing to prove or disprove, no doubt of our guilt.

Benjamin said, "I mean, there's no way we can even ask for an arbitration. We can't go in there and say, 'Gee, we had no freaking idea this thing mattered to anyone. It didn't *look* like it would'—"

"I don't think we want to say that to them," I pointed out. I didn't mention that since it was a criminal case, arbitration wasn't an option anyway.

"—and we'd be happy to pay for repairs. Hey, we'll scrape off the Wite-Out ourselves. And Jeff here's proven he can do things that blend in well. He could repaint the apostrophe in the wrong spot if you really want it there. We should be able to sit *down* with someone and *talk* about it, right? Honest communication, cooperative problem-solving . . . *some*thing."

"They've already decided that we are the problem." I didn't point out that *our* lack of communication—not asking permission—had led us here.

"This whole stupid scenario is making it difficult for me to feel much remorse."

That scared me. Our lawyer had taken us on at a single price with the understanding that Benjamin and I would be doing everything in full agreement. We'd accept the same plea agreement—which we *still* hadn't seen, despite repeated requests—and say "Guilty" in tandem. We'd be good little citizens and respectful of the court. Now I wondered what actions Benjamin was considering as he worked himself into a slow broiling rage.

We read *Red Mars* in adjacent seats on the flight, rather wishing that we were headed to that rust-dusted planet instead of Phoenix. Before we landed, the people behind us started talking about the election with their seatmates. They were all set on John McCain. One of them mentioned the "very informative" book on Obama by Jerome Corsi, the same guy who'd started the Swift Boat slander against Kerry. As we touched down in Arizona, McCain's home state, Benjamin whispered, "Enemy territory, dude. I have a *bad* feeling about how this is gonna go down."

The drive north to Flagstaff had a different temper from our original westward approach. Storm clouds closed in on both sides, as if preparing to slam together and make our compact car more so. Especially in the east the darkness neared, exhaling twisting winds that sent the dust up in swirls, suggesting tornadoes would burst forth at any moment. Still, I couldn't help but be fascinated by the dark majesty of the whole landscape, and a rainbow wedged itself between gray cloud and barren hills. We checked into a shabby hotel upon arrival. At least this time in Flagstaff, Benjamin wouldn't have to sleep on the floor. We unpacked our suits, then collapsed. Even with the time change and the exhausting trip, sleep eluded me. Were they seriously going to brand me a criminal tomorrow? Was this all TEAL would be remembered by?

In the morning we had breakfast at the diner where we'd corrected a set of typos. They had asked us if we charged for our services. We were glad to see the sign still in the window, all its spellings correct. Benjamin left a 30-percent tip. Whatever happened next, I was proud of what the League had done in that window. We returned to the hotel room, got into our suits, and went to court, where our lawyer had asked us to meet her an hour before the proceedings. We waited for half an hour in the lobby before she appeared. I'd thought we would go over the details of the plea agreement, but she informed us that the prosecuting attorney would be bringing the copies. In the meantime, she told us what a great job she had done on our behalf. For one thing, she'd persuaded them not to seek jail time as part of the punishment. Yes, a federal misdemeanor can earn someone up to six months in the clink. Our lawyer had also ensured we'd be charged "only" restitution. Benjamin shot me a glance. The prosecutor hadn't mentioned either jail time or fines beyond restitution when we'd first spoken with her on the phone.

The prosecutor arrived and handed over the finalized plea agreement. I restrained myself from pointing out the typos—"resitution" for *restitution* and "vandlaizing" for *vandalizing*—not out of discretion but because the document offered plenty more to upset us. Its aim was to ensure that we not vandalize National Park property, but they'd used broad strokes. In effect, it asked us to refrain from correcting typos, writing descriptions of correcting typos, or even encouraging others to correct typos. The contest I'd run to inspire others to take up the cause had gained the ire of our prosecutor, and she specifically referenced typo contests as a no-no. "This is way worse than we thought," I whispered to Benjamin as we sat on a back bench in the diminutive courtroom.

Our lawyer limped over. When we pointed out the offending passages, those barring us from typo correction and running the website, she took a better look, as if she hadn't quite known what was in our plea agreement. The two of us conferenced without her. "There's nothing we can do at this point," Benjamin said angrily. "I mean we *could* reject this, but then they'll run us through completely. It's too late to try to get it changed. We're trapped; we have to accept this."

To demonstrate how well justice was served in this courtroom, the real-live criminals, who'd have to return immediately to jail, went first. They were wearing correctional outfits and shackles. We watched a lawyer argue passionately for a one-month postponement on the judge's preferred trial date. It was the most valiant and energetic lawyering we saw all day, in defense of the attorney's own vacation plans.

Now the judge summoned us forward. Everything that follows is taken directly from the trial transcript. Immediately after we'd been sworn in, the judge's first question was, "All right. Who's Mr. Herson?" Against alphabetical logic, he would ask Benjamin to answer first every single time. This was helpful in one regard: it gave me a chance to temper my friend's replies. While I can't claim I wore my happy face, Benjamin had cast off his congenial nature, and I worried that his ability to show respect for the court wasn't far behind.

First, the judge reviewed the plea agreement we'd signed and asked us if we understood it. Benjamin said yes, and then I did the same, saying "Yes, Your Honor," rather than dropping a curt yes-bomb like my colleague. In case we didn't have as firm a handle on the plea agreement as we thought (and we didn't), the judge went over it anyway. He surprised me when he clarified what being forbidden from correcting "public signs" meant: "I interpret that to be not limited to national park signs, but any governmental sign anywhere. Am I correct on that?" Both the prosecuting attorney and our lawyer confirmed that he was. To me *public* signs had meant any signs out in public. While he'd made sure to check that it *extended* to all government signs, to me he'd kindly limited its scope.

"You would also be required to remove from any of your websites any information urging others to engage in such behavior. And that you're not to participate in public forums advocating this type of behavior." He paused, deliberately. "Now, let me ask the parties, obviously this is, from the Statement of Probable Cause appendix to the Complaint, aimed at their what could be deemed to be First Amendment rights." We had to agree to forfeit our freedom of speech, but for how long? Forever? At that point the judge began to utter what might have been the most important clarifying question for the future of the League: "Is there any objection on a First Amendment grounds to—"

The judge possibly wouldn't have concluded with "this condition *of the year's probation*" or any other explanation of how far this agreement would reach, yet his whole intent here was clarification. As adversarial as he came off, the man was careful, cautious, and precise about the details. He knew his stuff. How I wish I'd heard the end of that sentence. I wish I'd thought to speak up, but it was our lawyer's responsibility to speak for us, and speak she did. She cut the judge off, practically leaping forward to fling aside any concerns about the forfeiture of our rights. "No, Your Honor."

"All right," the judge replied.

No, not all right! But they'd moved on.

When the court asked how quickly we could post a required

notice on our website warning our readers of the dangers of vandalism and disrespecting the public parks, the prosecuting attorney stood up. She happily volunteered some kind words about us, saying how articulate and creative we were, and how therefore we could easily be expected to write said notice within thirty days.

The judge checked again that we understood everything. I considered clarifying the First Amendment thing, but Benjamin hurled another live "yes" at the judge, and I echoed it. The judge let us know that we didn't have to do this, of course. "You have an absolute right to go to trial on the charges in the Complaint." Sure, we did. Maybe if I had a trust fund. This whole thing was pre-decided. We were guilty by our own blogged admission. What we had done *was wrong*. We couldn't justify our actions or claim innocence, but these proceedings seemed disproportionate to our action. We'd have received the same treatment for an intentional decision to ruin the artwork on the tower walls, and they offered no way for us to even suggest that someone consider the differences and act accordingly. We corked our bitter laughter before it could leave our mouths and deface the court record.

After the court had made sure we weren't under the influence of any drugs and hadn't been coerced into our pleas by any outside parties, we were given the opportunity to officially answer that yes, we agreed to the terms of the plea agreement. From there, we moved to a confession, of sorts, by going over the events enumerated by the complaint. "Now, Mr. Herson, tell me what your participation was."

Benjamin answered, his voice calm and professional, but chilly. "We were driving across the border from New Mexico into Arizona. We were on a cross-country road trip to correct typos and educate people about typo awareness. And we also decided we would like to visit the Grand Canyon while we were coming through." I wondered if the judge had caught on to the fact that he'd explicitly separated the two intentions. The phrase "And we'd also decided" pulled the typo correction and the Grand Canyon visits apart. Even as Benjamin obliged them with a confession, he was disputing the fine point that we'd gone to the Grand Canyon to commit vandalism. "Though initially we had thought we would take a day off of correcting typos, which is remarked in the blog, we happened upon this sign, saw that it was missing one comma and had an apostrophe that we would like to move, and decided to go ahead and make those corrections."

"Who actually made the corrections?"

"I believe it was a combination of both of us," Benjamin replied. "I believe I used the marker to mark out the apostrophe that was in the incorrect place. Jeff used the Wite-Out to add the comma and the apostrophe."

"All right. Mr. Deck, tell me what you did."

While I appreciated what Benjamin had done on our behalf, I worried that he was aggravating the judge. He'd stated our actions in a detached manner: Mr. Spock saying, "I am attempting to correct a typo, Captain; it is only logical." There had been no hint of remorse in his statement.

"Well, I think," I said, decided *think* wasn't strong enough, and started over. "I mean, I agree with everything that Benjamin has stated. We thought—we thought that we were doing something positive by fixing typos around the country. I mean, I realize now that we were misguided, particularly in this instance, by correcting the sign without getting anyone's permission." I paused to take a breath; I didn't like how the words were spilling out of my mouth so fast. "We saw this particular sign and saw that there were two punctuation issues, and we corrected them."

"Sometimes historic artifacts have an importance all of their own," the judge intoned.

"Yes," I agreed.

But Benjamin wouldn't shut up. In his most respectful tone yet, and yet still with coldness, he added another little detail to the court record: "I'm afraid we hadn't realized the significance of the sign."

"Yeah," I added, trying to massage the tone, "we had no idea. I mean, that's no excuse, but we had no idea that it was historic."

"All right." Translation: enough of that. "Mr. Herson, how do you plead to the charge in Count 1, the conspiracy charge, guilty or not guilty?"

Benjamin paused long enough to set everyone on edge before replying, "Guilty."

"And Mr. Deck, how do you plead, guilty or not guilty?"

"Guilty."

The judge accepted our plea, and at last our lawyer acted on our behalf, restating ground that we'd already covered. "My clients, as they've indicated, did not have any idea it was a historic sign, and they thought they were doing good by what they were trying to accomplish. And they are very remorseful for their actions."

We were given three months, at Benjamin's request, to pay off restitution. Benjamin even said, "Thank you," while I went with a "Thank you very much, Your Honor."

The prosecutor rose again to say her piece. "Your Honor, this was an—I believe it's set out in the Affidavit. But this was—this all took place at the Desert Lodge Tower, which as the Court is aware was designed by Mary Colter, who is a unique and special individual to those of us who live in the Southwest.

"This sign was a 1932 hand-painted Mary Colter sign. Although the $3,000 will attempt to repair it, according to sources at the Park Service, the sign will never be back in the condition obviously that it was in. So they have inflicted damage on something that will ulti-mately never be fully repaired.

"I should also note the Park Service has a very small number of such signs that were obviously the caliber of somebody like Mary Col-ter. And so they are feeling this damage I guess in a very powerful way. So they're pleased to hear that the defendants were accepting respon-sibility and pleading guilty, and certainly hope that the defendants can understand the distinction between education and vandalism.

"And they clearly have the ability to educate and garner attention. But to direct people, which it appears they have done, to actually vandalize public signs is crossing the line into the criminal arena, and hopefully they will not go down that route again."

The judge accepted the sentence and dismissed the second count against us, the actual vandalism charge. We'd have to meet with a probation officer. It was unsupervised probation, so we wouldn't be getting visits from any officers; we just had to meet with one who'd go over everything with us. Then the judge had his say. "The Grand Canyon, in fact, most of our national parks are very special places. They have a tremendous influx of people, tourists year to year, and it is very difficult, simply because the number of feet on the ground, to protect them. But when individuals take it upon themselves to unilaterally affect what goes on simply because they think that—it's rather egotistical on your part, simply because you think you know the English language better than others, to go around and force people to conform to what you think is appropriate."

Benjamin glared back at him, perhaps causing him to lose his next words. I just wanted it to be over. No, that didn't characterize us correctly at all, but I didn't want to argue. "We recognize that, Your Honor," I said.

"It's kind of a crusade on your part, I can understand that. But now you see what's happened as a result of your crusade."

"Yes, sir," I replied.

Benjamin offered no vocal response.

"That was a course of conduct that you decided to engage in," concluded the judge before moving on to the final details of collecting our social security numbers and the rest. By the time we'd gotten to that guilty plea, I'd thought that had already been covered when we accepted the terms of the plea agreement: Paying $3,035 in restitution and a year of probation, during which we were banned from typo correcting and all National Parks. My head spun as we wandered out. The bailiff arranged for our meeting with the probation officer at 2:00 p.m. It was the earliest possible meeting, but it'd leave us barely enough time to get the rental car back to Phoenix without incurring charges for an extra day. I'd hoped to be screaming southward within minutes of leaving the courtroom and checking out of the hotel. No such luck.

I thanked our lawyer and shook hands with her. Her hand drifted toward Benjamin, but then dropped. He pointedly had not thanked her. He did not shake her hand. Once she'd walked away, he said, "Where's a customer feedback card when you need one? I want my money back."

We stepped out into the bright glare of a day nearing noon, the August heat attempting to get its licks in ahead of a line of fast-approaching clouds. We went back to the hotel and changed into civilian clothing, and then we stuffed our faces with roast beef sandwiches and curly fries at Arby's. As much as I protest the national landscape's saturation with the same handful of restaurants and stores, sometimes you need the comfort of knowing exactly what you're going to get.

We examined and reexamined the papers we'd been given. The site would have to stay down, for safety's sake. At every point when they'd mentioned us not correcting typos, both in the documentation and when the judge was speaking, they'd said directly *or indirectly*. They'd been targeting the website with that one. That's what they'd meant when aiming at our First Amendment rights, but how far did it extend? Plus, even though the judge had specified "public signs" as government property, Benjamin and I considered the safest route was to avoid fine lines and lie low altogether. No more typo correcting, and no more website, at least not for a year. "There's a clarity issue here," Benjamin said, "and I'm not talking about the 'resitution' in the plea agreement. How far does all of this extend?" Was the First Amendment ban only for the probationary period? That wasn't as spelled out as I'd like. We hoped the probation officer would be able to clarify some things for us. I was more concerned about the question of the National Park ban. It wasn't as if they'd hang wanted posters in every ranger cabin. Really, they included that so that if we did something on their territory again, they'd be able to hit us double-hard. But I wanted to stick to the letter of the law. Before we'd arrived here, I'd asked both my own lawyer and the prosecuting attorney if either could supply me with a list of territories designated as the jurisdiction of the National Park Service. Parts of the Freedom Trail, which runs through downtown Boston, could have been included, so I'd have to tread carefully. Likewise, Benjamin could still go to the Smithsonian museums, but he couldn't walk across the National Mall. No one ever obliged us with a clarification.

At two o'clock we arrived at the probation office, upstairs in the same building as the courtroom, and began a long wait. As we sat there, Benjamin sank further into dejection. "Ahh well," he said finally, "it's not like I could have afforded the AT now anyway, thanks to the lawyer fees." He'd put the Appalachian Trail off for a year for TEAL, but our ban from the parks extended into next August, way too late in the year to start. It had now been put off for two years, which is to say indefinitely. "That's the worst part about this thing, man. I'm one of their people. No one goes outside anymore, and their budget is continually under attack. I want to be with them in this fight, but here they are wasting money on a federal court case against us instead of keeping the concealed weapons out."[*]

Our probation officer, Julie, finished with the previous perp and summoned us in. We'd filled out some paperwork in the waiting room, and she now wanted to make sure we'd seen the part about what drugs and alcohol we'd used in the previous year or so. We'd left mostly blank space there. That brought us the first laugh we'd had all day. Benjamin added, "If you knew us better, you'd understand. This whole situation . . . isn't very us." She recognized that she wasn't dealing with hardened criminals and sailed us through the rest of the operation quickly and painlessly. Though she also didn't have a list of what counted as National Park territory, we both felt better that we'd be coordinating restitution (sorry, *resitution*) through Julie's office. Once we'd returned to the rental car, Benjamin held up

---

[*] Concealed weapons are now allowed inside National Parks. Any panther that tries to sneak up on your granny in a dark gully is in for a surprise.

her business card and declared that whenever possible, if he needed to check on anything, he'd definitely check with her first. Indeed, during our interactions with her over the next year, she remained as intelligent, professional, and helpful as ever. In our dismal experience with the court system, she was the shining exception, for which we very much thank her.

We sped down to Phoenix, checked in the car, barred ourselves in a hotel room, and ordered a pizza. In the morning, Benjamin's eye looked misshapen in a familiar way.

"I cannot believe this," he said as he grabbed a washcloth to put over his eye. "Now I've got a sty. I've never had a sty before. I'd never even heard of them until we got to Georgia!" Benjamin kept the washcloth as we left the hotel for the airport, adding theft to his rap sheet. The swelling had gone down by the time we touched down in Dallas–Fort Worth.

We rode an escalator to the airport's inter-concourse monorail. Benjamin, an inveterate train buff, was disappointed that he wouldn't be riding it himself, as his next flight was a few gates away. He ensured the washcloth was in his left hand as he stretched out his right. "Well, have a good flight."

"Yeah, you too." I'd already vaguely apologized, which he had brushed off, claiming I couldn't have known this would happen and that he took responsibility for his own actions, along with other predictable rejoinders. Still, TEAL had been my mission, and my friend being punished too seemed to be the worst part of my own punishment. "We'll figure something out."

"Yeah, we'll be in touch, man. Lucky thing the bookstore took me back so I can pay my half off fast."

"Right. How are things back at the bookstore?" Toward the end of the TEAL trip, Jenny had called to say that the district manager he'd so disliked had quit, so Benjamin had wound up back at the same place.

He shrugged. "I'd never been a training supervisor before, but I kinda like it." My shuttle arrived. "It's good to be surrounded by the books again, to know what's out and what's coming and what's readable. Anyway." He nodded to the opening doors.

"Yeah. Have a nice flight."

"You too," he said, already turning toward the escalator.

That should have been the end of things for a while, but our punishment apparently was not complete. Knowing full well that our own First Amendment rights had been inhibited, the federal prosecutor's office issued a press release, which led to a story in the *Arizona Republic* on August 22, 2008. The press release claimed we were "self-described 'grammar vigilantes,' " so the *Republic* repeated the assertion with only minor alteration: "Two self-anointed 'grammar vigilantes' . . ." We had in fact never described (nor anointed) ourselves as "vigilantes." But hey, the prosecutors knew they had a muzzle on us, so why *not* exaggerate the facts to make us into worthy villains? Accompanying the *Republic* article was the black-and-white photo of me from the complaint document; underneath the picture was Benjamin's name. "According to court records, Deck and Herson toured the United States from March to May, wiping out errors on government and private signs." Interesting, and here I thought we'd focused on public signs. Had we hit any other government signs? Had that Galveston security guard ratted us out for photographing the sign in front of the courthouse?

All in all, they got the gist of the story, though. Who could fault them for fudging the details, especially when their source material was suspect? Commenters on the newspaper's website suggested we be hired to help edit the paper itself. At least it was only a statewide rag. It's not as if this story was disseminating nationally.

Naturally, the Associated Press picked it up later that day.

As news has increasingly twisted toward entertainment, there's been a growing desire to open funny and close with a punchline at any cost. The AP story begins, "When it comes to marking up historic signs, good grammar is a bad defense." The addition of the joke was about all they took the time to change from the *Republic*'s intro. The next line begins, "Two self-styled vigilantes . . ." They knew not to claim that we'd called ourselves "grammar vigilantes," but they went ahead and charged us with full-on vigilantism. (Meanwhile *USA Today*, owned by the same conglomerate that owns the *Republic*, dutifully repeated the "grammar vigilante" meme.) But the AP did repeat the "government and private signs" bit. Their biggest addition, other than the description of the correction, was a new last line.

While I'd waited for the prosecutor's approval of the statement of contrition she'd forced us to write for the website, I had posted a quick announcement: "Statement on the signage of our National Parks and public lands to come". The AP concluded its article by noting that our website contained only that message . . . "without a period." Get it? The grammar guys forgot to punctuate their own sentence, *hyuk hyuk*. What baffles me is that someone at the AP apparently can't differentiate a sentence from a nonsentence. My announcement followed the same conventions as news headlines, which do not take periods (e.g., an AP headline from that very day, "Seinfeld to be pitchman for Microsoft"). More specifically, you'd think that the AP would be familiar with the common journalistic placeholder "to come". It even gets its own abbreviation in newspaper page galleys, marking places where text or photos will be filled in later: TK (no periods required for the acronym). When did reportage became synonymous with the cracks made by the class clown from the back row?

Still, the AP had nothing on the professional loudmouths from cable news; Keith Olbermann ranked us as two of the worst people in the world. Olbermann was the master of ending on a punch line, favoring style over substance in a way that would make Hortense from Miracle on Main Street proud. A former producer for Walter Cronkite said once that Olbermann was "not a newsman. He's not a reporter. I've never seen anything that he's done that was original, in terms of the information. It's all derivative."* Which explains how,

---

* The rest of the quote (this is from a *New Yorker* piece): "I like him, I agree with his perspective, and I think he's very, very good on television. But he's not a newsman. Ten years ago, if he had done at CBS what he does every day on the air at MSNBC, he would have been fired by the end of the day."

as a picture of us appeared, he said, "The silver [medal goes] to Jeff Michael Deck and Benjamin Douglas Herson, two self-proclaimed, twenty-eight-year-old grammar vigilantes—and you'd never guess it by looking at them." There it was again, "self-proclaimed grammar vigilantes"—he'd yanked that misstatement right from the *Republic* piece. Having finished his rip 'n' read, Olbermann concluded in his own riotous way, "Our sources say the judge was also going to order them to get a life, but apparently it's too late for that."

"Get a life? That O'Reilly wannabe needs to get a fact-checker," Benjamin said.

To be fair, the media couldn't exactly ask Benjamin and me for clarification, never mind our side of the story. Our court-issued muzzles were firmly in place. Of the many stories about the case, however, not one bothered to include "before" and "after" pictures of the watchtower sign. A side-by-side comparison would have shown how tiny our correction had been.

After temping around for a couple months, I found myself a new job in mid-September. Benjamin and his girlfriend decided to try life on the West Coast and began saving up. We paid our *resitution* with weeks to spare. As the weather turned cold, we settled into semi-hibernation. The country slid deeper into recession. For the first time, the guy we voted for won the presidency. We could do nothing but wait for the year to pass, but I knew I'd been onto something. On Inauguration Day I silently vowed that the president wouldn't be alone in bringing change, even if I had to come late to the fight.

Typo Trial Tally

Total found: 3
Total corrected: −1

19 | A Place for Starting Things

September 13-15, 2009 (Divers locations in and offshore from the Boston, MA, area)

Our Heroes, post-probates that they are, return to the Quest once reunited. Out to sea and back to school, they race to wherever Adventure calls them as they begin the bold task of charting a Course for TEAL's future exploits.

Remarkably, neither of our girlfriends abandoned us for returning from Arizona as debt-saddled criminals. Then again, every girl loves a bad boy. More than a year after our courtroom debacle, when Benjamin and I finally received notice in the mail that our probation had ended and all our civil rights had been restored, Benjamin came to Somerville for a proper celebration. The visit wasn't all champagne and cupcakes, for typo eradication is serious business, and we intended to pick up where we'd left off in May of 2008. We'd resurrect the website, and we would hold eloquent and furious discourse on the future of the League. First, though, we had one immediate thirst to quench. We decided, naturally, to visit the nearest National Park.

Living in the Boston area had posed special perils for complying with the National Park ban, which encompassed historic as well as natural sites. Walk down any given street and you'll inevitably blunder into a building that, 250 years ago, housed some fervid future hero with a blunderbuss and a dream. Did the Freedom Trail count as a national historical property? It's literally a line painted through downtown Boston, snaking through the brick and cobblestone streets for more than two miles. Each time I came upon it, which was often, I found it necessary to vault over the line rather than touch it, *just in case.*

But Queen Liberty had at long last planted her embrace upon our froggy mouths, restoring our sovereignty as whole citizens, who could tread whatever soil they pleased without fear of swift and bloody legal retribution. The Freedom Trail, Faneuil Hall, the Old State House, and various other historic and possibly nationally historic sites around Boston opened their arms out wide to me once more, but Benjamin and I desired to set foot in a true National *Park*, a natural setting rather than the constructions of ancient foremen. We decided on the Harbor Islands, thirty-odd patches of earth between here and Hull that had been collectively designated as National Park territory. Jane, an incorrigible outdoorswoman, happily joined our expedition. At noon on a fine September day, Jane and I bought our tickets at Long Wharf to travel to Spectacle and Georges, two islands in the collection that offered more to see than seagulls pooping on each other. Benjamin went to the window to claim his own, but as Jane and I walked toward the ferry, we heard a ticket agent proclaim that the ferry was now sold out. Had Benjamin made it? He sauntered over with a wry smile and an eyebrow waggle, holding up the last ticket. "You didn't think they'd leave a gent like me behind, did you?" We boarded a packed ferry and squashed ourselves up against the railing.

After a short ride, the dual mounds of Spectacle Island hove into view. We disembarked at the small, grassy island and found there to be little cover from the suddenly hot sun. Crickets sang their welcome. I regretted wearing jeans. Benjamin did not because he hadn't actually packed any shorts. We stopped in at the visitors' center near the pier to use the bathroom. Once we were back outside, Jane blinked in the strong light and turned to us. "Where would you guys like to go?"

"How about the trail winding up the North Drumlin," I suggested, pointing at the hill ahead of us, slightly larger and higher than the one at our backs. We headed up the path, alone now that the other visitors had scattered elsewhere on the island. Along the way to the North Drumlin, we stopped periodically to read signs that explained the history of Spectacle. It had indeed originally resembled a pair of spectacles, the northern and southern hills as two mismatched lenses with a narrower spit of land between them serving as the bridge. Now, with the spit thickened and expanded by additional landmass, the island looked mostly like a porkchop. I imagined that a corresponding name change would have been undesirable, though. Jane's nose wrinkled as she read about what served as the foundation for that extra land.

"Hate to say it," she said, "but the first park you decided to visit is where the city used to dump all its trash. We're hiking over a landfill."

That gave me pause until I looked back across the trails and grass, bright in the afternoon sun. The Park Service had done an excellent job landscaping over the sins of the past. "Nicest landfill I've seen in a while," I said.

We stopped to eat our packed lunches in the shade of a gazebo with a notably spectacular view out across the harbor. Then we continued on to scale the drumlin itself. The path up the summit, such as it was, wound in a spiral. Jane and I walked with intertwined hands as Benjamin scouted ahead. Along the way, we passed older tourists rooting in the bushes by the side of the path, perhaps seeking rare plants for tinctures.

We came to the top and took in another splendid view, this time covering 360 degrees. I wandered over to a lookout from which you could see the Boston skyline in clear detail. Directly below the skyline stood a sign with a corresponding picture of the skyline, with each of the notable elements labeled: Prudential Tower, Hancock Tower, and so forth. One label made me stop and read again: LONG WARF. That almost but did not quite capture the name of where we'd boarded the ferry to get here; it was a letter short.

Jane noticed that I had been standing in front of the sign for a few minutes, so she came over. "Jeff, did you . . . *find* something?" She sounded a bit apprehensive.

"It, uh, just popped out at me." I showed her the error. I'd known not to bring the Typo Correction Kit with me, as that would have been asking for trouble. The League would no longer be making corrections without permission, anyway. However, I couldn't leave the sign as it was without telling someone in charge about it. Our corrective mission had to carry on, and that started today.

Benjamin agreed with me in theory. In practice, though, he was nervous. The three of us held court in the summit's gazebo. No one else had felt the inclination to come up here, it seemed.

"So you do realize," I said, "we have to go and point that out at the visitors' office." I recalled seeing a grandmotherly ranger sitting at a desk in the center; I figured we'd be able to enlist her help.

"You have to be kidding," he said. Our year in exile had tempered his rages and enthusiasms. He'd lost his taste for trouble.

"Well, we have to stick by our principles," I said.

"Oh, can't we save it for the second tour?"

"Second tour?" I said.

"Second tour?" Jane echoed, alarmed.

He shrugged, pulling back. "Yeah, I was assuming we'd have to get out and do it again, man. Eventually. It's just a little soon right now to stir the pot."

I held firm, fixing my old colleague with a flinty gaze. "We're off probation now, we have all our rights back. We should be fully entitled to go down there and tell them about it."

"Yeah . . . I'm not looking forward to that," said Benjamin. "Don't get me wrong, I'm not trying to back down, but can't we give it some time, man?"

I stood. If I'd thought to bring my Santa Fe hat, I would have put it on then. "Don't worry about it," I said casually. "Jane and I will take care of it."

Jane got up, too. "Second . . . second tour?" she said. Her knees knocked together.

We turned and began to head back down the drumlin. A moment later, Benjamin tore by us, hollering, "I'll get there before you do, suckas!" He trotted down the stone-lined culvert along the path. Before long, we reached level ground and walked into the visitors' center. As we stepped inside, the kindly-looking old ranger got up from her station at the desk and ambled out to the front porch. A man in powder-blue with a sour expression sat down at the desk and leafed through a magazine.

Jane clutched my arm and whispered, "Oh no! What happened to Grandma?"

I assured her that we'd be fine asking this guy for help instead. Nevertheless, she suddenly took an interest in the historic displays several yards away from the ranger's desk. It would be up to Benjamin and me, then. We approached the desk, and the ranger looked up from his magazine. "What can I do for you?"

"Hi there," I said, giving him a friendly smile. "We were up on the North Drumlin, enjoying the beautiful view. While we were up there, we happened to notice a typo in a sign up there—the one that explains the view of Boston. 'Long Wharf' was missing its *h*."

The ranger peered at us dispassionately for a second, and then the weathered contours of his face described a smile. "Is that so? I must have missed that."

"Is there any way that somebody could fix that?"

"Tell you what," he said, "if you write down the mistake, and which sign it was in, I'll make sure to pass the note on to the right person."

"Great!" said Benjamin, tearing out a page from his ever-present poetry notebook. He checked the Spectacle Island brochure and found the sign's number, then noted that down along with the error.

"It may or may not take an act of Congress to get that fixed, though," the old ranger joked.

We thanked him, collected Jane, and walked out of the office, feeling a familiar brand of satisfaction wash over us. The ranger had been glad to hear about the error when we brought it up congenially and directly. Our conversation with him now reinforced my certainty that we had steered back onto the correct track. Stealth corrections had no place in the League, and probably never should have. As we waited for the ferry to arrive and convey us to Georges Island, I reflected that the most rewarding moments of the TEAL trip had not been when we successfully carried out covert alterations, but when we had engaged with people in honest conversations about spelling and grammar. Our countrymen hadn't always wanted to hear what we had to say, but the times that they did made it all worth it. Realizing this was one positive result to come out of the Grand Canyon disaster. We'd had as much to learn as anyone else.

"Are you really thinking about a second tour?" I asked Benjamin later that afternoon, as we toured Fort Warren, a Civil War–era POW camp on Georges Island.

"Haven't you been?" he shot back. He walked carefully along the stone borders of old gun emplacements.

I admitted that I had. I could already feel the barest tingling of a need to get back on the road, to dive once more into the murky pool of modern grammatical realities. Not right away, but sometime within the next year. And this time we'd arm ourselves with more tools to edify than just the Kit. Knowing what we knew now, we could make a bigger difference in American literacy. In fact, we could start working on our broader goals long before we hit the road again.

On Benjamin's second leg of my original typo hunt, we'd begun to reimagine TEAL's mission. A second quest would have to take that altered vision into account. Even if we hunted down typos and—with *permission*, of course—fixed them, that might not be our sole mission. I didn't know how it would look yet, but already I had visions of replacing "Typo Hunt" with "Editor's Quest" . . . or something like that.

Even as Benjamin spurred me to voice these ideas and recognize that I couldn't *not* embark on a second journey, we had to address the other half of TEAL's mission: education. People couldn't be their own editors if they didn't fully understand the mechanisms of grammar and spelling. Even as we worked to sharpen the editing skills of the present generation, TEAL had to proactively enable the next generation of communicators.

Benjamin had made this half a personal focus, as he related most to this part of the mission. He'd teetered on the brink of plunging into a teaching career, had brought up the possibility occasionally, back when we shared a Maryland apartment. During our year of probation he'd returned to spelunk the halls of research that had so consumed him during the trip itself. He'd emerged dusty and triumphant, telling me excitedly that he had found the solution to the nation's orthographic conundrum—and that it had been here all along, or at least for the last fifty years. Two days after we visited Spectacle Island, we joined with Callie and Authority in poignant reunion and drove a few miles over to Malden, Massachusetts. Benjamin had arranged for us to visit the Mystic Valley Regional Charter School.

We walked into a class of thirty children reading words aloud from a list in their books. It was a diverse crowd, for Massachusetts, anyway: besides the majority of white kids, there were also Hispanic, black, and Asian kids. Their fingers held their place in the books, and a teaching assistant continually refocused individual kids by moving a hand or an arm to make sure all fingers followed the action. In unison, the class spoke: "Dis-uh-pEEr!"

"My turn," the teacher said loudly and clearly, raising her hand in front of her as if she had called on herself. "Eyes on me." That's where the eyes went; it was almost like a game. She gave them a simple definition of *disappear*. This she read from the script she cradled in an arm while walking among the students, leading the children through their phonics-based reading lesson. Benjamin had found us a school that used Direct Instruction (DI), a teaching model with a scripted curriculum. The teacher's authority is explicit, the children respond when signaled, and feedback is both positive and immediate.

With a "your turn" the teacher let them know they'd be expected to answer again. Before each response, the teacher let them know exactly what they were supposed to do, paused for a beat, then said "Get ready!" It wasn't the "get ready" of "ready, set, Go!" but the wind-up of the ball being pitched, and the kids knocked it out of the park: "D-I-S-A-P-P-E-A-R." Well, I'd thought they'd hit it out of the park, but the teacher heard some hesitation and had them spell it again.

In my own school days, I'd answered questions about twice an hour. In this hour-and-a-half Reading Mastery lesson, these kids easily surpassed one hundred responses each. As they moved to the next word list, the teacher began asking the class to identify each word's first syllable before reading the whole words. They cruised along until they hit *remove*; an *mmm* slipped into one quadrant of the classroom. The teacher immediately took back over with "my turn" to explain that the first syllable of *remove* is just *re*.

Once the class had made it through all the words, the teacher switched to calling on kids by name to review them. "Good sound-

ing it out, Arlene," the teacher said. "Good sticking with it, Bret."
"Nice smooth reading, Cindy." She'd been inserting comments like
these all along, albeit not as often, when they were reading things
together. "Good knowing these hard words," she'd told them. To
close this part of the lesson, the teacher mentioned that there'd been
one word they'd need to return to tomorrow. Could anyone guess
what their one "goodbye word" was? More than two-thirds of the
kids raised their hands. "Yes, Don?" Don thought *monthly*, which
hadn't sounded crisp even on the class's second try, was the culprit.
Sure enough, *monthly* went up onto the board under *drank*, a previous goodbye word.

Pointing fingers went to the beginning of a story. "I like how Emily's pointing. I like how Franklin's pointing." Each child read three
sentences aloud. Their story was no absurdly repetitive narrative
like *See Spot run. Run, Spot, run! Oh! Oh! We can run and run and
run!* These stories actually made sense (even if you took the pictures
away). Ms. McKinnon, our administrator tour guide, explained that
the writers *did* try to keep the text unpredictable. After a sentence
about two people, a next sentence might start with *They*, but it starts
with *That* instead. Thus the reader must be actually reading and not
guessing from context. We were treated to the tale of a beagle who
had lost a little weight so he could bound higher up into the air.
We watched the boy who got to read a punch line pause to mug for
everyone as the class cracked up.

Ms. McKinnon directed our attention to the teacher and her
book. She took quick notes of how many errors the class made.
She'd said they would read this story making "less than nine errors,"
but she counted even the hesitations as errors, so I didn't think they
were going to make it. We had to move on, though.

As we left the room, Benjamin asked, "Those were *first graders*?"
We visited on September 15, so the school year had only begun three
weeks earlier. I tried to remember when I'd first heard the word
syllable.

The kindergarten class down the hall had been divided into three groups. We observed one group learning to connect sounds with letters. The *e* they were learning had the macron, or bar, on top to indicate that it was specifically the long *e*. They weren't naming the letters; they were making the sounds; *s* meant the hissing "ssss" sound, not "ess." We watched the end of the ritual. The teacher held up a sheet with the letters, pointed to one, and said, "Get ready."

"Goodbye *ssss*."

The teacher made an *x* over it. The pencil pointed to the next one. "Get ready."

"Goodbye *ee*."

We watched a different group blending sounds together.

"First you say *sssss*, then you say *at*. First you say *sssss*, then you say *at*," the kindergarten teacher sang, and with each sound came a gesture.

The child said *ssss* and *at* as instructed, and then the teacher requested it be said the fast way. "Sat."

"Yes, sat."

As we left, one of the boys who was returning to his seat held up his tickets. "I got three tickets!"

"Nice work," I said.

The tickets were a reward system that this school had created; DI did leave room for individual schools to add their own systems or tweak as needed. If schools used Direct Instruction as their primary program, they might be considered a "DI school." That needn't be the only way, though. There were teachers who'd completed the DI training and used the material themselves, alone. Of course, DI worked best when the kids could build on the same skills from year to year.

Our last stop was another first-grade class, at a different level of Reading Mastery than the first room we visited. The kids were placed by skill level early on. It was crucial that every child have a firm foundation in the basics, but kids who already knew them shouldn't be allowed to get bored. This solidified my support for DI. The first graders who were working on Reading Mastery level two rather than level three were getting more instruction time with the most important steps of phonics. Even if they were behind the other class, you couldn't call them remedial readers. Unlike "slower" reading students in other school systems, these guys would be caught up and integrated with their grade-mates somewhere around fifth or sixth grade at the absolute latest, when they'd all be independent readers.

DI has been around for quite a while. In the 1960s, marketer-turned-educator Zig Engelmann realized that what was most missing from elementary education was clarity of instruction. The kids would absorb whatever the teachers presented, but teachers might be vague, or they might not give enough examples—or enough counter-examples—to reinforce the points they were trying to make. Through continual testing, Engelmann and his colleagues built a scripted method of instruction designed specifically to enhance clarity, thereby accelerating learning for all children.

Benjamin had met with Jerry Silbert, a coauthor of several DI programs, at the National Institute for Direct Instruction, headquartered in Eugene, Oregon. Silbert had given him a teaching guide for Spelling Mastery, and Benjamin had randomly flipped it open to "Junction changes!" Those oft-awkward meetings of roots and suffixes (or prefixes) had been responsible for many a typo we'd found on the trip. Benjamin examined the page that went over all the rules of consonant-doubling and when *not* to consonant-double. There were example sets first teaching kids how, and then helping them recognize when to use the rule and when not to. These were basic mechanics of spelling.

Seeing it in action helped me understand how all the pieces fit together. The script gave the students recognizable cues that all of them understood the same way. In effect, they shared a classroom language, obliterating a legion of communication barriers, from lack of specificity to cross-cultural confusion. Better still, the cues fit into a rhythm of call and response that radically increased the number of times each child got to respond during the class period.

More practice with the material leads to better assimilation of that material. The positive effects compound as the call-and-response setting, along with the continual positive feedback, reduces the stigma of being called on in isolation. While these periods of study are intensive, they're sensitive to the psychology of the children. The call-and-response approaches a "Simon says" kind of game. Then, of course, there are the phonics drills.

A century ago, American educators began projecting their own emotions onto the educational process. Deciding that the repetition involved in learning phonics was too dull for them, they eliminated it for the kids who needed it. But as any parent who's had to sit through multiple consecutive viewings of *The Land Before Time XIII* can tell you, children love repetition. Unlike the chaotic, seemingly illogical world around them, repetition offers them the power of prediction, of guessing ahead and being right. In his book *The Tipping Point*, Malcolm Gladwell relates how the creators of *Blue's Clues* had a tough sell when they asked the network to air each episode five times. The whole week would be the same episode over and over again! They'd done their research, and kids had no problem with watching the same episode repeatedly, becoming more excited as they worked through the same puzzles, grasping the concepts better each time. Phonics instruction works in exactly the same way, both in allowing the children to build up their knowledge and apply it better with practice, and in appealing to the inner delight that comes from mastery.

Like *Blue's Clues*, DI is research driven. The first book that directed Benjamin's attention to DI was *Super Crunchers*; Ian Ayres used it as an example of his larger discussion on the battle between intuition and data. DI, of course, was in the camp representing data. While individual teachers with their varied methods may feel they know best how to teach their students, the abnormally high rate (for a First World country) of illiteracy (14 percent of American adults in 2003—30 million people) suggests that the school system has largely failed. In 1967, President Johnson initiated Project Follow Through, a long-term government study of seventeen different teaching methods. Eight years later, DI was the hands-down winner across multiple measures of success. DI students earned the highest test scores in core subjects like vocabulary and math, but Project Follow Through also checked students' ability to tackle higher-order thinking problems and even determined which students had the highest self-esteem. DI won in those categories too, proving that when students are given the chance to feel smart by actually understanding the material, everything else would fall into place. But thirty years after that revealing data, DI is still used by only a handful of schools in America.

Why? In part, because the program hasn't sold itself effectively. It still makes people uncomfortable, in spite of repeatedly proving to be a superior model. Teachers in particular worry over the loss of their autonomy, but the Hollywood ideal of the heroic rogue teacher succeeding amid widespread failure needs to be beaten back to make room for a school system where everyone wins together. While teachers might fight DI at the outset, the program often changes their minds, thanks to a couple of key factors. First off, since the lessons are scripted, there's no prep time needed. Teachers are overworked and underpaid as it is, and this can take some pressure off. Most teachers have to do their lesson planning on their own time. Second, and more significantly, DI *works*. Once the teachers see how effective it is, how specific changes in their method can make a huge difference, they tend to come around.

"What can we do?" I wondered as we drove back to my apartment.

"Somehow, we can help." My friend was silent a moment, but then erupted in typical Benjamin fashion. "Thing is, President Obama recently kicked off his 'Race to the Top' initiative. Grants for the K-through-12 schools that seem to be performing the best. Education's a huge priority because—like health care and energy—it's a game changer. They're the issues that dig tentacles into other issues and make it impossible to fix anything else first. This is a time of opportunity. Mark my words, a lot of things are going to change in this next decade—either by our being smart enough to change them how we needed to, or when we'll be acted upon by larger forces. This is everyone's moment to fail or succeed, and TEAL's gonna have to find its place in that. We've got to get the website back up soon so that we can find our people again."

I needed the blog, partly for opening my thoughts to feedback from everyone who cared like I did, but also for *writing out* my thoughts in the first place. That's the way my thought process worked best: text-based, writing and editing on the page.

As we worked to resurrect the website, reliving our typo memories one by one, I said, "For the second tour, we'll include more people from the start."

"Try to score corrections in all fifty states?" Benjamin suggested.

"That's an idea," I said. "But this time around, it's going to be about more than just the corrections. It'll be an Editor's Quest. We'll show everyone the marvels that can be wrought by simply taking a second look."

"By the way," said Benjamin, "you owe me at least one state on the Appalachian Trail. Keep some white space in your calendar for . . . 2011?"

I promised I would, then returned to my musings. The dimensions of the League's possibility opened wide, straining against the tissue of my frontal lobes. After all our adventures and misadventures, I could picture multifarious, multifaceted destinies for TEAL—the push for Direct Instruction, yes, and another tour, but there were additional promising actions that we could carry out even sooner. As she'd offered more than a year ago, Jane could help me put together compelling games and videos on the Internet that would spread education in the same viral fashion that typos themselves often operated. By jingo, I could craft entire narrative worlds around the concepts we had learned, the issues we had stumbled upon, such as clarity's vital role in communication and the importance of *awareness,* of patience and care. Everything that touched typos could be scaled out to universal proportions and eventually scaled back again, the way language itself functioned as both a tool and a bellwether of humanity. Like English itself, TEAL could swell its boundaries and encompass all that needed a place to belong.

We took a break from our website work and went on a walk around Somerville. Night had fallen. We wound up at the Prospect Hill castle, a monument built on the site where, on January 1, 1776, General George Washington raised the first flag of the thirteen colonies—in essence, the first American flag to fly anywhere across this land. The lights of Somerville, Cambridge, and Boston sparkled below us and before us in the darkness, a fabulous patchwork of gems that would not have made for a bad *Rocks & Minerals* spread. The tops of Boston's highest towers disappeared into cloud.

"Quite a different view than what Washington must have seen," Benjamin said, marveling at the electric panoply. Sirens sounded behind us somewhere in the thicket of Somerville streets. Beneath the parapet, homeless men mumbled and played in the trees.

"If you look straight ahead, you can see where I used to work at MIT." I indicated a squat tower in the foreground of the river with a golf-ball-shaped atmospheric radome on top. "You know, once upon a time," back when I'd felt like the only one stuck in place, surrounded by people with purpose. Then I'd headed to Hanover, where my classmates had roused me to action. Strange that by now they must have all heard that I was a criminal. I could finally laugh about it now: ten thousand dollars for a comma and an apostrophe. And we didn't even get to keep them.

Contrary to what the Park Service thought about us, both Benjamin and I had a sharp interest in bygone times. My friend noted wryly that this castle had been built in 1903 to celebrate a historic site—the commemoration itself decades older than the supposed priceless artifact at the Grand Canyon. Still, while Benjamin was upset that fellow outdoorsmen had considered him an enemy, I'd been disappointed by the mutual shortsightedness. We'd made one mistake, and they'd trumped it. It had left me with a sense of an error uncorrected, a resolution never quite reached.

"Think Paul Bunyan ever played golf?" Benjamin asked, still eyeing the MIT building. Well, that's one way to shatter a reverie. Once he'd brought me back to the present, though, he chuckled and said, "You really did it. Do you even realize that?"

My journey *had* shaken things up, had lit furious conversations among all the various factions and individuals who still cared about spelling and grammar, and that was a start. It had also revealed telling patterns about the mistakes people were making. All of that was more than I even should have hoped for from such a quixotic venture. I congratulated myself for these modest gains, and Benjamin laughed at me.

"C'mon! Going around the country correcting typos? I didn't think you were serious, dude. Then I remember reading the blog with Jenny and saying, 'Oh, he wasn't kidding.' You actually were committed. Why? How?" His laughter echoed off the stone crenellation.

I told him exactly what I'd decided two summers prior: "I wanted to change the world somehow, but editing was all I had."

"And that's what slays me. You started with what you had, and you . . . rolled with it, Deck. You started the mission, and the mission is what found you the real purpose." Benjamin stopped. He must have seen the realization alight. I'd known the effect I wanted (fewer typos), and I'd let that effect—and my own small methods of working toward it—find its own causes. My hope pulled me into action, and the action had led me to comprehension and vision. I could never have worked this all out from the beginning.

"I figured out TEAL's purpose is increasing clarity in communication," I said slowly. "But the clarity of that *purpose* is obvious to me only now." Benjamin, standing beside me on the battlement, had become a believer somewhere along the way. TEAL's mission owed its new two-pronged approach to his determination, as he'd dug out the deeper educational import. I wondered what we could accomplish now.

Could we change the way the country communicates, honoring

the power of the edit? If we are our words, we deserve to be the right ones.

Could we change the course of education, bringing that phonics component back? Our unkempt world needs a generation of problem solvers, and literacy is an absolute prereq.

"This is a place for starting things," I said, gazing out at the starlight poking through the haze, the office buildings shouldering elder architecture, the city pocked with remnants of a revolutionary spirit. "I'm not sure what we can do, or what we can be." Benjamin nodded, primed for the next adventure and already agreeing with my chimerical notions. "What do you say we find out?"

Appendix: A Field Guide to Typo Avoidance

Genus: Apostrophe Errors

Species: Missing Apostrophes

HOW TO SPOT—Whenever you see a possessive word or a contraction that lacks an apostrophe, you'll know that this shy creature has gone into hiding once again—to the detriment of its parent word.

Dont touch that dial!

The Worlds Only Soybean Palace

HOW TO HANDLE—You must track the spoor of the Missing Apostrophe and return it to the bosom of its owner. Contractions always need an apostrophe and, except for the possessive form of pronouns, possession always needs an apostrophe, too.

Don't touch that dial!

The World's Only Soybean Palace

Species: Unnecessary Apostrophes

HOW TO SPOT—Unnecessary Apostrophes like to wedge themselves into plural words right before the *s*. These mischievous pests can't take a hint.

We sell panini's and gyro's!

HOW TO HANDLE—Be cautious when approaching Unnecessary Apostrophes, but be firm and drive them out of plural words before the little critters can multiply. It's important to keep all plural words apostrophe-free; they'll be grateful for the delousing.

We sell paninis and gyros!

Species: Possessive/Contraction Confusion

HOW TO SPOT—Some contractions and possessive forms of pronouns sound like each other. If you are aware of their auditory camouflage, though, you can still *see* them when you look at the words.

Why did the cat chase it's tail?

Your my best friend.

HOW TO HANDLE—Familiarize yourself with the most commonly confused pairs of words: its/it's, your/you're, their/they're, whose/who's. In case of doubt, see if you can break the word into two words: e.g., will "it is" or "you are" work in place of the word? If you can break it into two, it's a contraction and needs the apostrophe. If it can't break in two, it doesn't need the apostrophe because it's the possessive form of a pronoun.

Why did the cat chase its tail?

You're my best friend.

Species: Misplaced Apostrophe

HOW TO SPOT—These well-meaning critters have a poor sense of direction and just plunk down wherever when they find the end of a plural possessive word. They are often found sitting in front of the *s* when they should let the *s* connect to the word to show that it's plural. Or, some Misplaced Apostrophes sit down after the *s* without considering that the word is already plural.

The girl's uniforms were dirty after field hockey practice.

the womens' secret society

HOW TO HANDLE—First decide if the possessive word is supposed to be singular or plural. For a possessive word that already has an *s,* just tack the apostrophe on to the end to make it possessive as well. If the word is a plural that doesn't have an *s* (the word itself is a plural form), add an apostrophe and then an *s,* just like you would to a singular word.

The girls' uniforms were dirty after field hockey practice.

the women's secret society

Genus: Misspellings

Species: Junction Errors

HOW TO SPOT—These mutants are the result of word experiments gone terribly awry. Two word parts, such as a verb and a suffix, have been incorrectly joined together. With an understanding of phonics, you can recognize Junction Errors right away, because their misspelling leads to mispronouncing them.

Dinning room

Next-day shiping

HOW TO HANDLE—There are rules for determining how a root connects to a suffix. Though there are exceptions, here's the general set of rules:

For a word ending in a **double-consonant**, just add on the suffix

befriend + -ing = befriending

friend + -ship = friendship

For a word ending in **e,** drop the **e** if the suffix begins with a **vowel** (this eliminates a confusing double-vowel sound)

loose × -en = loosen

loose + -ly = loosely

For a word ending in a **consonant-vowel-consonant**, double the **last consonant** if the suffix begins with a **vowel** (this is so the short vowel sound can be indicated by the double-consonant)

> ship × -ing = shipping
>
> ship + -ment = shipment

Hence:

> Dining room
>
> Next-day shipping

Species: Homophone Errors

HOW TO SPOT—These insidious sirens lure an inattentive speller to the rocks of blundering with their familiar song. Homophone Errors happen in writing when a word is confused for another perfectly valid word that *sounds* just like it.

> Don't slam on the breaks!
>
> I've got a splinter in my heal.

HOW TO HANDLE—Since the "wrong" word is still spelled correctly, spell-checking software will overlook these mistakes. So might your eye. The only way to spot these is by carefully rereading your work (see "The Art of Editing," below). Simply checking over what you've written is a grate, er, great way to catch these mistakes.

> Don't slam on the brakes!
>
> I've got a splinter in my heel.

Species: Common Misspellings

HOW TO SPOT—The horde of Common Misspellings is diverse indeed: words with transposed letters, single letters instead of double letters, wrong vowels, and so on.

> Restaraunt, cappucino, independant, definately, Sahara Dessert . . .

HOW TO HANDLE—Assuming you weren't taught with phonics (and sometimes even if you were), you'll need to have memorized the antidote to every individual Common Misspelling, of which there are hundreds. Until we're capable of adding "extra memory" to our brains like we do with computers, why clog up precious mental resources? Instead, have a dictionary ready. This is the weapon that can neutralize the hobgoblins of misspelling. First, merely notice whenever you're unsure of a word spelling, then consult the dictionary to help you cast the proper spell . . . ing. If no dictionary is available, at least consult another person nearby. Sometimes multiple people can determine what "looks right" to the computer-brains we already have.

Restaurant, cappuccino, independent, definitely, Sahara Desert . . .

Genus: Agreement Errors

Species: Article/Noun Disagreement

HOW TO SPOT—Article/Noun Disagreements are mischievous imps that specialize in tripping up the tongue. The wrong choice of *a* v. *an* before a noun will sound funny.

a apple

an banana

HOW TO HANDLE—To make *a/an* agree with the noun it precedes, you want to avoid a double-consonant or double-vowel sound. If the noun begins with a vowel sound, it takes *an* (which ends with a consonant sound) in front of it; if it begins with a consonant, it takes *a* (a vowel sound). This is why words beginning with a silent *h* also take *an*. The sound combination makes the words flow together better when spoken.

an apple

a banana

Species: Subject/Verb Disagreement

HOW TO SPOT—Subject/Verb Disagreements sow discord between the two most important parts of a sentence. They are tricksters that cause a singular noun to wind up with a plural-form verb, or vice versa.

The lime are tasty.

Lemons is good for you.

HOW TO HANDLE—Don't let your nouns make the wrong choice for their verb mates, or things are likely to get nasty. If the noun is singular, be sure that the verb that goes along with it is in singular form as well; if the noun is plural, give it a plural-form verb.

The lime is tasty.

Lemons are good for you.

Bonus: Style and Savvy

Care and Feeding of the Common Comma

When it comes to clarity of communication, commas are vital companions. An omitted comma in a list will cause confusion (such as the perplexing item in the middle of this shopping list: "bread, lasagna, turkey carrots, milk, O.J."). An extraneous comma can change the meaning of a sentence entirely ("Give me a piece of that apple, cobbler").

However, to stop at the comma's purely technical usage is to discredit the surprising power of this humble breed of punctuation. Commas can be a marker of an individual writer's style and voice just as surely as the words she is using. When you want the reader to rush through sentences, use commas sparingly. When a more leisurely, intricate pace is called for, plant more commas. Wherever you'd like the reader to take a breath, deploy a comma. You are shaping the voice the reader hears in his head.

The Art of Editing

It's a good policy to go back and read over what you've written. You'll easily spot true typographical errors, and you're likely to spot other mistakes, too. A general check is helpful not only for catching misspellings or grammatical mistakes, but also for enhancing general readability. The first look back is a chance to ensure that your text says what you want it to, which is about more than just catching technical errors. Were you clear in what you meant? Is your message easy to follow?

Reading through your work again after that first technical edit, you can scrutinize your sentences and sharpen your message. This next edit is more focused on technique and style as you refine phrasing and word choice. There's no such thing as a perfect first draft, just as in writing there's no single "right" answer; use a second edit (or more!) to improve the clarity and power of your words.

References

"Albany Tulip Festival in Washington Park." Albany.com, http://www.albany
.com/news/tulip-festival.cfm

Amador, Xavier. *I'm Right, You're Wrong, Now What?: Break the Impasse and Get
What You Need.* New York: Hyperion, 2008.

Associated Press. "Grammar Police Punished for 'Fixing' Rare Sign." MSNBC
(and elsewhere), August 22, 2008. http://www.msnbc.msn.com/id/26351328/

———. "Iowa College Apologizes for Offensive Typo." MSNBC, September 25,
2008. http://www.msnbc.msn.com/id/26891761/

Ayres, Ian. *Super Crunchers: Why Thinking-by-Numbers Is the New Way to Be
Smart.* New York: Bantam Books, 2007.

Balmuth, Miriam. *The Roots of Phonics: A Historical Introduction.* New York:
McGraw-Hill Book, 1982.

Bauer, Laurie. *Watching English Change.* New York: Longman, 1994.

Boyer, Peter J. "One Angry Man: Is Keith Olbermann Changing TV News?" *The
New Yorker,* June 23, 2008.

Bryson, Bill. *The Mother Tongue: English and How It Got That Way.* New York:
Harper Perennial, 1991.

Burnley, J. D. "Sources of Standardization in Later Middle English." *Standard-
izing English: Essays in the History of Language Change,* edited by Joseph B. Tra-
hern Jr. Tennessee Studies in Literature, vol. 31. Knoxville, TN: University of
Tennessee Press, 1989.

The Chicago Manual of Style, 15th Edition. Chicago: University of Chicago Press, 2003.

Cletus, Seabiscute, Al Cyone, et al. Comments from "No Typo Is an Island," *Typo Hunt Across America*, March 20, 2008, http://www.jeffdeck.com/teal/blog

Conan Doyle, Arthur. *A Study in Scarlet*. London: Penguin Classics, 2001.

Copeland, Larry. "Casino Proposal Bets on Underground Atlanta," *USA Today*, February 2, 2009. http://www.usatoday.com/travel/destinations/2009-02-02-underground-atlanta_N.htm

Crystal, David. *The Fight for English: How Language Pundits Ate, Shot, and Left*. Oxford, England: Oxford University Press, 2007.

————. *Txtng: The Gr8 Db8*. Oxford, England: Oxford University Press, 2008.

Dello Stritto, Mike. "Paraplegic Man Suffers Spider Bite, Walks Again." CBS 13, March 12, 2009. http://cbs13.com/watercooler/Paraplegic.Man.Suffers.2.958151.html

Dixon, Robert, and Siegfried Engelmann. *SRA Spelling Mastery Series Guide*. Columbus, OH: SRA, 2007.

"Domestic Names—Frequently Asked Questions (FAQs)." U.S. Board on Geographic Names. http://geonames.usgs.gov/domestic/faqs.htm

Drabble, Margaret and Jenny Stringer. "Francis of Assisi, St. Giovanni Francesco Bernardone." *The Concise Oxford Companion to English Literature*. Oxford, England: Oxford University Press, 2003.

"Fell's (Not Fells) Point." *Baltimore Magazine*, April 15, 2009. http://www.baltimoremagazine.net/eyesonthestreet/index.php/2009/04/fells-not-fells-point/

Finegan, Edward. *Attitudes Toward English Usage: The History of a War of Words*. New York: Teachers College Press, Columbia University, 1980.

Flesch, Rudolf. *Why Johnny Can't Read: And What You Can Do About It*. New York: Perennial Library, 1955, 1986.

————. *Why Johnny Still Can't Read*. New York: Harper Colophon, 1983.

"Friday's Quote of the Day," *BBC Magazine Monitor*, June 27, 2008. http://www.bbc.co.uk/blogs/magazinemonitor/2008/06/22-week/

Gladwell, Malcolm. *The Tipping Point: How Little Things Can Make a Big Difference*. New York: Back Bay Books, 2002.

"Governor Isaac Stevens' Territorial Library Collection." Washington Secretary of State. http://www.secstate.wa.gov/library/territorialcollection.aspx

Grossen, Bonnie, ed. "The Story Behind Project Follow Through." *Effective School Practices* 15, no. 1 (winter 1995–96). Association for Direct Instruction.

"History of Underground Atlanta." Underground Atlanta website, http://www.underground-atlanta.com/about-us/history-of-underground.html

Kleiner, Art. *Who Really Matters? The Core Group Theory of Power, Privilege, and Success.* New York: Currency/Doubleday, 2003.

Larson, Erik. *Isaac's Storm: A Man, a Time, and the Deadliest Hurricane in History.* New York: Vintage Books, 1999.

Lerer, Seth. *Inventing English.* New York: Columbia University Press, 2007.

Lissner, Caren. "So, Does Veterans Day Have a Fucking Apostrophe or What?" *The Black Table*, October 18, 2005. http://www.blacktable.com/lissner051018.htm

Liu, Irene Jay. " 'Barack Osama' absentee ballot sent to voters in Rensselaer County." *Albany Times Union*, October 10, 2008. http://blog.timesunion.com/capitol/archives/8953/

Mikkelson, Barbara and David P. "Niger Innis." Snopes, February 19, 2008. http://www.snopes.com/inboxer/outrage/innis.asp

Miles, Elaine. *English Words and Their Spelling: A History of Phonological Conflicts.* London: Whurr Publishers, 2005.

Milgram, Stanley. *Obedience to Authority: An Experimental View.* New York: Harper & Row, 1974.

Monaghan, E. Jennifer. *A Common Heritage: Noah Webster's Blue-Black Speller.* North Haven, CT: Archon Books, 1983.

Mountford, John. *An Insight into English Spelling.* London: Hodder & Stoughton, 1998.

Mueller, Andrew. "Linguistic Pedants of the World Unite." *The Guardian*, April 14, 2008. http://www.guardian.co.uk/commentisfree/2008/apr/14/linguisticpedantsoftheworldunite

Mugglestone, Lynda, ed. *Lexicography and the OED: Pioneers in the Untrodden Forest.* Oxford, England: Oxford University Press, 2000.

National Assessment of Adult Literacy. National Center for Education Statistics, U.S. Department of Education, http://nces.ed.gov/naal/kf_demographics.asp

O'Conner, Patricia T. (3rd ed.). *Woe Is I.* New York: Riverhead Books, 2009.

Office of the United States Attorney, District of Arizona. "Pair Sentenced for Vandalism to Historic Work in Grand Canyon National Park." U.S. Department of Justice press release, August 21, 2008.

Osselton, N. E. *Chosen Words: Past and Present Problems for Dictionary Makers.* Exeter, England: University of Exeter Press, 1995.

———. *The Dumb Linguists.* Leiden, Netherlands: Leiden University Press, 1973.

Pinker, Steven. *The Language Instinct: How the Mind Creates Language.* New York: Harper Perennial, 1995.

Shafer, Jack. "Weasel-Words Rip My Flesh!" *Slate,* September 20, 2005. http://www.slate.com/id/2126636/

Shea, Ammon. "The Price of a Self-Righteous Holiday." OUPblog, August 28, 2008, http://blog.oup.com/2008/08/emense/

Swift, Jonathan. *Polite Conversation in Three Dialogues,* edited by George Saintsbury. Chiswick Press: London, 1892.

Toffler, Alvin. *Future Shock.* New York: Bantam Books, 1971.

Truss, Lynne. *Talk to the Hand: The Utter Bloody Rudeness of the World Today, or Six Good Reasons to Stay Home and Bolt the Door.* New York: Gotham, 2005.

United States District Court for the District of Arizona. *United States of America v. Jeff Michael Deck & Benjamin Douglas Herson.* Case number: 08-04086M-002-PCT-MEA. Flagstaff, AZ: August 2008. Transcribed by Candy Potter: Phoenix, AZ, July 2009.

Venezky, Richard L. *The Structure of English Orthography.* Netherlands: Mouton & Co., 1970.

"Venomous Spider Bite Cures Paraplegic." *The Week,* March 19, 2009. http://www.theweek.com/article/index/94426/Venomous_spider_bite_cures_paraplegic

Wagner, Dennis. "Typo Vigilantes Answer to Letter of the Law." *Arizona Republic,* August 22, 2008, http://www.azcentral.com/news/articles/2008/08/22/20080822grammarcops0822.html

Wanjek, Christopher. "Spider Bite Cures Paralyzed Man: Miracle or Bad Reporting?" LiveScience.com, March 24, 2009. http://www.livescience.com/strangenews/090324-bad-spider-bite.html

Waterhouse, Ben. "Restaurant Apocalypse 2008: Elmer's, Sal's, Hartwell's." *Willamette Week,* Portland, OR, November 10, 2008. http://blogs.wweek.com/news/2008/11/10/restaurant-apocalypse-2008-elmers-sals-hartwells/

Watkins, Cathy. "Follow Through: Why Didn't We?" *Effective School Practices* 15, no. 1(winter 1995–96). Association for Direct Instruction.

Weinstein, Lawrence A. *Grammar for the Soul: Using Language for Personal Change.* Wheaton, IL: Quest Books, 2008.

Winchester, Simon. *The Meaning of Everything: The Story of the Oxford English Dictionary.* Oxford, England: Oxford University Press, 2003.

———. *The Professor and the Madman: A Tale of Murder, Insanity, and the Making of the Oxford English Dictionary.* New York: Harper Perennial, 1998.

Wolman, David. *Righting the Mother Tongue: From Olde English to Email, the Tangled Story of English Spelling.* New York: Collins, 2008.

"Worst Person in the World." *Countdown with Keith Olbermann,* August 22, 2008.

Acknowledgments

Many thanks to Julia Pastore, who believed in this project from the start, for all of her careful attentions. She promised an editorial style of raising important questions, offering gentle guidance that led us to find the book we wanted to write. Also to Domenica Alioto, who makes sure Julia doesn't leave her office without her head firmly attached.

We'd like to extend a thank-you and a hearty hurrah to everyone at Harmony Books; you saw what was significant about our struggle for orthographic justice—and got the joke, too. To Kira Walton, associate director of marketing, Campbell Wharton, director of publicity, and Penny Simon, executive publicist, for patiently helping two neophytes to introduce their book to the world in a way that would best connect it to readers who'd love it. To Shaye Areheart, publisher of Harmony Books, for welcoming us into the fold and for assembling such a fantastic team. To David Wade Smith, for superior copyediting. To Patty Shaw, production editor; Jessie Bright, jacket designer; and Elina Nudelman, text designer.

A special thanks to our agent, Jeff Kleinman, the man who never sleeps. You tracked us down, told us we "had to be writing a book," and introduced us to the folks at Harmony. We couldn't have gotten here without you. Thanks also to the whole team at Folio Lit.

We're very grateful to everyone who was kind enough to host us and other TEAL associates during our typo hunt across America: Alice and Brian, Raisha Price, Diane and David Herson, Abby Horowitz and Eli Rosenberg, Paula and Ben Sides, Stephanie Bortis, Christine Laliberte, Frank Yoshida, Katie Lynch and Lisa Torrey, Jon Schroeder, Michelle Grimard, Marie and Terry Huizing, Jessica Deck, R. Jerry and Toni Deck, Grandma Mary Jane Deck, Dan and Rachel Herson, Bill Bortis and E. Kristen Frederick, and Susan Deck. We would never have made it without such a surfeit of hospitality.

Thanks so much to everyone who wrote in to express their support for the TEAL trip while it was happening and in the months that followed. You were a constant reminder that the trip was worthwhile, so crucial during those days when our efforts met blank stares and brush-offs. You (and those who thoughtfully purchased this book) are the future of the League. We can't wait to work with you in further campaigns for improvement of spelling and grammar education.

We would also like to thank Dr. Joe McCleary, Chris Finn, Gina McKinnon, Nicole Gregory, Kelly Flynn, and Bridget Sheehan at Mystic Valley Regional Charter School for demonstrating to us the marvels of Direct Instruction. Thanks also to Jerry Silbert of NIFDI. Thanks as well to Tim Cahill, a creative collaborator and good friend who gave chapter 18 a read-through and then explained to us what had happened in that courtroom; to Kevin Allen, who let us use his personal story; and to Chris Collins.

Jeff Deck

Special thanks to Uncle Pat for rousting the local media in Erie, and to Uncle Danny for the free food at his sports bar, On Deck. Thanks to Gary for the free sandwiches in Ellensburg, Washington. Thanks to Lisa Watson of Cupcake Jones in Portland, Oregon, for the free cupcakes. Thanks to my friends in Somerville who presented me with a generous gas card at my birthday/farewell party: Krystina and James Bruce, Tim Tufts and Ainsley Ross, Emily Perry and Joe O'Brien, and Sonya Grabauskas. Thanks to Dana Tellier and Carol Stamnas Tellier for an equally generous offering. Thanks to Aunt Carol and Uncle George for the road-trip assistance. Thanks to Uncle Bill and Aunt Kristen for lending me a hand in times of legal trouble. Thank you to Josh Roberts for participating in the West Coast leg of the trip, including a lot of driving. Also thank you to Erin Donovan for putting up with Benjamin and me as we finished the book.

Thanks to Professor Ernie Hebert, teacher, writer, and adviser at Dartmouth College, for offering so many helpful insights into the craft of writing. Thanks to Mr. Joe Sullivan of West High School in New Hampshire for sparking my interest in writing in the first place. As for my training in editing, copyediting, and proofreading, I can credit the instruction and example of my supervisors at (now-defunct) Heldref Publications: Paul Skalleberg, Marie Huizing, Jennifer Pricola (Horak), and Abby Beckel.

I'm indebted to Jane Connolly for designing the TEAL website, patiently enduring my long absence during the trip, accompanying me through the northern plains, and later patiently enduring my summons to Arizona (and branding as a criminal). Her love and support sure helped the writing of this book, too. Much love, bear.

Thanks to my mom for offering suggestions on the manuscript and for consistently supporting my dreams and endeavors. I've been continually inspired by her strength and savvy; singlehandedly raising me could not have been an easy task. Thanks to my dad for the assistance during the trip and for doing his best to scout out typo territory in Hudson, Ohio, and its environs. Don't worry, I won't tell anyone what the "R." in R. Jerry Deck stands for, because I do want to live until my next birthday.

Benjamin D. Herson

Thanks first to David and Diane Herson for causing me to exist. Oh, and I suppose thanks also for all their tremendous, unwavering love and support over the next thirty years and counting. To Dan Herson, the awesomest little brother a boy could have. To Jenny, about whom I'm thoroughly crazy, thanks hardly begins to suffice; in fact, if someone could invent a better word for love that isn't so clichéd, I could really use it about now. Thanks to Jenny and my mom for reading through the book and offering suggestions.

Keeping up with Jeff required some serious skills, developed over a long time thanks to an improbably good run of excellent teachers. Most notable for the creation of this book are Teacher Janis (for getting permission to teach me how to read, and for using phonics to do so), my four amazing First Colonial High School English teachers, Mrs. Daugherty, Mr. Kaminski, Mrs. Haring, and Mrs. Antley (really, I was going to be a mathematician before you guys showed me how I could play with language more than I could with numbers), and many more in between. Excellent teachers really do make all the difference. Further sharpening my writing (directly and indirectly) at Dartmouth College were Professors Hebert, Garrod, Pfister, and my thesis adviser Professor Susan Ackerman.

Other assorted thanks: To Borders, both up the ladder where everyone has supported one of their own, and among my many friends (it's going to be weird knowing you guys are handing off my book—at least you'll always have something to recommend). To Lisa and Katie for letting me show up early and helping me pull off a fun surprise. Also to the folks at the San Diego Point Loma hostel who helped with my April Fool's Day typo correction. To Chris Baty for National Novel Writing Month (nanowrimo.org), which Jeff and I have participated in annually since '03, which helped us put in the writing time so that when this opportunity arose, we were ready for it.

More random thanks yet: To Stephen Colbert for what he said about Keith Olbermann on the 11/6/08 show; we sincerely hope that you too will be selected one of Olbermann's Worst in the World, and we agree that his glaring oversight of not honoring you thusly is as absurd as it is insulting. To Jon Stewart for getting me through eight very long years.

Special final thanks: To Allen White and my whole Unity in Silver Spring family; you always believed. Melissa, Doug, Peter, Justin, and all my amazing Rally friends, there when I needed you most.

About the Authors

JEFF DECK has worked in Washington, D.C., and Boston as an editor. He enjoys speculative fiction books and role-playing games, as well as drawing comics. He grew up in Manchester, New Hampshire, and now lives in Portsmouth, New Hampshire, with his girlfriend, Jane. They have zero cats.

BENJAMIN D. HERSON grew up in Virginia Beach, Virginia, attended Dartmouth College in Hanover, New Hampshire, and lived in the D.C. area for seven years. He now lives in Beaverton, Oregon, with his symbiant, Jenny; they are happily unmarried to each other. They work at rival bookstores, read a lot, and have zero cats. He is also an Eagle Scout and a fan of science fiction.

www.greattypohunt.com